GLOSSARY OF POLITICAL SCIENCE TERMS: Islamic and Western

ABDUL RASHID MOTEN

EL-FATIH A. ABDEL SALAM

THOMSON™

Australia • Canada • Mexico • Singapore • Spain • United Kingdom • United States

THOMSON™

GLOSSARY OF POLITICAL SCIENCE TERMS: Islamic and Western
By Abdul Rashid Moten, El-Fatih A. Abdel Salam

For more information, please contact:
Thomson Learning
(a division of Thomson Asia Pte Ltd)
5 Shenton Way
#01-01 UIC Building
Singapore 068808

Or visit our internet website at *http://www.thomsonlearningasia.com*

Thomson Learning offices in Asia: Bangkok, Beijing, Hong Kong, Kuala Lumpur, Manila, Mumbai, Seoul, Singapore, Taipei, Tokyo.

Printed in Malaysia
1 2 3 4 5 06 05 04

When ordering this book, please use **ISBN 981-254-529-8**

PREFACE

This book had its origins, almost four years ago, in the preparation of another project, the International Conference for the Islamization of Human Sciences, organized by the Kulliyah (Faculty) of Islamic Revealed Knowledge and Human Sciences, the International Islamic University Malaysia, which took place in August 2000. One outcome of that conference was the felt need for dictionaries covering the terms in various disciplines. In the department of Political science, we felt that the discipline has evolved a colourful and extensive vocabulary. Although these specialized terms greatly facilitate discussion among those who understand the language, they can impede discussions between specialists and non-specialists, and even between experts in different subfields. There is a need for concerted efforts to break down these communication barriers by providing clear and succinct definitions of key terms used by policymakers, journalists, commentators, and analysts, in discussing national and international politics. A plan and outline were soon prepared. We divided the work between the two of us, each one of us, thus, became responsible to account for the meaning of terms he would be treating and to track its political and societal context.

The purpose of this book is to provide a clear and lively introduction to selected Islamic and Western political science terms. It is the first of its kind combining Political Science terms from the two streams. It provides succinct definitions and explanations of around 2000 key concepts in political science in an engaging style, cross-referenced, and easily accessible to readers new to the subject. Following the practice of the compilers of the Oxford dictionaries, entries are listed in strict alphabetical order. As a work of reference, this glossary will be useful for students and teachers of political science.

This glossary has been compiled with considerable study and labour in the hope that it will be an inexpensive source book which will be of use, to students in particular, and also scholars and layman alike. As authors, we are very much aware that the compilation of any glossary, particularly of one which claims to be popular, is a highly subjective matter. Everyone has his or her own ideas about what is crucially important and the compiler is thus a hostage to his reader's interests, preferences and scholarly emphases. We have tried to present the bare minimum of what is an immensely rich and vitally important subject. Our approach has been, in so far as it is humanly possible, objective and phenomenological which does not, however, preclude immense respect for all the terms and concepts here treated.

The selection of our terms is inevitably arbitrary. We started with a list, conjured up with the help of many sources, primarily Political Science text-books. Writing each entry one uses terms that themselves turn out to require definition, so a chain reaction starts, and it stops when the rate of reaction has slowed down and the sheer length of the book is at a publishing optimum. We really operated with rules for exclusion, not inclusion. Most entries in this glossary refer to various aspects of political science. We have given definition of events, organizations, their historical significance and terms pertinent to the twenty-first century. The names of specific politicians and political parties are not included. However, exceptions have been made for policies or movements which have a general significance.

We believe that the outcome is a collection of definitions of political terms that is authoritative without being dull or stereotyped. But the attentive reader will soon become aware that few political definitions can be given a simple, straightforward definition, nor can there be uncontroversial definitions of political movements and ideologies. We submit that this is an uncomfortable terrain for those who believe that to every political term there is one right definition. If, besides being informative, we have succeeded in communicating something of the open-endedness of the meaning of political terms in the pages that follow, we shall feel doubly pleased.

We are, of course, responsible for all errors of commission, omission, misinterpretations and misprints which may unwittingly have crept into the text. Since a work covering such an immense field can only reach perfection through collaboration, users are invited to notify us of any mishaps; we will do our best to rectify them in possible future editions.

We both owe debts to our home institution, the International Islamic University Malaysia, whose environment allowed us to plan and produce what we feel an outstandingly interesting and distinguished work. We are equally indebted to our families for providing us the needed incentives to finish the work. This work is dedicated to our students from whom we have learnt a lot.

There remain two things we wish to say about this glossary. We have learned a lot in the process of researching it. We have enjoyed writing it far more than anything else we have written, and even if nobody learns anything from it, we hope someone enjoys it. It is a modest work which is not meant to be an encyclopaedia, a biography or a complete reference book on political science terms, although it may serve one or all of these purposes in a small way.

All praises are due to Allah Alone, Who is our source of inspiration and to Whom we shall return.

Abdul Rashid Moten
armoten90@hotmail.com

El-fatih A. Abdel Salam
elfatih70@hotmail.com

Glossary of Political Science

A

Abbasids

A Great dynasty ruling (37 caliphs) from 750 (132H) until the Monghols conquered Baghdad in 1258/656H . The Abbasids were all of one big family that claimed to descend from Abbas, an uncle of Prophet Muhammad (SAAS). The second 'Abbasid caliph, al-Mansur (reg. 754–775) can be considered the architect of the medieval Islamic empire, and he moved the administrative capital from Damascus, in Syria, to Baghdad on the Tigris River in Iraq. For the first 100 years, Abbasids were leaders, both of Islam and of the Muslim community. Soon, the Abbasid caliphs became puppets in the hands of the Turkish military troops. The Persian Shii Buwayhids were the real rulers from 945 until the 10th century. As the caliphs lost the grip of power, the unity of the caliphate also fell apart, and independent states were formed. Harun al-Rashid is the most famous of the Abbasid caliphs. The Abbasid period is recognized for the most elevated scientific works. The Abbasid era is often regarded as the golden age of Muslim civilization.

Absolutism

A system of government, popular with medieval kings, in which the authority is absolute and unchecked. There is no legal limit on what a government may do and there is no group outside of government which is allowed to resist the government. Islam does not condone absolutism of any kind.

Accountability

The requirement for an individual or public organization (usually an executive) to render an account to parliament or some other source of legitimate authority. This conception of accountability implies that some powers have been delegated and that the agent must later justify its actions to the source of those delegated powers. Those in authority must prove that they have exercised their power and performed their duties as per legal requirements. Accountability is a generalised system for evaluating and improving performance in the public sector, or as a prospective means of specifying responsibility.

Act

An Act is a specific body of law that is passed by the parliament and is given assent by the head of state (king, president, or governor general). An act does not become a law until it has received the assent of the head of state. Proclamations of Acts which have received the assent are published in the government Gazette.

'Adālah

(*root, adl*). *'Adl* literally means to straighten and be upright, to move from a position of wrong to a position that is desirable, it also means to equalise, and, finally it means balance and equilibrium. *'Adl* in Islam has several dimensions. First, it has a Divine basis, rooted in morality, and guidance revealed by God. So the first principle of *'adl* is to relate to and recognise God, the Creator, Cherisher and Sustainer of the universe. Second, the equality of man and social, political and cultural life to be based upon a set of moral values and principles. These moral values are not merely moral imperatives but they also become legal and political norms. Finally, justice is a process through which people redress injuries and grievances, establish rights and struggle for the removal of exploitation, oppression and injustice from society. The term is much more comprehensive than the word "justice". *'Adālah* in Islam is not simply legal but pervades every matter in life including oneself. The aim of an Islamic state is the fulfilment of justice on behalf of Allah on earth. Many Muslim scholars agree with Ibn Taymiyyah that Allah will help a just state even though it be composed of non-Muslims, while He might not help a tyrannical state that happens to be composed entirely of Muslims. See JUSTICE.

Adjournment

Discontinuance of the sitting of a legislative assembly, either by the speaker of the House or on a resolution passed by the members present. A legislature may adjourn if the deputies are disorderly, or when there is no quorum. In other cases, adjournment may be invoked to block the adoption of a resolution.

Adjudication

One mechanism for settling a dispute amicably, by submitting it to determination by an established court of law. Other mechanisms of pacific settlement include good offices, mediation, conciliation and arbitration.

Administration

The ways in which the activities of an organization are managed. It connotes the management, supervision, surveillance, command, superintendence and directing the decision-making of public policy.

Administrative law

The total body of canon, decree, rules and regulations made by executive and administrative agencies within certain specified limits. Administrative law has grown to considerable size.

Administrative Tribunal

A special court outside the judicial system that decides conflicts in a particular area such as tax or labour issues.

Administrator

A person appointed to executive agencies to enforce laws and carry out policies and whose tenure and promotion depend on professional merit rather than on political affiliation.

Advanced Capitalism

Economic system characterized by private ownership but with a major role played by the public sector. Most developed market economies like those in North America, Western Europe, Japan and Australia are examples of advanced capitalism

Affirmative action

Pro-active efforts to redress social inequalities. Affirmative action produces structural change which should, ideally, obviate complaints of discrimination. Affirmative action can be introduced in a number of domains: in the labour market, in systems of political representation, in higher education, in other kinds of associations such as trade unions and political parties. In the United States, "affirmative action" program was designed to increase the number of minority group members or women in jobs or schools from which they were previously wholly or partly excluded. This programme was meant to correct past practices redundant against disadvantaged groups.

African National Congress (ANC)

The first African liberation movement formed in response to the creation of the South African Union which institutionalized the racist white minority rule in the Republic of South Africa. Initially, this organization had little impact until it expanded its base in the 1940s. In 1943, Nelson Mandela and Oliver Tambo espoused a radical programme which became the basis of the Defiance Campaign of the 1950s. This shift coincided with the adoption of apartheid in 1948. Following the Sharpeville shootings in 1960, the ANC was banned and forced into exile and the organization in response reorganized a clandestine military campaign. With the white minority regime coming under increasing pressure at home and abroad, the ANC was the principal focus of opposition. In 1989 F.W. de Klerk became president of South Africa. The following year he released Nelson Mandela, decided the unbanning of the African organizations, and opened talks with Mandela to enfranchise the African majority in a new constitution. In the April 1994 elections, the ANC emerged victorious and Mandela was installed as the first non-white president of South Africa.

'Ahd

Testamentary designation; covenant, agreement. The term occurs frequently in the Qur'an. It is used there to denote Allah's covenant with men and His commands and in the sense of religious engagement which believers have agreed. It may also refer to a political agreement and undertakings of believers towards certain obligation, among people, and finally it may mean ordinary civil agreements and contract in transactions. *'Ahd* has sometimes been used interchangeably with *ittifāq* or *ittifāqiyyah* (the former may mean "contract", while the latter means, more strictly, "agreement"). Its employment in the sense of "treaty" appears to have been borrowed from 19th century Ottoman usage by officials and scholars concerned with international relations.

Ahl al dhimmah

From *dhimmah*, a covenant of "protection." A non-Muslim citizen who is protected and cared for in his or her minority status when living under Muslim rule, in exchange for certain obligations such as paying the "poll tax" (*jizyah*). Throughout Muslim history, people of the book, whether Jewish, Christian, or Zoroastrian (in the Iranian regions), were granted *dhimmī*, "protected" status with their community rules governing internal matters. *Dhimmis* were not required to bear arms or serve in the military; they were granted protection from enemies of the state. For many generations in the early centuries of the Islamic movement, the *dhimmis* often occupied high and honoured positions in government. They were treated with justice and respect by the Muslims, far more so than could be said of non-Christians in predominantly Christian lands over the same centuries (the Western Middle Ages down to modern times) or even of minority Christian bodies that lived independently of Rome. The Jews, especially, flourished under Muslim rule in such places as Iraq, Egypt, the Maghrib, and especially Spain.

Ahl al Badr

Muslims (about 300) who fought at Badr under the leadership of the Prophet (SAW) in 2AH/624CE and emerged victorious against the polytheists of Quraysh, who numbered about 950 men. They are also known as *Badriyyūn* and came to be regarded as an aristocracy of merit. They enjoyed respect because of their heroism in the battle.

Ahl al-Bayt

Literally, "the people of the House"; also referred to as *Āl al-Nabī*, "the family of the Prophet." The phrase *ahl al-bayt* occurs twice in the Qur'an. Once it is applied to the house of Ibrahim. The second, it was applied to the house of Prophet Muhammad (SAW); it was here that the precise interpretation of the phrase gave rise to differences of opinion. The shi'ah apply it to mean the Prophet, Ali, Fatimah, al-Hasan and al-Husayn. Sunni Muslims extend the term to include all the Banu Hashim. Some Sunni Muslims, though, use it to mean the entire community of Muslims.

Ahl al Ijma'

"Scholars of consensus" on religious matters. They are the scholars whose competence and piety are beyond question; they provide legal opinion on a subject not directly ruled upon in the Qur'an or the Sunnah of the Prophet (SAW).

Ahl al-ḥall wa al- 'aqd

Literally, "those who loosen and bind"; influential people: the qualified representatives of the Muslim community who act on their behalf in appointing and deposing a ruler (*khalifah*). These influential people must enjoy certain qualities: they must be Muslims, male, of age, free, and capable of judging who is best qualified to fill the office. The current orthodox view would identify these electors with the whole of the nation, with Parliament, or with the body of religious scholars and jurists.

Ahl al ikhtiar

Commission set up to choose certain group argued to do something. Usually, the term is used for those that choose the ministers traditionally based on certain criteria. Furthermore, the term may be used for those who have been chosen amongst others on the basis of certain criteria. Literally, the term itself (*ikhtiar*) means one's intention to do an act which manner between existent and non-existence and which is within the doer's power of preferring one alternative to another. Hence, it means "will" or volition.

Ahl al-sunah wa al-jamā'ah

Literally, people of the Sunnah. The Sunnites i.e., the orthodox Muslims. Refers to the vast majority of Muslims united behind the Sunnah of the Prophet and the precedents of his rightly-guided successors. Used in contradistinction to the shi'i (heterodox) sect who believed that 'Ali, the Prophet's cousin and son-in-law, should have been his immediate successor.

Al Anṣār

Helpers, adherents, followers, partisans, sponsors, patrons, friends. Specifically, it refers to the Muslims of Madinah who helped the *Muhajirin* (immigrants) of Makkah in the process of the latter's settling down in the new environment.

Al dabt al siyāsī

Political order in Islam. Sometimes, it is used to mean precise and accurate in reproducing reports pertaining to hadith terminology.

Al ḥaq

The truth, righteousness, justice, state of being just, proper, correct and valid. In a technical sense, it is an attribute of Allah as is used in variety of context in the Qur'an. See ALLAH.

Al Maṣālih al-Mursalah

"*Maṣālih*" is the plural of "*Maṣlahah*", which means interest, benefit. When the word is used with *Mursalah*, it means unrestricted, undefined or independently-judged interest. This term owes its origin to the conception that *Shari'ah* is for social utility and that its function is to promote benefit and prevent evil. The famous jurist, Imam Malik approved that public interest as one of the sources of *Shari'ah* and named it *al-Maslahah al-Mursalah*. But the jurist, Imam Abu Hanifah, considered it to be too vague and general in making legal deductions.

Al-Qāedah

An Arabic word meaning "the base." *Al-Qāedah* is a network of many different organizations in diverse countries. It was established sometimes between 1988 and 1989 by Osama bin Laden and Muhammed Atef. It is not an Islamic movement like Jama'at-e-Islami of Pakistan or al-Ikhwan al-Muslimoon of Egypt with a well-articulated ideology and a programme. It is a Muslim movement to champion the cause of Muslims all over the world who consider themselves, for good reasons, to have been oppressed and exploited by America and American interests. Its objectives are: to fight against America and Israel; to drive the "American crusaders and their allies" out of Saudi Arabia, the "land of the two Holy places", Iraq, Afghanistan and the Gulf; and to bring about an awareness of the people, Muslims and non-Muslims alike, to the consequences of the US policies on Muslim population all over the world. It uses violence as it is too weak to use conventional military force against the super powers.

Until the American bombing of Afghanistan in 2001, the Al-Qaedah was based in Afghanistan. It grew out of the Afghan war against the Soviets. Its members, including its leader Osama bin Laden, were armed and trained by the Americans. The CIA launched a US$ 500 million per year campaign to arm and train the Mujahideen who later joined the *Al-Qāedah*. *Al-Qāedah* became the target of US fury after the September 11, 2001 incidence in which thousands of innocent people living in America died, New York's twin tower were razed to the ground, and part of the Pentagon destroyed. The September incident was widely, and justifiably, condemned by Muslims and non-Muslims all over the world as an inhuman act of terrorism. Islam is against such an act as it is a religion of peace. The United States launched a war against terrorism with a good deal of support from the people all over the world. However, the best solution to the problem of global terrorism is to remove the causes of terrorism like the unqualified American support for Israel.

Al Rāshidūn

Those following the right way, having the truth and rightly guided people (leaders). The term is used to refer to the first four caliphs who followed the Prophet (SAW). These orhodox caliphs are Abubakr, 'Umar, 'Uthman and 'Ali.

Al Sunnah

Literally, "the beaten path," the collections of recorded words, actions, and sanctions of the Prophet (SAW) commonly referred to as *Hadith* or *Sunnah* and established as legally —binding precedents immediately next in importance to the Qur'an, a recommended deed as opposed to *fardh* (i.e., a compulsory deed). See *ḤADĪTH*.

Al Wassi

An authorized agent, a successor. In politics, it is used for commissioner, executor, legal guardian, administrator. Legally, it may be used to refer to a caretaker.

Alien

A person who resides or travels outside of the country of his or her citizenship or nationality. An alien, who owes allegiance to another state and whose loyalty and sympathy belong to a foreign country, is denied the enjoyment of political rights, and the laws of the state in which he or she temporarily resides do not permit the person to participate in the politics of that country. When a country is at war, restrictions on aliens become pretty stringent, particularly on the citizens of the belligerent countries, who are called "enemy aliens" as distinguished from "friendly aliens," that is, citizens of states that are not at war.

Alienation

An abstract and complex concept common among Hegelians, Marxists, Existentialists, and psycho-analysts. Defined as a sense of the splitting asunder of what once held together, a sense of "estrangement" from oneself, from society, and particularly within the context of living in modern, large-scale societies. Conceptually, alienation has five meanings: powerlessness, meaninglessness, norm-lessness, isolation, and self-estrangement. Alienation is the key concept in Marx's early critique of capitalist society. It is seen as being generated in the process of production. Marx argued that in a capitalist system, ownership is divorced from the act of production and objects are produced for profit in distant markets. Capitalist production is explained as setting human beings against the process of production, the object they produce, their fellow human beings and their generic identity as creative beings who can produce freely and according to general, non-limited criteria.

Allāh

"God." A contraction of Arabic al-ilah, "The God." According to Islamic belief, *Allāh* is one in His essence, one in His attributes, and one in His works. There is none worthy of worship except *Allāh*. He is the Lord, the Creator, Cherisher and Sustainer of the universe. Sovereignty in an Islamic state, and in fact over the entire universe, rests with Him and Him alone. As His creation, Muslims believe that they are responsible to *Allāh* to help create a humane society living fully and truly according to the will of *Allāh*. See *TAWḤĪD*, SOVEREIGNTY.

Alliance

Voluntary association of two or more states to advance or protect their shared interests. The association is not meant to be permanent and is directed at some generally defined purpose. Many alliances are founded on some type of formal agreement, such as a treaty, wherein members pledge specific obligations for fixed periods of time. As instruments of international law, treaties impose certain obligations upon their parties. Less formal arrangements also may serve as the bases of alliances, including pacts, protocols, and charters. In all cases, the alliance partners agree to unite in addressing a common concern. In the domestic level, alliance refers to an agreement between two or more groups and political parties to co-operate.

Almohads

Anglicized form of *Al-Muwaḥḥidūn*, literally, "The Unitarians." In its singular form, the term *muwahhid* refers to a believer in *tawḥīd*, divine unity and making the unity constant in thoughts and actions. However, Almohad refers to the dynasty that flourished in Morocco and Spain from 524/1130 – 667/1269. Their inspiration was the reformist Berber scholar Ibn Tumart (470/1077 – 474/1081 – 524/1130). The dynasty, with its reforming zeal and piety filled the vacuum left by the declining Almoravids in the Muslim West. However, the Almohads were defeated by the Christian Kings at the Battle of Las

Navas de Tolosa in 609/1212. They were followed in Morocco by the Marinids.

Almoravids

Anglicized form of *al-Murābiṭūn*, literally "those who line up together (in defence of the faith)". It may also refer to those who were connected with a *ribāt* i.e., "a frontier post." The Almoravid dynasty lasted from 448/1056 to 541/1147.

Amān

Security, safety, peace, shelter and protection. In some cases, it may denote safeguarding and immunity from punishment.

Amānah

Trust, trusteeship, moral responsibility, honesty. It has meaning not only in interpersonal dealings, but also in the dealing between man and Allah (SWT), that Allah (SWT) has made man His vicegerent commissioning him with the trusteeship of *khilafah*; this responsibility of *khilāfah* is called *amanah.*

Ambassador

A senior diplomatic officer stationed at an embassy in another state. Before an ambassador is sent to a foreign land, the host state needs to agree to recognize that person as the legitimate delegate. Upon arrival in the host state, an ambassador and all accompanying staff are considered representatives of their state. Prior to the advent of modern communications, a country's ambassador and staff were a critical part of the decision-making process. Treaties and agreements were often negotiated and agreed upon by ambassadors without prior approval of their superiors. In more recent times, the role of the ambassador has become more ceremonial and less critical to the decision-making process.

Amendment

An addition to, or alteration of, a statute or constitution. It is a provision added to a law or rule in order to change and improve it. Like the related device of repeal, it is an instrument of law reform aimed at serving the true and best interests of the people. The means by which the fundamental political institutions and power relationships of a constitution are formally changed is known as amendment process.

'Āmīl

Government agent or official, particularly the collector of taxes. The Prophet (SAW) appointed representatives among the tribes or in the areas under his authority in order to collect *zakah* from Muslims and the tributes from non-Muslims; some of them had political and military duties. Later on, it was used to mean a provincial governor or administrator. By the 4th century A.H., *'āmil* had normally come to mean a finance officer. The *amir* of a province had beside him an *'āmil* whose major function was to collect revenues and to submit balance sheets of their areas.

Amīr al Mu'minīn

A title variously translated as "Commander of the Faithful," "Prince of the Believers" and "Prince of the Faithful," among others. Initially, *Amīr al Mu'minīn* meant someone given military leadership. The title was then assumed by the second Khalifah Umar b. al-Khattab, and from his time onwards it became a title reserved for a caliph alone. It was sometimes used by the Sultans in the early period of the Ottomans. By contrast, the Almoravids preferred to use the title *Amīr al-*

Muslimīn which meant "leader of the Muslims."

Amīr al-umārā

Chief *amīr*, commander-in-chief of the army. Originally, the term was confined to the military command. However, with the gradual weakening of the caliphal authority, the amir also handled all civil matters.

Amr

(plural *Awāmīr, Umūr*): this term refers to command, matter, and affair. Sometimes, it is used in the Qur'ān to denote "be" (*kun*) that translate possibilities into the manifest. Hence, the Qur'ān indicates two stages for the creation of anything: the divine plan for that entity and the actual process of bringing it into being.

Amnesty

A pardon granted to a group of people, usually for political offences. Amnesty is usually granted during a major national celebration.

Amr bil ma'rūf

A classical Arabic phrase meaning "commanding the good." This was one of the five principles of the *Mu'tazilah*. In other words, the phrase means promotion of good deed. This is a duty of all Muslims as prescribed in the Qur'ān.

Anarchism

Used rather loosely as a synonym for disorder, but which in fact refers to the doctrine which counsels the absence of formal government. It is a political philosophy that rejects all forms of coercive authority. It believes that all governments are evil and unnecessary. Governments should therefore, be replaced by voluntary groups. It envisions a society without a state. This anarchist society would be a collection of free individuals, each having sovereignty over his or her own life, exercising his or her own judgment to decide what is best to do. Modern anarchist philosophy originated in William Godwin's analysis of authority. Critics have argued that anarchism would result in chaos, that the state is necessary to maintain order. Anarchists have replied that the state, far from maintaining order, is the greatest producer of social discord.

Androcentric bias

Pervasion of a male-centered or androcentric bias in people's thoughts and actions. This bias, according to Feminists, is due to the fact that males have, far too long, dominated social, political, and economic arenas of life.

Anomie

A term popularized by Emile Durkheim, a French sociologist, to explain why men decide to commit suicide. He conceptualized anomie as the breakdown of the individual's connection with society. He saw anomie as a result of the speedy pace of industrialization which dismantled the existing moral order.

Anomic groups

More or less spontaneous groups that form suddenly when many individuals respond similarly to frustration, disappointment, or other strong emotions. Without previous organization or planning, these groups rise and subside suddenly; their actions may lead to violence, but not necessarily.

Anṣār (sing. *Nāṣir*)

Adherents, sponsors, patrons. Specifically, it refers to "the helpers" i.e., the Madinan followers of the Prophet (SAW) who joined with Makkan Muslim followers in establishing the Ummah.

Anticlericalism

A political outlook strongly opposed to the churches wielding any direct political influence or power. Anticlerical parties or politicians have played an important role in most Western polities at one time or another. The debate between clericalists and anti-clericalists continues in Italy.

ANZUS

Agreement signed in 1951 by Australia, New Zealand and the United States which pledged mutual security. Its major aim was to discourage communist incursions in the South Pacific region. It was part of the U. S. strategy of global containment. Though still technically operative, the organization has little strategic relevance in the post-cold war era.

Apartheid

Afrikaans term meaning, literally "apartness" or "separateness." A system in which strict racial separation laws are enforced by the white minority over the black majority. A policy of racial segregation was officially followed by the government of South Africa between 1948 and 1989. The system separated whites from non-whites. The policy also involved the "separate development" of 10 Bantu homelands, where the majority of the population lived on a very small portion of poor land. This policy was imposed by denying the rights to vote, own land, travel, or work without permits. Dissent led by the deprived majority of the population coupled with nearly worldwide economic sanctions led, in the early 1990s, the South African regime to dismantle the system, and to introduce democratic structures. By 1994, a black majority rule was established. Political parties appealing to racism have appeared in Australia, Austria, France, Germany, Norway and other places.

Apparatchiki

Literally "the men of the apparatus," from Russian. Full-time party officials in communist party states who acted as watchdogs and troubleshooters, enforcing party control over all areas of policy.

Appeasement

A policy of acquiescence to an aggressive enemy in order to gain peace. Today, this term is used in a pejorative sense because it connotes sacrificing other people's rights by acceding to hostile demands of an aggressor. Many critics of this policy believe that it does not work since the aggressor will ask for more and more concessions. Historically, this policy refers to the policies of the British and French governments during the 1930s as they were too afraid of the growing strength of Nazi Germany and Japan. Appeasement was abandoned with the Anglo-French declaration of war in September 1939 when Hitler invaded Poland.

Appropriations

The earmarking of money by governmental officials for specific projects. This is an essential requirement of democratic government as the legislature is empowered to raise revenue and control the expenditure of public funds. In Britain, for instance, control over appropriations lies with the executive; whereas in the United States Congress is in full legislative control over appropriations.

'Aqd

Knitting, knotting, tying, joining, junction, locking and holding. In its legal sense, *'aqd* is properly a legal act, whether it relates to a contract or to a simple unilateral declaration, such as a will. Jurists distinguish between the *'aqd* or contract and simple promises and allowances, which are not binding.

'Aqīdah (Pl. *'Aqā'id*)

Creed, but sometimes also doctrine, dogma, or article of faith. Astandard account of a Muslim's *'aqīdah* include the belief in the following: (1) tawhid: the Unity of Allah and His attributes; (2) the angels, as Allah's creation crom light and His servants; (3) the books of Allah. The revelation Allah sent through His messengers; (4) the prophets and messengers of Allah; (5) the *ākhirah* (the hereafter); (6) the *qadr*, Allah's power over His creation; (7) the meaning of Islam and the basic duties of a Muslim.

Arab League

League of Arab states was founded in 1945 with its headquarter in Cairo, Egypt. The League is the outcome of a national awakening of the Arabs, following the fall of the Osmanli caliphate in the first World War. Its objective is to promote economic, cultural, political and military cooperation among Arab states. It has 22 Arab states and the Palestine Liberation Organization as its members. The League expelled Egypt in 1979 after the country signed a peace treaty with Israel, and the seat of the League was moved to Tunis. Egypt, however, rejoined the League in 1989. The League has failed to achieve its stated goals due to rivalries and political differences among Arab leaders.

Arbitration

The hearing and determining of a dispute between parties by a person or persons chosen or agreed to by them. This is a kind of third party conflict resolution mechanisms. In arbitration, the parties to a conflict willingly submit to a third party for a decision on their dispute, and agree in advance to be bound by the decision. They also specify in advance what the issues of the dispute are and the procedure to be followed.

Aristocracy

The term, coined by Aristotle, comes from the Greek "aristos," meaning best and "archia," meaning rule. It is a government composed of a hereditary elite. Aristotle's meaning, however, was "rule by the best." Later, the term was used to refer to political rule by a small elite. Membership in this elite is often based on wealth, nobility, or office in a religious organization. During much of the nineteenth century, politics in many areas of the United States and Europe was dominated by a few wealthy families. Today, it refers to a class of persons holding exceptional rank and privileges, especially the hereditary nobility. See OLIGARCHY.

Arms control

The overarching concept of weapons control in terms of number, type, and deployment. It includes arms limitation, reduction and elimination. Specifically, it refers to the regulation of armed power and weapons at a particular level to improve the security of states.

Arms Limitation

The setting of a cap or limit on the number, type, and deployment of weapons systems. The first practical efforts to limit armaments by international agreements were made at conferences held at The Hague in 1899 and 1907 but without success. A major attempt was undertaken by the League of Nations when it convened in 1932 in the World Disarmament Conference, Geneva. However, after three years of negotiations, the gathering ended in failure. More efforts followed WWII and were dominated by the Cold War alliances. More serious and notable agreements were signed this time such as SALT of the 1970s and START of the 1980s and 1990s. See SALT, START.

Army

The military forces of a nation exclusive of the navy and in some countries the air force. In a specific sense, army is a large organized group of people who are armed and trained to fight on land. Armies usually are organized and controlled by governments. As an extension of the civilian government, the military normally takes on the attitudes of the government. If the government is aggressive, the military will take on more strident tones. If the government is more benevolent, the military remains in a more preparatory state.

'Arsh

Literally, it means throne. The word acquired considerable mystical and symbolic overtones and significance among some groups in medieval Islam especially the Ismailis. In the Holy Qur'an verse 54 of *sūrah* of *al-A'rāf*, Allah is portrayed as being on a throne.

Articles of confederation

The instrument of government that served as the basic document for the American states prior to the adoption of the U.S. Constitution. In that system each of the thirteen states was nearly autonomous. They were equally represented in Congress, which had virtually no taxing, regulatory or military powers. The Articles of Confederation could not be amended without the consent of every state.

Aryan supremacy

The Nazi doctrine that their definition of the Aryan race (of which the Germans are representative) is the culturally, intellectually, and technologically most developed race of people and the naturally strongest, so that it should subjugate or destroy all others. See NATIONAL SOCIALISM or NAZISM.

'Aṣabiyyah

Group solidarity, kinship ethos. However, the term was popularized by Ibn Khaldun who made it the basis for his theory of rise and fall of dynasties. Whether it is based on blood ties or on some other social groupings, *'asabiyyah* for Ibn Khaldun is the force which impels groups of human beings to assert themselves, to struggle for primacy, to establish hegemonies, dynasties and empires. The Prophet (SAW) condemned *'asabiyyah* as contrary to the spirit of Islam.

Ash'arites

Followers of Abul Hasan al-Ash'ari, the founder of a theological school. Important members of this school include: al-Baqillani, al-Juwayni, al-Ghazali, al-Razi and al-Jurjani. Ash'arites formed the dominant school in the Arabic-speaking parts of the Abbasid caliphate.

Asia-Pacific Economic Forum (APEC)

A group of 18 states which agreed in November 1994 to create a loosely-knit trade association that would span the Pacific. Members have agreed to scrap all tariff barriers by no later than 2020. APEC's pessimists argue that the vastness of the Pacific makes such integration difficult; in addition, they point to the fears of both a resurgent Japan and a revitalized China which have both traditionally exerted hegemony over most of East Asia and Southeast Asian sphere.

Asian Democracy

A new variant of democracy embedded in Asian values practised in some of the countries in Southeast Asia. It is characterized by direct representation of the people; majority rule; periodic elections contested by a multitude of political parties; and responsiveness of the elected government to public opinion. These characteristics are accompanied by "Asian values" of predisposition towards stable leadership; preference for collective welfare over individual rights; and respect for authority and social harmony to boost economic prosperity.

Asian Economic Crisis

It refers to the economic crisis that began in early 1997, when South Korean and Thai businesses defaulted on their foreign debts. The contagion quickly spread to other Asian countries such as Indonesia, Malaysia and even Japan. The quick withdrawal of international investments accentuated the crisis. The amazing thing about this crisis is that the countries which experienced the sudden economic collapse had, over a period of 30 years, experienced the highest levels of continuous growth in history. By 1999, the worst effects of the crisis had passed.

Asian Tiger Economies

The collective name given to the great "Asian economic success stories" of Singapore, Taiwan, South Korea and Hong Kong.

Asian Values

The idea that there are ways of doing things, ideas, forms of government, values and traditions that are specific to, and shared by, cultures and nations in Asia. The idea of Asian values was coined and propagated by Senior Minister Lee Kuan Yew of Singapore and Prime Minister Mahathir Mohamad of Malaysia.

Assembly

A body which considers questions of public policy, and with constitutional powers to make law. Assemblies (or legislatures) traditionally performed the function of making laws. As the scope of government has grown, effective control of law-making has moved to the executive and the bureaucracy. Today, assemblies pass laws without really making them. The key function of the modern assembly is representation: to stand for the people and to act for them. The other functions are making and dismissing governments, passing laws and scrutinizing the executive, and recruitment and socialization of political leaders.

Associational groups

Organizations that characteristically represent the expressed interests of a particular group, employ a full time professional staff, and have orderly procedures for formulating interests and demands. Examples include trade unions, chambers of commerce and industries, ethnic associations, religious associations, and civic groups.

Asylum

Sanctuary or place of refuge. It refers to a temporary or permanent haven granted by a country to people who have fled their countries of origin because they fear persecution due to their race, religion, ideology or views, thus losing the protective benefits of citizenship. Political asylum is given to people under life-threatening situations.

Athār

Literally, impact, trace, vestige, also deeds and precedents of the Companions of the Prophet (SAW). The majority of jurists have upheld the precedent of the Companions as one of the transmitted proofs. In cases where Qur'ān and Sunnah are silent, jurists followed the precedent of the Companions. Among the Companions, the opinion of the first four caliphs received precedence over others.

Authoritarianism

A political philosophy or belief in a political system that emphasizes authority and tradition instead of individual liberty. It calls for giving unlimited power to a single leader or small leadership group. Citizens have no right to resist government. Some authoritarian governments demand total obedience, others seek to use government power to regulate and reshape the behaviour of all their citizens. In an authoritarian system, governmental repression is habitual, the role of the military is commonly great, and use is made of such practices as torture, imprisonment without due process, and summary, anonymous execution. Spain under Franco (1939–1975), Argentina under Peron (1946–1955), and absolute monarchies are examples of authoritarian states in the twentieth century.

Authoritarian government

An authoritarian government is based on principles hostile to democracy, such as rule by a select few, suppression of the opposition, and reliance on physical coercion rather than law. These features are totally opposed to the principles of an Islamic political system.

Authority

Legal power. Power vested in a position or person that ensures obedience from others. Thus, a police officer has the authority to stop cars and pedestrians. The authority may be personal or in a formal position. A leader such as Nelson Mandela possesses personal authority. The prime minister of Malaysia derives authority from the office he holds. The obedience to authority may be rooted in habit, tradition, or even rational choice.

Autocracy

Literally, "self-authorized rule." It is often used to refer to the rule by a single, powerful individual who governs without constitutional limits. An autocrat is basically the same as a dictator. Cuba, Chile, Zaire and Russia with their dictatorial systems are some of the examples of autocracy.

Autonomy

Self-rule or self-government. Derived from the Greek "auto-nomous" meaning literally, to give the law to oneself or to be self governing. An individual is considered autonomous when he or she is able to act according to his or her own accord; this is closely linked to the concept of freedom. An institution or a province is considered autonomous if it is able to regulate its own affairs.

Āyāt al-aḥkām

Revealed verses of the Qur'ān that have legal values and ordinances or revealed verses from which laws and rules could be deduced.

Ayyubid

The name of a dynasty founded by Salah al-Din ibn Ayyub, known to Europe as Saladin. From 1169/564 H to 1250/648 H, the Ayyubids ruled Egypt and Syria. In some regions of upper Mesopotamia and the Yemen, their rule continued till the end of the 15th century.

Ayatullah

Literally, a sign, a mark, an exemplar of God. A title in the religious hierarchy, of twelver shiis, achieved by scholars who have demonstrated highly advanced knowledge of Islamic law. An *Ayatullah* is a *mujtahid*, capable of formulating independent judgements based on the Ja'fari school of jurisprudence. Such a *mujtahid* came to be regarded as representing the will of the hidden Imam, and as his deputy until his return. Ayatullahs, because of their knowledge and piety, enjoy the status of a privileged elite in contemporary Iranian politics and society.

B

Bai'ah

Contract, agreement, homage; oath of allegiance to a ruler, especially a Caliph. The act by which a certain number of persons collectively or individually recognise the authority of another person. Thus, the *bai'ah* of a Caliph is the act by which one person is proclaimed and recognized as head of the Islamic state. *Bai'ah* has two principal aims: the first is that of adherence to a doctrine and recognition of the authority of the person who teaches it e.g., in this sense the relations between the Prophet (SAW) and his followers who accept Islam was a *bai'ah*. The second aim of the concept is to recognize the authority of a person and to promise him obedience e.g., the election of a person to a post of command and, in particular, the election of a Caliph, when a promise of obedience is made.

The legal doctrine analyzes the *bai'ah* as a contractual agreement: on the one hand, there is the will of the electors expressed in the designation of the candidate, which constitutes the offer, and on the other, the will of the elected person which constitutes the acceptance. The *bai'ah* is made on condition that the elected person remains faithful to the divine prescriptions; if he deviates, the electors are released from their commitment to him.

Bai'ah al 'ammah

General oath of allegiance. This is a specific type of *bai'ah*. The suffix "*'ammah*" show specifically the collective recognition of somebody's authority and collective obedience to his commands.

Bai'ah al-khāṣṣah

Oath of allegiance by leaders representing the *Ummah.*

Bait al māl

The treasury or public money which is the property of Allah (SWT) and the Muslim nation, and, as such, no one has any right of ownership or right of expenditure of it for his personal use. Like all the affairs of the Muslims, the management and expenditure of *bait al mal* should be conducted through consultations with the freely-elected representatives of the people. Whatever is collected from the people, and wherever it is spent, it must be done lawfully according to the code of the law of the Shariah and the Muslims should have full rights of examination and accounting of the money thus received and spent by the government.

Balance of power

Refers to a condition of equilibrium among states or alliances, a rough equality of internationally relevant power that governments of affected states generally accept. Also used to label policy of trying to create or maintain such an equilibrium.

Balfour Declaration

A statement of British policy issued on November 2, 1917 by Foreign Secretary Arthur Balfour. It stated British support for a Jewish national home in Palestine without prejudice to the civil and religious rights of the then existing non-Jewish communities.

Balkanization

Originally referred to the division of the Balkan region into several small, mutually hostile and frequently warring states. Now applied to any country, region or organization characterised by fragmentation with destabilising consequences.

Ballot

Derived from the term "ballotta," a round bullet. This word eventually came to mean a voice or a lot used in the act of voting, usually in secret, by written or printed tickets or slips of paper.

Barā'ah

This terms is used to denote the immunity and innocence of someone from guilt and blame. Sometimes it may denote free, clear and discharge from any suspicion.

Barā'ah al-dhimmah al-aṣliyyah

Presumption of original freedom from liability. It means freedom from obligations until the contrary is proved. No person may thus be compelled to perform any obligation unless the law requires so. Similarly, no one is liable to punishment until his guilt is established through lawful evidence.

Ba'athism

A pan-Arab ideology based on Arab socialism and nationalism. The ideology was developed by two French-educated Syrian activists in the early 1940s: Salah al-Din al-Bitar and Michel Aflaq. According to Aflaq, Arabs are a cultural community united by a common language. The ultimate goal of the doctrine was Arab unity. As an ideology, Ba'athism had little confidence in gradual reform through pluralistic politics. Rather, Ba'athists believed that revolution was the correct way to awaken the Arab spirit and the renaissance of the Arab nation. Although a Greek Orthodox Christian, Aflaq viewed Islam as part of Arabism. The party began in Syria but it soon spread to other Arab countries. Dreams of Ba'athists to forge political unity never materialized because of deep-seated animosities and rivalries.

Basic Democracies

A scheme in Pakistan wherein people were allowed to choose an Electoral College that would elect legislatures, local government councillors and the country's president. The Basic Democracies scheme, according to President Ayub Khan who introduced it in Pakistan, aimed at developing local leadership at the grassroot level, so that democracy was not foisted on the people from above but grew from within. The scheme consisted of a four-tier structure was dismantled in 1969 when President Ayub was forced to step down due to protests and demonstrations.

Bāṭil

Invalid, null and void of something in juridical sense. It refers to the performance of an act that disagrees with commands as desired by the lawgiver. When the performance of the rituals, for instance, disagrees with his commands as desired by him, they are invalid. According to al-Shafii, *bātil* and *fāsid* are synonymous terms denoting what is not valid. The majority of the jurists are of the view that an act, whether ritual or a transaction, is either valid or *bātil*. There is no other category between the two. The Hanafis divide transaction or contract into three kinds: *sahih* (valid), *fasid* (irregular) and *batil* (invalid).

Behaviouralism

A movement in post-World War II political science, concerned with shifting the emphasis of political studies away from its traditional legal-institutional manifestation and generating theories about the political world. It emphasizes the systematic understanding of all identifiable manifestations of political behaviour. It stresses the application of rigorous scientific and statistical methods to standardize testing and attempt value-free inquiry of the world of politics. In short, it aims at rendering the study of politics more scientific.

Bicameralism

Refers to the principle that legislature should consist and often do consist of two houses. A legislative body made of two separate houses (sometimes called upper and lower house) is bicameral. A single-house legislative body is unicameral. Today, unicameral legislatures outnumber bicameral assemblies by a ratio of three to two. Bicameralism permits a system of dual representation for the constituent parts of the union; prevents concentration of legislative power in one assembly, and provides a second forum for deliberating legislation. The US, Canada, and Malaysia, among others, have bicameral legislatures. The largest number of unicameral legislatures is found in Africa, Asia and the Middle East.

Bicameral legislature

A legislature that is divided into two houses or branches.

Bid'ah

Innovation, a belief or practice for which there is no precedent at the time of the Prophet (SAW). It is the opposite of sunnah. A clear distinction must be made between a *bid'ah* which is "good" (*ḥasanah*) or praise worthy (*Mahmudah*) and the one which is "bad" (*Sayyiáh*) or blameworthy. Al-Shafii maintains that any innovation contrary to Qur'an and Sunnah is an erring innovation.

Bill

A bill is a legislative document in the form of proposed Act that is introduced to parliament for discussion and consideration. Explanatory memoranda are usually released when a Bill is introduced to parliament. Explanatory memoranda detail the purpose of the bill and the proposed sections or clauses.

Bill of rights

Refers to the first ten amendments made to the constitution of the United States. These amendments were ratified in 1791 in response to fears over a too-strong national government and provide numerous restrictions on the national government. Important rights include protection against government limit on speech and the press, unreasonable searches and seizures, and the right to a speedy trial.

Bipolarity

A world configuration in which there are two centres of power. Analysts describe global politics between World War II until 1989 as bipolar: a division between two contending and enormously powerful superpowers, the United States and the Soviet Union. Many analysts have argued about the relative stability of bipolar world. The nuclear balance of terror between the two superpowers was the best guarantee against instability and a general nuclear war.

Black Market

A situation in which there is illegal selling of goods at prices above a legal maximum set by the government. It occurs due to relative scarcity of the goods concerned and the existence of an excess demand for them at the established price.

Bloc voting

Members of a group voting pretty much alike for a candidate or party. When an organized labour overwhelmingly supports a candidate of a particular political party, for instance, this is considered bloc voting.

Bolshevism

Political doctrine and practice of the Bolshevik party which, under the leadership of V. I. Lenin, seized power during the Russian revolution of 1917. The Bolsheviks were the proponents of the wing of the Russian Social Democratic Labour Party (RSDLP) led by Lenin. The name originated in 1903 when the central committee of the RSDLP split over the criteria of party membership. Lenin called his supporters Bolsheviks (from the Russian word for majority) and his opponents Mensheviks (from the word for minority). The party seized the state in the revolution of October 1917. In March 1918, the name was changed to Russian Communist Party. The Bolsheviks later founded the Third (Communist) International, while the Mensheviks remained affiliated to the Second (Socialist) International.

Bonapartism

Following the practices of Napoleon Bonaparte (1769–1821), general and emperor of France (1804–1814). Historically, Bonapartism stood for strong leadership and conservative nationalism. The political legacy of Bonapartism includes two basic concepts. One is "benevolent dictatorship," or strong leadership that serves the interests of the state. The second is the presumed ability of such strong leadership to overcome parliamentary paralysis or parliamentary responsibility. However, it was Karl Marx who gave the term its specific meaning. To him, Bonapartism was an opportunistic alliance between part of the capitalist class and working classes in order to secure legitimacy for the Bourgeois regime.

Boundaries

The outer perimeter of a defined area, especially one established for political purposes. In politics, the term refers not only to the circumference of a state's defined territory, but also more widely to other spatially defined circumferences (such as those of sub-state units and tracts of private property). Boundaries have become increasingly important in recent centuries as competition for land has increased and the nation-state has become a dominant player in the world economy.

Bourgeois hegemony

Bourgeois rule usually by means other than brute force. According to Antonio Gramsci, an Italian communist, the bourgeoisie rules not by force, but through a widely proliferated ideology that legitimizes its rule through processes of education, socialization, and mass communication in a variety of institutions, thereby destroying proletarian class-consciousness and the possibility for a genuine revolutionary change.

Bourgeoisie

A term that originally referred to "those who dwell in the city" (and are middle class). Karl Marx used it to refer to that socio-economic class in capitalist society that owns the means of production (land, banks, factories, natural resources, etc.). Usually bourgeoisie consists of factory owners, bankers, merchants, and lawyers. See PROLETARIAT.

Brinkmanship

The technique or practice of manoeuvring a dangerous situation to the limits of tolerance or safety in order to secure the greatest advantage. This technique or policy is usually associated with the cold war practice of the two superpowers where one of them would initiate a conflict involving a potential escalation into a general thermonuclear war. Such a policy of going to the brink of war was followed in the hope that the rival would be forced into making concessions on the issue in question e.g., the Cuban Missile

Crisis of October 1962. See INTERNATIONAL RELATIONS.

Broker parties

Parties whose main goal is to win elections and who therefore appeal to as broad a spectrum of interests and ideologies as possible. Leading examples of such parties are the Democratic and Republican parties of the United States. They are also known as catch-all parties. They measure their success not by looking if their ideology is rigidly followed by their rank and file but by the number of candidates they have succeeded in getting elected.

Budget

An estimate, often itemized, of expected income and expenditure, or operating results for a given period in the future, usually one year. The budget is annually prepared by the executive branch of government and then is presented to the parliament for its approval.

Budgeting

The method of deciding on the financial resources necessary to meet the cost of given policy goals. The process of modern budgeting originated in France at the time of the restoration of the monarchy in 1815, when the old system was replaced by a systematic method of presenting to legislature an evaluation of government fiscal needs and ways of raising the required finances. Following that, it was agreed that this process should take place annually and that by the end of the fiscal year, the accounts of an implemented budget should be verified by official audit.

Bureaucracy

It refers both to a way of conducting business in an organization and to organizations in government ("the bureaucracy"). In a bureaucracy a clear division of labour exists; power is organized hierarchically; the qualifications for each are specified; and rules are well defined and administered objectively.

Bush Doctrine

The **Bush Doctrine** refers to the set of new foreign policies adopted by President of the United States George W. Bush in the wake of the September 11, 2001 terrorist attacks. The salient elements of the Bush Doctrine include: (1) A policy of preemptive war, should the US or its allies be threatened by terrorists or rogue states that are engaged in the production of weapons of mass destruction (2) The right for the US to pursue unilateral military action when acceptable multi-lateral solutions cannot be found. (3) A policy that "America has, and intends to keep, military strengths beyond challenge." (4) A policy of actively promoting democracy and freedom in all regions of the world. The new policy was fully delineated in a National Security Council text entitled the *National Security Strategy of the United States* issued on September 17, 2002.

Buwayhid or Buyid

The most important dynasty to control the Iranian plateau and Iraq between the early Arab conquest and the Turkish conquest of the 11th century. Its name derives from the Buwayh (also written Buyah), the father of the three brothers who founded the dynasty.

C

Cabinet / cabinet government

A group of the most senior and powerful ministers in a government or advisors to the president, who meet regularly to discuss and take policy decisions. The cabinet is usually not spelled out in the constitution and membership can be changed.

Cadre

A military term that refers to the key group of officers and enlisted men, necessary to establish and train a new military unit. Later, this term was applied to communist political parties to refer to a cell of professional party leaders, or to a member of such a cell. Within the context of the Russian Revolution the initiation of that concept reflected the need of the revolution's leadership to create a disciplined, hierarchically organized, and swiftly responsive system to control the revolutionary change.

Cadre party

A type of a party in which a small group of notables dominates party decisions, such as securing nominations and dispensing patronage. The Communist party of the Soviet Union is an example of a cadre party.

Campaign

Organized efforts that link a variety of components together to achieving specifically defined objectives especially that of winning an election. A typical election campaign would include programmes for fund raising, volunteer recruitment, and voter contact. See ELECTION.

Camp David

The US presidential retreat outside Washington D.C. where numerous Middle East negotiations have been held. The location became famous for the 1978 Camp David peace accords, brokered by President Jimmy Carter, between Israel and Egypt. In the resulting compromise Egypt recognized Israel as a nation and Israel withdrew from the territory captured in 1967. In the context of the Palestinian-Israeli conflict, Camp David is commonly a reference to the failed attempt by President Bill Clinton to achieve a similarly historic final settlement between Israel and the Palestinians.

Candidate

The person seeking election to office. The candidate is at the core of the election campaign and is most effective in contacting voters, contributors, volunteers and others.

Capitalism

The economic system of free enterprise based on private ownership producing for profit in the open market. In it, productive property such as land and factories is privately owned and individuals have extensive liberties to work, invest, trade, and consume as they like, constrained only by their natural capacities and economic resources.

Caste

Division of society into closed groups, primarily by birth, but usually also involving religion and occupation. Deriving from the Portuguese word "casta," the caste was originally used to designate traditional divisions within the Hindu population. The Hindu caste system divides the society into four social divisions, the Brahman, the Kshatriya, Vaisya, and Sudra. The system exhibits several characteristics. It is endogamous, limiting marriage to partners of one's own caste. It is also hereditary and restrictive, limiting other kinds of social contact between members of different caste. It is a hierarchical system in which Brahmans occupy the pyramidal position. Members of the high castes could be contaminated by touch or other association with persons from lower castes. Each caste has its own privileges and limitations and is transferred by inheritance from one generation to the next. The caste system dates from 3000 B.C. and plays an important role in the Indian political system.

Castroism

Theory and practice associated with Fidel Castro, Cuban Lawyer, revolutionary and the Cuban premier since 1959. Castro led an abortive revolution in 1953 against dictator Fulgencio Batista, and was imprisoned and exiled. In 1956, he invaded Cuba with about 81 men, overthrew Batista's government, and established himself as premier. As a doctrine, Castroism emphasizes nationalism, democracy, and social justice. This translated itself in the nationalization of industry and collectivization of agriculture, becoming increasingly dependent upon the Soviet Union for financial support. The continuous U.S. attempts to isolate Cuba and to overthrow the Castro regime have not achieved success.

Catch-all parties

The parties that have no clear or specific ideologies. They direct their appeals for votes at all major population groups. They are more concerned with winning elections here and now than with eventually making permanent converts. See BROKER PARTIES

Caucus

In general, a political meeting. In reality, it refers to a closed meeting of the members of a political party, either to select a candidate for office or to discuss a legislative position. Though once the most popular method of selecting nominees for public office in the U. S., caucuses were strongly criticized as being undemocratic.

Caudillo

Translated as "strong man" or "man on horse back." A characteristic form of leadership in Hispanic nations, in which authority attaches to the individual, rather than to the institutions which he or she represents.

Cell

A small group of people who have been specially trained and organized to work together as part of a larger organization. For instance, a Trotskyist cell within the labour organization.

Censorship

The practice by government of limiting the expression of ideas before they are expressed. The policy of prohibiting the circulation of any printed matter or the production of books, plays, films, or reports considered by the government to be prejudicial to the interest of the people or the country. In mature democracies, censorship is very rare and is usually permitted in wartime and where national security or criminal prosecutions are involved.

Central Intelligence Agency (CIA)

U.S. government agency created as an adjunct of the National Security Council by the National Security Act of 1947. The CIA superseded the U.S. National Intelligence Authority and Central Intelligence Group created in 1946. Its objective is to coordinate, evaluate, and disseminate intelligence from other U.S. agencies and to advise the President and the National Security Council on security matters. The CIA has done much in terms of clandestine activities to further U.S. interests, particularly, during the Cold War years. It has been involved in overthrowing legally established governments, assassinating political personalities and undermining the legitimacy of governments if they go against the U.S. dictates. Over the decades its power has grown and it has developed a large staff to carry out its activities. The CIA operates in almost all countries of importance. Every U.S. embassy houses a CIA station whose personnel pass as State Department people. Part of their duties include keeping tabs on underground happenings in the host country and trying to influence them, contacting opposition groups, funding local friends, and maintaining a surveillance of hostile embassies.

Centralisation

The concentration of administrative authority in a central government as opposed to the sharing of power and responsibilities between national, regional, and local authorities.

Centralised Planning

The determination by the state of what shall be produced and how factors of production shall be allocated among different uses. In a free enterprise economy, consumers decide what shall be produced through their demands. While maximum amount of capital planning is found in socialist economies, less developed countries and developed countries do show an increasing state planning in an attempt to maintain full employment. Central planning is done at the "center" and then dictated to various sections in the economy.

Charisma

A personal quality to attract, influence, and inspire deep political loyalty in large number of people.

Charter

A state law or specific legal document that creates a local governmental unit such as a town or city. Charters spell out the powers and responsibilities of these units, their jurisdiction and their method of operation. Sometimes it is understood to include pertinent judicial decisions and constitutional and statutory provisions.

Chartist movement

A group of reformers who sought further to democratize English politics during the nineteenth century. Among their goals were less restrictive voting rights (approaching universal suffrage), equal electoral district, and abolition of property qualifications for holding office.

Chauvinism

Excessive, almost obsessive, patriotism expressed in the phrase "my country right or wrong." A strong and unreasonable belief that one's own country or race is more important and morally better than others.

Checks and balances

Checks and balances are the means by which the principle of separation of powers in the constitution is implemented. The constitution in general separates the powers of government into three different kinds of activities: law making, administration or enforcement, and judging. However, the distribution of power is so devised that one element of government exercises some degree of power over the other. Its purpose is to prevent one part of government (for instance, the executive) from dominating another part of government (for example, the legislature). The system of checks and balances prevents unilateral and quick action and thus ensures that policy decisions are fully deliberated.

Christian democracy

A postwar political movement in Western Europe, and to a lesser degree, Latin America.

Its ideological roots lie in the galvanization of Catholics in reaction to the rise of liberal capitalism in the nineteenth century. Catholic interest groups emerged to defend such institutions as the family and a harmonious social order against the onslaught of industrialization and liberalism. This ideology was promoted at the end of World War II by the Allies partly to counter communism. Consequently, Christian Democrats won office in Italy, Germany, France, Austria, Belgium and Holland. As the danger of communism receded, the tide of Christian Democracy weakened by the 1970s. However, by the 1980s, these groups enjoyed resurgence as part of the general conservative swing of European electorates.

Church and state

Refers to the relationship between church and state. In theory, the Western governments follow the principle that there will be no overlap between the powers of organized religion and of government. Thus in the U.S., the First Amendment prohibits the government from either establishing a religion or limiting religious freedoms. In practice, however, a complete separation of church and state has been impossible. Therefore, in some countries the two are closely tied together – the government enforces religious laws, financially supports the religion, and favours one religion over all others. Islam, being an organic religion, does not compartmentalize the human life into temporal and spiritual domains. Islam governs all aspects of the believer's life and it also constitutes the essential basis and focus of identity of the follower and his loyalty to the community. The emphasis in Islam is on unity, which explicitly refers to the oneness of the Creator and His Lordship but implicitly provides for the totality and universality of the Islamic belief system. See SECULARISM.

Citizen

A person who has the legal status of being a full member of a particular nation. He or she is loyal to the nation, receives its protection and enjoys the right to participate in its political process.

Citizenship

The conception by which individuals are given membership, rights, and responsibilities in a political community, a city or a nation-state. It is conferred upon individuals by governments, which retain the sole authority to determine the criteria for citizenship and the benefits that flow from that status. Citizenship is of two kinds, natural and naturalized. Natural citizenship is governed by the principles of **Jus Sanguinis** (in which a child follows the nationality of his parents or one of them), and **Jus Soli** (in which a child born within the state becomes a citizen). Majority of the states follow the principle of **Jus Sanguinis**. There are, however, some states, like Britain and the United States that follow both principles. A citizenship acquired by an alien through application and fulfilment of certain requirements is called naturalized citizenship. Citizens in democracies have both rights and responsibilities as active participants within the civil community.

City government

A state-defined unit of government that has certain legal responsibilities and rights. See UNITARY GOVERNMENT

Civic culture

A system in which a participant political culture is balanced by the survival of subject and parochial attitudes. In the civic culture, the citizen is active enough in politics to express his or her preferences to government but is not so involved in particular issues as to refuse to accept the decisions made by the elite. The citizen feels capable of influencing the government but often chooses not to do so, thus giving the government a measure of flexibility. The term was popularized in the early 1960s by Gabriel Almond and Sidney Verba in their now classic five-nation study called *The Civic Culture*.

Civil defence

Public safety activity of governments which is designed in the event of an enemy attack to minimize damage, provide essential services and information, maintain law and order, and reconstruct damaged areas.

Civil disobedience

A purposeful and public defiance of an established law or norm, undertaken with the intent of altering state policy. Non-violent disruptive actions, usually based on moral principles, are used to emphasize presumptive injustices. Civil disobedience is an intermediate step between dissent and resistance. The best known practitioner of this doctrine is Mahatma Gandhi in his struggle for independence of India from British rule in the 1940s. He called it *satyagarha*. Its leading American practitioner was Dr. Martin Luther King. In the 1960s, civil disobedience was used by Vietnam protesters and by the legendary boxer Muhammad Ali. The purpose of Muhammad Ali's action was both to protest the government's "morally wrong" Vietnam policies and to generate public sympathy for a cause. Those who commit civil disobedience are willing to accept the punishment for their actions. Muhammad Ali was stripped of his boxing championship belt. Civil disobedience is frequently used interchangeably with similar concepts such as non-violent resistance, non-violent direct action, and passive resistance, in discussions of structured opposition to laws or governmental policies that are perceived to be unjust or immoral.

Civil law

A body of statutes (laws) regulating relationships among private individuals. Civil law is in contrast to criminal law, in which an individual is prosecuted by the government for an offence, in principle, against the people.

Civil liberties

Rights that protect individuals, opinions, and property against arbitrary interference by government. A law that prohibits government from taking private property without proper procedure and just compensation is an example of civil liberty. Many civil liberties are usually spelled out in the constitution or in laws, but some are protected on the basis of a long legal tradition (such as the right to privacy). Like all rights, civil liberties can be restricted under certain conditions.

Civil rights

Governmental guarantees to protect individuals against discrimination or arbitrary action by other individuals or groups. A law that provides freedom from racial or sexual discrimination in employment is an example of a civil right. It is also used to refer to those rights that assure minority groups equality before the law.

Civil service

Non-military administrators paid for implementing the policies of governments. The institution dates back to ancient China. Modern theory of civil service emphasizes basic principles: entrance and promotion on merit; full-time, life-long career; division of tasks into intellectual and routine; and, a tradition of political neutrality.

Civil society

Set of intermediate organizations occupying the space between the state and the family. It consists of all associations bigger than the family but smaller than the state such as the market, private or voluntary organizations, activities and associations. The standard usage is derived from Hegel. Building civil society has been seen as an important prerequisite for democracy.

Civil war

A war fought between different geographical areas, political divisions, or ideological factions within the same country. A civil war is a war taking place within the borders of a single nation. Minor or isolated civil wars have the potential to lure in major powers, thereby escalating the destructiveness of the conflict and even at time endangering international peace e.g., Korea, Vietnam, Cambodia, Lebanon, Nigeria and Sudan. One variety of civil war is guerilla war.

Class

For Marx, it is vertical groupings based on the ownership of the means of production (Marx). In general usage it refers to the level of social stratification e.g., upper, middle, and lower class. Classes lack the rigid boundaries characterizing caste, so that mobility between classes is possible.

Class conflict

Historical conflict between the ruling class and the oppressed class. According to Marxist social theory, the struggle between these classes accounts for social and historical development. Class conflict is the motive force behind history.

Class-consciousness

The awareness of social divisions in society and the acceptance that class strongly determines life chances. At the individual level, it refers to the awareness of belonging to a definite class and a conscious knowledge of the political interests of that class.

Classical liberalism

Often called "nineteenth-century liberalism" to distinguish it from contemporary liberalism, this worldview emphasizes individual liberty, free-market or capitalist economies, limited government, and representative democracy. See LIBERALISM.

Classless society

Marx's vision of the post historical society in which there will be no distinguishable socioeconomic classes, because the division of labor that establishes such classes will no longer exist. The society will be based on the principle: "From each according to his ability, to each according to his needs." Every person will be free to labor in the creative, nonalienated manner that Marx envisions as natural, desirable state for human beings. In such a society the state will "wither away."

Clientelism

A symbiotic relationship between governmental or political elites (patrons) and groups of privileged clients within the polity or society. The word is of ancient derivation: in Rome, "cliens" denoted a plebeian under the patronage of a patrician, in this relation called a patron, "patronus," who was obliged to protect his client's interests. The clientele relationship is one of mutual (though not equal) benefits. The patron provides desirable jobs and job security, or various other kinds of political favours (such as preferential treatment by governmental agencies) in exchange for political and material support from clients. In some countries, clientelism strengthens the basic political or societal structures. Political scientists discuss modern clientelism under a number of different guises, including patrimonialism and patronage.

Coalition

Individuals and groups whose members cooperate with one another to realize common political objectives. A coalition may be formed by several groups that work in the same general policy area.

Cohabitation

Cooperation between parties for specific goals without actually forming a coalition. It represents a conflictual relationship, but one involving collaboration where there is an overlap of responsibilities. Cohabitation took place in France in 1986 between a socialist president F. Mitterand and the government, dominated by the right under J. Chirac. It was a critical test for the Constitution of the Fifth Republic which withstood it successfully. Likewise, the socialist Prime Minister Lionel Jospin was forced to cooperate with the conservative President Jaceques Chirac after the 1997 legislative election ended the parliamentary rule of Chirac's Gaullists and ushered a left-wing coalition into government.

Cold War

The period between 1945 and 1989 in which the world was basically bipolar and marked by loyalty to either the United States and its allies or the Soviet Union and its allies. It involved intense hostility which verged upon, but never deteriorated, into a "hot" war. The Cold War began in the 1940s when the U.S. believed it was imperative to check Soviet expansionist designs on Western Europe. It reached its height during the 1950s and the 1960s, when the threat of nuclear annihilation hung over the world, particularly during the Cuban missile crisis in 1962. The Cold War made itself felt all over the globe; it was as if the entire world was divided into two units, East and West. No small regional Third World conflict was insignificant. The U.S. backed any regime that was anti-communist; while the Soviets tried to expand their influence anywhere they could, from Cuba and Central America to the Middle East and Africa. The Cold War eased slightly in the 1970s as a result of the U.S.-Soviet policy of détente. It finally began to wind down in the late 1980s. In 1985, Mikhail Gorbachev came to power in the Soviet Union and began his policies of *glasnost* (openness) and *perestroika* (restructuring). The Soviet Union and the U.S. agreed to wide-ranging arms control measures. Then, when communism crumbled in Eastern Europe in 1989, without resistance from Moscow, U.S.-Soviet relations warmed dramatically. By 1990, the Cold War was virtually over.

Collective Leadership

Leadership provided by a collective body. A practice of the Communist Party of the Soviet Union following the death or ouster of the party leader. The purpose being to avoid any sense of a power vacuum until a new general secretary is nominated. This was used after Lenin's death in 1924, after Stalin's death in 1953, and following the ouster of Khruschev in 1964.

Collective Responsibility

Practised in a parliamentary system where all members of the cabinet are collectively held accountable for the acts of any single cabinet member. If a cabinet member cannot support the decisions of the government, he or she is expected to resign.

Collective Security

A machinery for joint action in order to prevent or counter any attacks against an established world order. Collective security is the peace keeping doctrine of both the League of Nations and the United Nations, which held that an attack against one was an attack against all and should be defeated by the collective action of all. The logic of the concept is simple and well-founded: no state can stand up to all of the other members of the system together, and that aggression will be permanently deterred. Collective security requires certain conditions to be met: one, all states must accept the status quo; two, all states must agree on a clear definition of aggression; three, all states must be willing to commit part of their armed forces to be used against aggression; and four, all states must prevent any breaches of sanctions imposed on an aggressor. The League of Nations failed to implement this policy because of the inability to meet these conditions. For most of the cold war period, the United Nations failed to apply this principle because of super power polarization. It was only after the end of the cold war, and after a lot of arms twisting by the US, that the international organization effectively applied the principle e.g., against Iraq in 1991.

Collectivisation

A view that private ownership of land would be replaced by public ownership or control.

Collectivism

A political system in which factories, farms, offices, etc., are owned and controlled by the state or all the people in a country.

Collectivist Soviet state

Refers to the state Joseph Stalin established in 1929 in the Soviet Union, in which all industrial property was nationalized, all agricultural activities collectivized, and the national economy was controlled by a powerful, centralized bureaucracy.

Colonialism

From the Latin word for farmer "colonus." The practice by which a powerful, technologically advanced country controls less powerful countries and exploits their resources in order to increase its own power and wealth. Often the rulers and colonial subjects are of different races and belong to different cultures. Colonialism dates to the Phoenicians; Rome was the largest ancient colonizer. As a vehicle for European imperialism and expansion, modern colonialism dates from 1500. The late-nineteenth century imperialists, the Western nations, conquered large tracts of Africa and Asia in search of cheap raw materials, cheap labour and new markets.

Command economy

A system in which decisions about production and distribution are centralized in the hands of the government or of a few monopolists. See COMMUNISM.

Commission

A document issued to an officer in the army, navy, and air force by the government giving him or her authority to serve in the armed services and give military orders.

Committee

Committees are small workgroups of members, set up in almost all legislative assemblies to cope with the volume of business. Their functions include the detailed consideration of legislative measures and examination of financial proposals. They also scrutinize government administration and past expenditure, and investigate matters of public concern.

Common law

A collection of customs and principles based on previous judicial rulings. It is usually contrasted to statute law, which is made by legislatures. Common law grew out of English custom and became established mainly by the adherence of judges to precedents. Common law can be incorporated into statutes, but some common law remains outside of official codification. A statute, however, always prevails over a common law or customary law.

Commonwealth

Derived from the phrase "common weal" (meaning public good) which the English philosopher Thomas Hobbes used to describe the collective interests of the members of a society. The term commonwealth signifies a collection of countries (or other entities) that regularly and formally consult each other, coordinate their policies, and otherwise join in association for mutual benefit. Some form of historical, cultural, or ideological ties typically bind the various members together. In this sense, the best example is the Commonwealth of Nations, which comprises the United Kingdom and almost fifty states which were once colonies, of the British Empire. The purpose of this organization is to coordinate policies and otherwise consult on issues of concern. It was created after World War I as the British colonies were increasingly granted political equality and ultimately independence. The Commonwealth might therefore be seen as a kinder and gentler successor to the British Empire. Membership in it is strictly voluntary; several former colonies have chosen to remain outside of it.

Communalism

A society divided along ethnic, linguistic and religious lines and that such divisions colour various social, economic and political institutions. People carry out their daily activities within their respective subcultures. Each community has separate schools and associations such as trade unions and political parties reflect the diverse pattern. The classic case is India where different subcultures live in different quarters of cities. Conflicts are more often expressed in communal riots. Communalism also refers to a theory or system of government according to which each commune is virtually an independent state and the nation is but a federation of such communes.

Communism

A collectivist social system in which the means of production are owned by the state and in which the products of society are distributed according to need. Karl Marx and his followers held that communist revolution was historically inevitable. With material abundance and property held in common, communism should be untainted by the exploitation and class conflict inherent in capitalism. In its final stage, communism means a classless and, therefore, stateless society.

Communist Manifesto

The most influential political document written by Karl Marx and F. Engels which ran into over a thousand editions. It is polemical in tone denouncing the rottenness of Western capitalism and civilization and attacking the socialists for opposing Marxism. Most importantly, it is a revolutionary call to the working class to win the world since they "have nothing to lose but their chains." The Manifesto also explains the necessity of establishing "proletarian internationalism" as a programme of world order and peace. The Manifesto has long out-lived its validity and purposes since 1848, and its value is chiefly historical.

Community

A group of people within a larger society sharing similar customs, interests, characteristics or beliefs. Biologists define communities as ecological entities consisting of interdependent populations of flora (plants) and fauna (animals). Traditional conservative thought emphasizes the idea that community is based upon commonality of origin—the blood, kinship, and historic ties—of a people living in a particular location as the Polish community in Chicago. Liberals, on the other hand, see communities as based on the freely chosen congregations of individuals bound together by common interests and needs e.g., the "financial community" or the "medical community."

Community power

This relates to the question of where political power resides within a community. Who makes authoritative decisions for the community? The debate over this issue proved sterile and inconclusive. Some authors suggest that power in a community is dominated by business elites; others (the pluralists) suggest that power within a community is dispersed among interested communities.

Comparative Government

The part of the discipline of political science that concerns making comparisons between and among the institutions, constitutions, processes, policies, and functions of governments.

Comparative Politics

The sub-discipline of political science that involves a search for similarities and differences between and among political phenomena including political institutions (such as legislatures, political parties, interest groups), political behaviour (such as, voting, campaigning, or demonstrating), or a set of political ideas (known also as ideologies like liberalism, nationalism, or Marxism).

Compulsory Voting

Electoral participation by qualified voters that is required by law as used in Australia, Belgium, the Netherlands, Austria, Brazil, Italy, and other states.

Confederacy

A loose-knit cooperative alliance among essentially independent political units whose major purpose, as a rule, is effective common defense. The minimal common government deals only with the unit governments and not with individual citizens.

Confederation

A loose association of regional units in which sovereign power is retained by the regional units rather than residing in the central government. The central government has no direct jurisdiction over individuals, consequently. Prior to the adoption of the Constitution, for example, the United States was governed as a confederation. To a considerable extent, the United Nations and the Organization of Islamic Conference may be classified as a confederation today, since power and sovereignty are retained by the countries that make up the membership of the two organizations. The Commonwealth of Independent States—composed of twelve of the republics that made up the old Soviet Union – is the most recent example of a confederation.

Conflict Resolution

A set of practices and procedures available to any government that serves to defuse, reduce, settle, or even to avoid disputes and tensions with other governments. Methods for handling conflict involve various procedures, which are usually classified by the number of conflict management agents or parties involved. In unilateral conflict resolution, one party tries to resolve a conflict without negotiating with another party. Bilateral conflict resolution can involve mutual coercion, including force or threats of force. Multilateral conflict resolution occurs when third parties intervene into ongoing conflict situations to assist in conflict resolution. The three forms of third-party conflict resolution are pacific settlement, collective security, and peaceful change.

Congress

The legislative branch of the United States federal government. The US Congress consists of the House of Representatives and the Senate. It also includes several agencies created by Congress to help formulate legislation and monitor the implementation of laws.

Consensus Democracy

A political system in which power is diffused throughout the government and the parties. It is the polar opposite of Majoritarianism. Under consensus democracy, executive authority is shared among members of a formal or informal coalition, drawn from various parties. The executive does not dominate the legislature as it does under majority democracy. There is a multi-party, rather than a two-party, system. The party system reflects several dimensions of cleavage rather than only one. Elections are typically held under proportional representation rather than first-past-the-post.

Consent

Assent, approval, acquiescence or agreement. It is the approval or attachment of an individual's will to a proposal, such that the individual accepts responsibility for the consequences. In the absence of consent, an action or state of affairs would be void and lack legitimacy and legality. The presence of consent has been a critical test of political legitimacy e.g., an authority would have no right to direct an individual's behaviour unless his/her consent to be governed had been granted.

Conservatism

Less an ideology than a cast of mind. Conservatives reject social engineering for its own sake; they accept that people are imperfect, different and unequal. The wisdom of the past is secreted in society's traditions and institutions; these should be respected. Change is therefore justified only where it is clearly necessary. Conservatism has endured for approximately two centuries as a major branch of political philosophy. It emphasizes traditions, authority, legitimacy, and the concept that government reflects human nature.

Conservationism

Conservationism is a homocentric approach to the environment that emphasizes the rational management and use of natural resources. Wilderness, for example, is to be protected, because it provides enjoyment, employment, and resources for humans.

Consociational democracy

A system of democracy applicable in societies characterized by cultural, religious, or ethnic differences. In consociational democracy, majority rule is replaced by consensual rule. In such a system, the working principles are grand coalitions, proportionality, segmental autonomy and mutual veto. Consociational systems exist, for example, in Austria, Lebanon, Netherlands, Malaysia, and some other countries.

Constituency

A legislative district from which an individual or group of individuals is chosen to represent in a public fashion the interest of people, known as constituents.

Constitution

The basic rules of a political system or organization. A set of rights, powers and procedures regulating the structure of, and relationships among, the public authorities, and between the public authorities and the citizens. The constitution could be written or unwritten. The first written constitution of the world is provided by Prophet Muhammad (SAW) and is known as "The Constitution of Madinah" or *Dastur al-madinah.*

Constitutional Democracy

A government in which freely expressed public opinion and free elections provide both the foundations of governmental authority and the basic institutionalized restraints on the exercise of governmental power.

Constitutional Law

Section of the law that interprets and enforces the provisions of the Constitution of the state. It is the set of rules that define the distribution of governmental powers. A wide range of matters fit into this definition e.g., law relating to the legislative, the executive and the judicial branch are all relevant to constitutional law. Two guiding principles distinguish constitutional law: the legislative sovereignty of parliament, and the supremacy of the constitution over ordinary law.

Constitutional Monarchy

A political system that has a royalty as ceremonial head of state, but assigns political power to the leader of a majority within parliament as in the United Kingdom and Malaysia. This concept is a result of the survival and adaptation of the figure of the monarch to modern democratic forms of government.

Constitutionalism

A system that limits the power of government, respects individual rights, and subjects both governors and governed to the same laws. In a constitutionally—governed state, government is limited by laws and institutions to make sure that the fundamental rights of citizens—such as freedom of speech and religion and freedom from arbitrary arrests and imprisonment—are not violated. An effective constitution, written or unwritten, is an essential ingredient of the legal order which may be called constitutionalism.

Containment

The strategy by which the United states attempted to restrict Soviet expansion through economic, political, and military means. George Kennan, an American diplomat who was in Moscow, coined the term in 1947. He advocated selective containment policy targeted on these regions of the world—western Europe, Japan, and the oil-rich Middle East—that were of vital geo-economic and thus geopolitical importance to the US. That became the official U.S. foreign policy under President Harry Truman. This policy was based on the premise that if the U.S. did not hold the anti-communist line everywhere, it would be challenged and eventually overrun everywhere. Containment as a policy translated itself in supplying massive aid to U.S. allies to help them resist communism and to sign a number of bilateral as well as multilateral defence pacts to fight international communism. Containment dominated the U.S. foreign policy for most of the years of the cold war. The policy, which remained intact for more than four decades, was apparently successful in that the Soviet empire dissolved and communism as a viable ideology was discredited.

Contemporary Conservatism

A prominent ideology that emerged after World War II and that is defined, in large part, by its opposition to communism, democratic socialism, and contemporary liberalism. It believes that strong liberal and socialist governments fail to solve the problems they address and, instead, create new economic and social problems, such as economic stagnation, bureaucratic red tape, a loss of individual initiative, and moral decay.

Contemporary Liberalism

A political outlook that both retains and modifies the ideals of classical liberalism. It celebrates certain older liberal values and goals such as individual freedom, expanding economy based largely on private initiatives, and a democratic political system. However, it departs from the classical liberal principle of limited government by believing that an active, problem-solving government can stimulate economic being for all citizens and enhance individual liberty. It also asserts that democratic institutions should represent the diversity of group interest that prevails in modern pluralist societies.

Contextualism

The view that the meaning of political ideas can be understood only by relating them to the historical contexts in which they were generated.

Convention

A meeting or formal assembly, as of representatives or delegates, for discussion of an action on particular matters of common concern. In the United States, it refers to a representative party assembly to nominate candidates and adopt platform and party rules.

Conventional Arms

All non-nuclear arms. It is divided into heavy weapons such as tanks, aircraft, heavy artillery, ship, and light weapons, such as rifles, side arms, and shoulder-held missiles that can be transported by one or two men. During the cold war era, the preponderance of conventional weapons remained in the hands of the two superpowers and their allies. Opposite of conventional arms, there are also weapons of mass destruction (WMD).

Conventions of the Constitution

Customs, precedents, and understandings which have resulted in rules concerning matters of fundamental political and constitutional importance. These conventions are not law. Yet they are being observed as though they were laws.

Convergence Thesis

The idea or belief that socialist and capitalist societies would inexorably grow more and more alike. The thesis is based on the argument, among others, that planning is essential for all societies and that planning and administrative control are, irrespective of their ideological complexion, essentially the same. Hence, all societies would eventually converge. This idea was formally developed by political scientists in the 1950s but foreshadowed by Max Weber and others much earlier.

Co-operatives

Associations of producers and consumers for the purpose of sharing among the members of profits that would otherwise go to intermediate businesses and individuals. The organized cooperative movement dates from the first half of the nineteenth century. Social reformers protested the exploitation of the workers associated with the Industrial Revolution and urged collective self-help. This socialist tradition flourished across the world: in farming, industry, and the service sector, and in the form of consumer societies and housing associations. Paradoxically, cooperatives are more common and successful in capitalist societies than under socialist systems.

Corporatism

A doctrine that refers to a system of interest intermediation linking producer interests and the state. The system recognizes the centrality of concerned interest groups and draws them into the policy-making process, both in the negotiation of policy stage and the stage of securing compliance from their members with the policy negotiated. Although the modern debate started in the 1970s, the idea of corporatism has a long history. After World War I, Mussolini placed the term at the centre of the Fascist Italian regime. As a result, corporatism suffered disrepute. The new generation of neocorporatists worked hard to strip corporatism of its fascist associations. They made a clear distinction between societal corporatism exercised in countries such as the Netherlands, Sweden and Switzerland, and state corporatism found in countries such as Mexico, Portugal and Spain as well as Fascist Italy. Much of the debate since the 1970s has focused on societal corporatism.

Coup d'etat

A French word for "a sudden strike, or blow, of a nation." Originally referred to illegal seizure or extension of power by an officeholder. Now includes any forceful overthrow of an existing government, whether by members of its own military forces or by armed revolutionaries. The term coup can also be used in a casual sense to mean a gain in advantage of one nation or entity over another; e.g. an *intelligence coup*. Coups have long been part of political tradition. Many Roman emperors came to power through coups. In the late 20th century, coups occurred most commonly in developing countries. Coups have often been a means for powerful nations to assure favourable outcomes in smaller foreign states. In particular, the American CIA is known for engineering coups in smaller states. See MARTIAL LAW.

Courts

Judicial tribunals established to administer justice. Courts are created by governments through constitutions or legislations for the purpose of applying and enforcing the law. The courts are established to be impartial forums for the resolution of controversies between parties.

Cuban Missile Crisis

The 1962 showdown between the United States and the Soviet Union over the latter's construction of nuclear missile bases in Cuba that were capable of attacking the United States, and much of Latin America. President Kennedy responded by placing all ships going to Cuba under quarantine and threatened retaliatory measure if attacked by the Soviet Union. Kennedy called for the prompt dismantling and removal of any offensive weapons in Cuba. Finally, after negotiations with Kennedy, Soviet Premier Khrushchev agreed to dismantle the missile sites and remove all weapons if the United States promised not to invade Cuba. It was a good face-saving solution, but it hurt Khrushchev in Kremlin politics and he was voted out of office two years later. See DIPLOMACY.

Cube Law (elections)

A mathematical relationship often purported to govern the relationship between seats and votes in a plurality electoral system. The cube law states that each party's share of seats will be proportional to its share of votes cubed. Cube law is not really a law but it may serve as a useful rule of thumb for understanding plurality elections.

Cult of personality

The promotion of a leader as the epitome of the revolution. Adulation of the wisdom and greatness of the leader on an all-embracing scale. A cult of personality develops when a political leader attracts followers because of his or her charisma, rather than because of the leader's views or opinions. Such leaders often have a dangerously strong hold on their subjects, since the public follows them for emotional rather than logical reasons.

Culture of Permissiveness

A critical appraisal of western culture during and after the 1960s by contemporary conservatives, who assert that contemporary liberalism has destroyed morality and authority by failing to assert an absolute standard of the good.

Cumulative Vote

A system of voting where voters have as many votes as there are representatives to be elected from a multimember district. The system allows a voter to cast one vote to each of a number of contestants or else to accumulate these votes upon one candidate. If every voter uses his rights ingenuously, this system of voting can be a critical test to judge the magnitude of the voter's support for different candidates. See VOTING.

D

***Dalīl* (pl. *adillah*)**

Literally, proof, evidence, indication. Technically, it is indication in the sources from which a practical rule of shari'ah is deduced. The indication of a proof is sometimes decisive (*qāt'ī*) and sometimes speculative (*ẓannī*) depending on the nature of the subject, clarity of the text, and the value which it seeks to establish.

Dār al 'ahd

Besides *dār al-Ḥarb* and *dār al-Islam*, some scholars of Islamic canon law recognize the existence of a third division, dar al-sulh, or al'ahd, which is not under Muslim rule, yet is in tributary relationship to Islam. One historical example of such a status is the Najran Christians with whom the Prophet (SAW) entered into treaty relationships, guaranteeing their safety and laying on them a certain tribute regarded by some jurists as *Kharāj* and by others as *jizyah*. See *DĀR AL ṢULH, DĀR AL-ISLAM*.

Dār al Ḥarb

In Muslim constitutional law, the World is divided into *dār al-ḥarb* and *dār al-Islam*. 'Abode of Islam' is that which is already under Muslim rule; "Abode of War" is that which is not, but which, actually or potentially, is a seat of war for Muslims until by conquest it is tuned into "Abode of Islam." Thus, to turn *dār al-ḥarb* into *dār al-Islam* is the object of jihad, and, theoretically, the Muslim state is in a constant state of warfare with the non-Muslim world. But practically, this is now impossible.

Dār al Sulh

An "abode of Islam" is a country where the ordinances of Islam are established and which is under the rule of a Muslim sovereign. Its inhabitants are Muslims and also non-Muslims who have submitted to Muslim control and who, under certain restrictions and without the possibility of full citizenship, are guaranteed their lives and property by the Muslim state, i.e., Dhimmis.

Dār al-Islam

It refers to the "Abode of Islam," meaning territories that are under Muslim control, territories where the divine responsibility of man could be performed according to the rules of *fiqh*. This is in contrast to *Dār al harb*, territories which have not enjoyed the benefits of shari'ah rule. This division of the world into two abodes is not found in the Qur'an or in the hadith. It was systematized by Muslim jurists during the development of *fiqh* (jurisprudence) and the enlargement of Muslims territories in order to specify the territories within which this juristic scheme could be applied. Such a division should not be regarded as a declaration of permanent war between the two abodes as some Orientalists argue, because according to Islam the normal and permanent state in international relations is the state of peace.

Ḍarūrah (pl. *darūriyyāt*)

Necessity, exigency, essentials. According to jurists, the essentials are those on which people's lives depend and their neglect leads to chaos and total disruption. There are five essential values: religion, life, intellect, lineage and property. These must be protected from threats of all kinds and must be promoted vigorously by an Islamic state.

Dustūr al Madīnah

Constitution of Madinah. A valuable document that has been preserved since Madinan times which is considered to be the first written constitution of the world. In it is spelled out the organization and structure of the newly formed Muslim polity in *Madīnah*. It restructured political life in Madinah according to the Islamic conception of the Ummah (section 2); recognised the Prophet (SAW) as the head of the new commonwealth (sections 23, 42), and defined his role as that of maintaining peace and order, arbitrating among groups in conflict; and of providing security from external attack (sections 37, 39, 40, 44). The Constitution confirmed the principle of equality, rejection of tyranny and equal protection of the law even to the humblest of believers (sections 15, 17). The Jews were considered a religious community (ummah) alongside the Muslims, sharing in the privileges as well as duties of life in a secure society. The remarkable thing about the Constitution of Madinah is that it transformed the warring and fractious tribes and clans into a solid community bound together not by kinship but by a common religious faith. See CONSTITUTION.

Da'wah

Literally, it means "to call" in vocation such as seeking Allah's (SWT) help. Generally, *da'wah* means the communication of Islam to Muslims as well as to non-Muslims. It is, in the words of the Qur'an, an invitation "to all that is good," and should be carried out with humility, wisdom and kindly manner. *Da'wah* can take different forms and levels. It can be through a profound intellectual discussion between two individuals. It can be through simple manifestation of Islamic behaviour in day to day activities. Islam definitely rules out *da'wah* through force. In the absence of a Church or clergy, *da'wah* becomes the responsibility of every Muslim man and woman. See ISLAM.

Dawlah

Alternations, rotation, change, dynasty, state, country, and empire. Generally, *dawlah* is used as an Arabic equivalent of the concept of nation-state. *Dawlah*, meaning a state, is neither used in the Qur'an nor was it in vogue at the time of the Prophet (SAAS). The early scholars used the terms *khilāfah* or imamah to denote the idea of a political order. The term dawlah gained currency in the early seventh century AH, and was employed with reference to the Muslim dynasties owing nominal allegiance to the powerless caliph. Another eight centuries had to elapse for the idea of an Islamic state to gain currency as an alternative to the caliphate. Although the term *dawlah* does not occur in the Qur'an, the essential elements that constitute a political order were referred to in the Qur'an which clearly indicate that the concept, if not the term, was meant in the Qur'an. See ISLAMIC STATE.

Decentralization

The distribution of power to lower levels in a territorial hierarchy whether the hierarchy is one of the governments within a state or offices within a large-scale organization. Or, more briefly, it refers to the aerial division of powers. So defined, the term encompasses both political and bureaucratic decentralization, federal and unitary states, and decentralization between levels of government and within units of government. See FEDERALISM, UNITARY GOVERNMENT.

Decision-Making

A process of identifying problems for decision, devising alternative courses of action, and choosing one alternative. It is distinguished from problem solving by requiring that problems and alternatives be formulated rather than given. It is also distinguished from policy making by (a) presence of sanctions to compel compliance with the decision and (b) including not only policy making in governmental or political organizations, but all kinds of decisional units.

Decision Theory

A theory of how individual actors should rationally behave under conditions of uncertainty and risk. It presupposes that individuals would make choices that would maximize their interests. The axioms of this theory have been widely challenged on theoretical and empirical grounds, however, so far no solid alternative has been formulated.

Declaration of the Rights of Man and the Citizen

A key philosophical document of the French Revolution, adopted by the French National Constituent Assembly in August 1789. It reflects the French Enlightenment's rejection of the role of absolute monarchy in favour of natural rights. The rights included equality, popular sovereignty, and individual rights to liberty, property, and freedom from arbitrary government abuse. This document inspired many democratic constitutions all over the world.

Deconcentration

Sometimes referred to as field administration. It involves the redistribution of administrative responsibilities within the central government.

Decree

An ordinance or edict promulgated by civil or other authority. In legal terms, it refers to judicial decisions. See LAW.

Decolonization

The forces of national self-determination that led to the rapid dwindling of empire and the birth of new, independent nation-states. See SELF-GOVERNMENT.

Deficit spending

An economic policy in which more money is spent than is received. The deficit (or money owed) is made up by government borrowing. Deficit spending is regarded as a cure for unemployment and underutilization of industrial capacity.

Deism

A religious and political philosophy during the seventeenth and eighteenth centuries, Deism holds that the human mind, through the study of nature, can discover the truth needed for a good life. With its emphasis on freedom and natural law, Deism anticipated the English, American, and French revolutions. While some scholars trace the antecedents of Deism to either the Renaissance Humanists or the left wing of the Protestant Reformation, most regard Edward Herbert (1583–1648) as its real father. Herbert propounded the five pillars of Deism. These principles are the existence of a Supreme Being, who created and governs the universe by natural law; the need for humans to worship this deity in whatever fashion their individual consciences dictated; toleration of religious diversity; repentance, the need for each person, using a rationally-informed conscience, to try to make good the wrong he had done to others; and a belief in immortality, grounded in the moral necessity for each person to be rewarded or punished in the hereafter for deeds done in earthly life. In simple terms, Deism is a religion without revelation, dogmas, churches, or formal worship and is based on the self-evident truths of nature as discovered by reason.

Delegate

An individual on whom another person or group confers the authority to act on his or their behalf. A delegate, therefore, is a representative. Delegation involves the notions of authorization, accountability and responsibility. One view concerning the particular character of the representative is that the delegate must represent the interests of his or her constituency whether or not he or she agrees with those interests. The other view holds that the representative is a trustee who votes on the basis of conscience in legislative considerations for those principles in which he or she believes. In short, the delegate is closely bound to reflect the wishes of those who elected him or her. The trustee, by contrast, uses independent judgement on behalf of the voters. Edmund Burke expressed the trustee approach.

Delegated Legislation

The authority delegated by the parliament to the executive arm of government or head of a department to make rules, regulations and by-laws connected with an Act of parliament. These rules do not pass through the full legislative scrutiny to which Acts of parliament are subjected. This is also known as "secondary legislation" as opposed to "primary legislation," legislation by parliament. Delegated legislation is accorded in order to administer and implement the requirements of primary legislation. In modern times, the amount and scope of delegated legislation has expanded due to the increasing pressure on parliamentary time. Proponents of secondary legislation suggest that it is an efficient way of assisting parliament; however, opponents suggest that it detracts from legislative autonomy.

Demagogue

A Leader who relies on highly emotional and usually irrational appeals to attract the immediate approval of the masses rather than to serve the needs of the country. Demagoguery is a political leader's use of strong emotional and personal appeals to call for political action, usually against a scapegoat of some sort.

Democracy

Derived from two Greek words: kratos (rule) and demos (people), Democracy literally means "rule by the people." In ancient and medieval times, referred to control of government by assembly of all citizens: direct democracy. In the modern world, it means constitutional, representative government in which top decision makers are elected in open and competitive elections, with almost all adults entitled to vote. Requires effective protection of basic political rights and liberties and effective restraints on government officials. Democracy may exist without formal written constitutions, as in Great Britain. It is also possible that a single political party, such as the Conservative Party in Britain, may govern the country over a long period of time. A country is democratic so long as elections are conducted freely and fairly and the possibility of change exists. Democracy is the spirit of the Islamic governmental system, even though it rejects philosophical assumptions about the people's sovereignty. See *SHŪRĀ*.

Democratic Capitalism

A term that is synonymous with "classical liberalism," it emphasizes the individual freedom that occurs when the economy is structured by the principles of free enterprise and when governments are based on political rights, including the right to vote and the right to oppose existing policies and regimes.

Democratic Centralism

Leninist concept of communist party organization. In theory, it means that party leadership and policies are decided by elections and criticisms from lower ranks of party. It means inner party democracy, criticism and self-criticism. However, once a decision has been made, every party official must support it. All nominations and elections are controlled from the top within the party structure, and all lower officials and members are expected to accept without question all their superiors' decisions.

Democratic Socialism

Also called Social democracy. A prominent twentieth-century ideology that believes that a more egalitarian society can be achieved, not by revolution as Marx specified, but by evolutionary means. Socialists call for citizens to acquire "deeper" understandings than liberalism provides of individuality, equality, democracy, and communal harmony; to elect politicians committed to these values; and for popularly-elected socialist governments to then tame the worst aspects of capitalism.

Democratization

The transition from authoritarianism to democracy and the consolidation of democracy. See WAVES OF DEMOCRACY.

Demonstration

Unconventional technique for displaying dissatisfaction and sometimes satisfaction and support with government officials or public policy and urging the authorities to change them. Demonstration include such activities as marches, picketing, and sit-ins.

Demonstration Effects

The effects of transfers of alien ways of life upon nationals of a country. Such effects are mainly cultural and attitudinal in nature, e.g., consumption habits, modes of dressing, patterns of education, leisure and recreation.

Deontology

The general idea that it is fruitless to try to define the true natures of the universe, societies, or humans. More particularly, many liberals believe that there is no objective knowledge of "the good" or "the bad" life other than the subjective understandings of individuals. A deontological approach to political theory attempts to define what people's rights are independent of any conception of what constitutes the good.

Dependence

A corollary of dominance; a situation where developing countries adopt developed countries' education systems, their technology, economic and political systems, attitudes, consumption patterns, dressing, etc. In the economic sphere, dependence means that developing countries have to rely on developed countries' domestic and international economic policy to stimulate their own economic growth. See INDEPENDENCE.

Dependency, Dependency Theory

suggests that the whole international economy operates to the disadvantage of the less developed world, because ex-colonies remain economically tied to and dependent upon former imperialist powers. The theory argues that the developing world has been systematically "underdeveloped" by advanced capitalist nations for their own benefit.

Deposit (Elections)

A sum of money paid as a precondition for a valid candidacy in an election. Sometimes a deposit is non-refundable, but typically a candidate will have his or her deposit returned on receiving a specific share of the vote or on being elected. Deposit is imposed to discourage frivolous candidacies.

Despotism

Absolute government by one person who rules without any constitutional controls. A despot need not necessarily be a tyrant. Indeed, in the eighteenth century, the concept of "benevolent" or "enlightened" despotism came into fashion. The theory was that people were not capable of governing themselves and needed a ruler who would look after their interests. For instance, Frederick the Great of Prussia considered himself an enlightened despot. In modern times, Western theorists reject despotism as an evil form, the inverse of the evil of anarchy, and it is not distinguishable from tyranny.

Détente

A French term meaning "relaxation," name given to the policy of easing tension between the US and the Soviet Union that occurred in the late 1960s and 1970s. It was particularly associated with President Richard Nixon and his national security advisor, Henry Kissinger. During this period, the Strategic Arms Limitation Treaty (SALT) 1 was signed. Détente was continued by President Gerald Ford who signed the Helsinki Accords. In 1979, however, tensions between the two superpowers rose again as a result of the Soviet invasion of Afghanistan and détente was temporarily abandoned. Although the term was associated with the cold war, it has a generic connotation which allows analysts to use it in describing any easing of tension between states. See ALLIANCE.

Deterrence

A primarily psychological approach to defense based on the goal of avoiding damage to oneself and on the perception of the retaliatory capability of the enemy. Theory of deterrence is based on the belief that each superpower possesses the capacity to destroy the other; neither side would use its nuclear weapons, because this would in effect guarantee its own destruction as well. The widely used acronym for this theory is MAD (Mutually Assured Destruction) which introduced what has been called the "Balance of Terror." The effectiveness of MAD depended on the belief by both sides that nuclear war was both unwinnable and unthinkable. However, in the late 1970s a rival theory of deterrence flourished. The proponents of this new theory claimed that nuclear war was survivable and thus thinkable. This led to what became known as Nuclear Utilization Theory or NUTs, according to which a nation must be prepared to fight, survive, and win a nuclear war. See WMD.

Development

A multidimensional process that leads to growth or change from a less to a more desirable state of affairs. One dimension of this term is economic development which indicates an increase in the level of economic activity in a nation, often measured by GDP or per capita GDP. Generally, this involves structural changes, with populations moving from agricultural (primary sector) to manufacturing (secondary sector) to services (tertiary sector). Other writers emphasize that development should translate into reductions in poverty, inequality, and unemployment. This process should also be characterized by the increasing satisfaction of basic needs. It should also translate into substantial improvements in social indicators such as housing provision, and physical quality of life, such as life expectancy. To another group of analysts development meant a reduction in dependency and increased self-reliance and self-determination. Development should also go beyond merely physical indicators of welfare to embrace spiritual and cultural attainments, individual dignity and group esteem. Political participation, accountable government, and a respect for human rights, have recently come into vogue as important features in the development discourse.

Devolution

The delegation of power by higher level of authority to a lower one. A devolved authority remains inferior constitutionally to the authority which gave it its power in the first place and the latter retained the right to revoke the power so devolved. Among the reasons for the devolution are that it will increase the efficiency level of government and help meet demands from special sections of the community for a degree of control over their own affairs.

Dialectical materialism

Marx's term for the historical changes in economic or material conditions of life that lead to class conflicts that, in turn, lead to new social, political, and ideological conditions. See COMMUNISM.

Dictatorship

A political system of arbitrary rule by an individual or small group that is not constitutionally responsible to the people or their elected representatives. Dictatorship is derived from a practice of ancient Rome in which extraordinary power was entrusted to a single leader for a term of no more than six months to promote public order or guarantee military security in a situation of great emergency. At the conclusion of the stipulated period, the dictator would relinquish his power, and constitutional government would be restored. In the twentieth century, it has come to mean a regime of unchallenged privilege for the leader or leadership group. Dictators usually argue that there is no need for the trappings of democracy because they and they alone are in tune with the people, the embodiment of the people's collective hopes and desires. See DEMOCRACY.

Dictatorship of the Proletariat

In Marxist doctrine, a short transition period between the destruction of capitalism and the establishment of the new order. This dictatorship of the proletariat exists to eliminate the last vestiges of capitalism. Once this "moping up" operation is complete, the state withers away, and everyone would accede to universal communism.

Difference Principle

The claim by John Rawls that, in a liberal society, social goods should be distributed equally unless unequal distributions benefit the poor and unless all members of society have equal prospects for acquiring greater than average shares of such goods.

Dīn

The word is from '*Dana*' which means "to owe," or be "indebted to." The word *din* has several meanings. The first is sovereignty, power, lordship, kingship, or rulership. The second is submission, obedience, service or slavery. The third is to bring to account, to judge, or to dispense reward and punishment for actions. All these three definitions are found in the Qur'an. In the Qur'anic language, *din* means the following:

1. To acknowledge God as Lord, Master and Ruler.
2. To obey and serve only Him.
3. To be accountable to Him, to fear only His punishment and to covet only His reward.

Islam is the name of that *dīn*. See ISLAM.

Diplomacy

Conduct of negotiations and maintenance of relations between sovereign states. It is a means used by nations to achieve their desired goals through peaceful means. It may involve multiple activities: face-to-face negotiations between belligerents or allies, economic deals between partners, or media posturing at international conferences. The conduct of diplomacy may include correspondence, discussions, lobbying, diplomatic visits, consultations, treaties, and even coercion. The Congress of Vienna, 1815, regularized a system of permanent diplomacy as an important aspect of relations between states. That early system was primarily bilateral in nature. Today, however, diplomacy has become increasingly multilateral: supra-national organizations often conduct diplomacy on behalf of their members and provide a forum for diplomacy of all sorts.

Diplomatic Immunity

Exemptions applied to diplomatic representatives of one country that protect them from certain internal civil and criminal jurisdictions of the country to which the representatives are accredited.

Direct Democracy

Government in which all citizens are entitled to participate in the supreme law-making assembly. Executive and judicial functions may also be conducted, at least in part, by ordinary citizens. This system was practiced in most part of the Muslim world during the pre-colonial era. Ancient Athens and New England town meetings are also best known examples of direct democracy.

Directive

An instruction issued by a higher authority to a subordinate asking a person to do something as detailed in the instruction. See DECREE.

Disarmament

A process that would remove the possibility of nuclear war by abolishing nuclear weapons altogether. Today, the term is used primarily in conjunction with nuclear weapons. Despite all the possible pitfalls, the superpowers have negotiated an important series of arms limitations and disarmament agreements. These treaties generally fall into two categories: treaties or agreements that deal with specific regions e.g., the Antarctic Treaty (1959), which internationalizes and demilitarizes the entire continent; and treaties or agreements that are applied to specific types of weapons e.g., Strategic Arms Limitation Treaties (SALT), and Strategic Arms Reduction Talks (START). See SALT, START.

Discretion

The power or right to decide or act according to one's own judgment. Freedom of judgment or choice allowed to those implementing laws. For instance, a police officer has the discretion to warn a driver over a parking offence or to proceed with prosecution. At the highest level, discretion may be exercised under the terms of an Act allowing a minister to issue more detailed supplementary regulations. Critics argue that discretion is a breach of the rule of law. Others argue for discretion to be accompanied with mechanisms to right the wrong decisions made.

Discrimination

The act of drawing a distinction. In social and political terms, discrimination denotes separating or setting people apart based on sex, ethnic origin, or class. Discrimination in a political system could be overt or official policy pursued by the state as did South Africa under apartheid. However, discrimination can be covert, or implicit based on gender, as feminists claim that women are discriminated against in work opportunities. However, covert discrimination refers to informal and non-institutionalized exclusions.

Dissolution of the Legislature

To dissolve a legislature before its term has lapsed. In parliamentary system of government, the Head of State, on the advise of the Prime Minister, dissolves the legislature, that is followed by a general election. The right of dissolution is a powerful weapon of the executive, allowing it not only to choose the occasion of the election, but also to some extent the issue on which it is fought. See PARLIAMENT.

Distributive Justice

A theory which sees the distribution of wealth and goods in society as involving justice, and which sets out a just scheme of distribution.

Divide et Impera

Latin phrase meaning "divide and rule." It is a strategy used by colonialists to gain and retain power by breaking up larger groups or territories into smaller units. In this way, the newly-created groups individually would have lesser power than the colonialists implementing the strategy. Effective use of this technique allows those with little real power to control those who collectively have a lot of power. See COLONIALISM.

Division of Labour

The division of tasks and functions, often leading to specialization and increased productivity, but associated with alienation and fragmentation.

Dīwān al-Nazr fī al-Maẓālim

The Islamic body which historically exercised judicial as well as supervisory functions over the conduct of the administration. Intended to set right cases of miscarriage of justice and tyrannical behaviour of the members of the ruling elite, the *diwan* served as a court of appeal as well as a court of first instance. It has the power to hold public officials, including the chief executive, to strict legal accountability for their acts. Nobody, not even the head of state, could secure or demand any preferential treatment.

Diyat

Financial compensation or "blood-money' paid in cases of homicide or other injuries to physical health committed upon another person. The historical origin of *diyat* lies in pre-Islamic Arabia, resting upon tribal basis. The tribe as a whole was obliged to share in the payment of *diyat*, an expression of the strong tribal solidarity. Basically, Islam confirms this institution with some modifications.

Dominance

In international affairs, a situation in which developed countries have much greater power than the less developed countries in decisions affecting important international political and economic issues; e.g., decisions in the security council of the United Nations, the prices of agricultural commodities and raw materials in world markets.

Dominion

A self-governing colony in the British Empire. The Balfour Report in 1926 described dominions as autonomous communities within the British Empire united by a common allegiance to the Crown and freely associated as members of the British Commonwealth of Nations. Dominions exchange high commissioners and not ambassadors.

Dual executive

A system of government, especially France under the Fifth Republic, headed by a popularly-elected President and a Prime Minister responsible to parliament. The Prime Minister determines and conducts the policy of the nation but the President appoints the Prime Minister, presides over the Council of Ministers and has powers to take the measures required in a national emergency.

Due Process of Law

Constitutional guarantee of fairness in the administration of justice. This concept can be traced back to the Magna Carta. Due process has two aspects: Procedural process which guarantees fair trial in the courts, and substantive due process which places limitations on the content of the law. It is under the latter heading that the U.S. Supreme Court has struck down many state laws restricting civil liberties as infringements of the Bill of Rights.

Dūstūr al-Madinah

Statue, regulation, by-laws, constitution of a city. Specifically, it refers to the first written constitution of the world which provided the basis for the Islamic political system established in Madinah. It restructured political life in Madinah according to the Islamic conception of the Ummah (section 2); recognized the Prophet (SAW) as the head of the new commonwealth (sections 23, 42), and defined his role as that of maintaining peace and order, arbitrating among groups in conflict; and of providing security from external attacks (sections 37, 39, 40, 44). The document confirmed the principle of equality, rejection of tyranny and equal protection of the law (sections 15, 17). The Jews were integrated into the body politic without depriving them of their religious freedom. See CONSTITUTION.

Dyarchy

The structure of British colonial government introduced under the Government of India Act 1919 in some of the Indian provinces. According to this structure, the British colonial government retained control over financial and security matters while other departments of government were assigned to Indian ministers responsible to the provincial legislature. The system was abolished in 1935. See COLONIALISM.

E

E-Government

Derived from "electronic government" which introduces the notion and practicalities of "electronic technology" into the various dimensions and ramifications of government. The most frequent use of the term e-Government is related to: (1) the delivery of public services via "online" or Internet; (2) the conduct of government business by those in authority (ministers, legislators etc) via "online" or electronic means; and (3) "online" voting, or where some online aspect is under consideration for voting.

Economic Determinism

Also called "historical materialism," orthodox Marxists attribute this doctrine to Marx. It claims that the ultimate realities in human life, and the basic causes of change and conflict, are not intellectual or spiritual, but economic and material, and that they are essentially beyond intentional human control.

Efficacy

The perception of an individual that personal activities can effect change. Political efficacy is the perception that the individual can influence political events.

Egalitarian Society

A group of people who are committed to the idea of intrinsic equality among themselves, who question the legitimacy of existing inequalities, and who seek to redress unjustified inequalities.

Egalitarianism

A belief in the equality of all men in wealth, status and power. It also involves identifying inequalities and attempting to remedy them through various means including distributive justice, education, and participation in decision-making activities.

Election

Derived from the Latin verb "eligere," meaning to pick out, to choose. Election is an organized process in which people vote to choose a person, to a position of public importance such as presidency, or group of people to represent them in national or state assemblies. Elections are the primary way of achieving popular goals and of orderly change in the personnel who run the administration. Elections to be meaningful must take place regularly within prescribed time limits and must be free and fair. All adults must have an equal opportunity to vote; they must have a choice between at least two candidates; they must be able to register their choices accurately; and that they should be informed of the results accurately and on time.

Electoral College

Group of people specially appointed, nominated, or elected in order to choose or elect individuals to political positions. This is an indirect method of electing people to some significant political positions. In the American context, voters choose electors and these electors then meet in their state capitals and elect the president and vice president. The electors are collectively known as Electoral College. Critics of the electoral college system describe it as undemocratic and, in this age of technology and communication, no longer necessary.

Electoral System

All the customs, laws, procedures, and institutions used to elect representatives in a political system. A comprehensive electoral system would include the customs and practices of campaigning and voting, the rules regulating the behaviour and funding of candidates, the methods of calculating and representing the popular vote, and the institutions that administer, recruit, and compete when elections are held.

Electorate

All those people of a country or an area who are legally qualified to vote in an election.

Elite

The best or the noble; in contemporary usage it is generally applied to those who have high status or high positions in politics, religion and society.

Elitism

The belief that political power is, or should be concentrated in the hands of a few most qualified leaders and that ordinary citizens are, or should be, without significant political power. Elite theory can be traced to Europe and the works ofVilfredo Pareto (1848–1923) and Gaetano Mosca (1858–1941), both of whom wrote about the inevitability of a ruling elites governing in any society. Elites are often viewed as essential and necessary for society. Some ideologies—like democratic socialism—make the empirical claim that power is concentrated among a few elites while stressing the normative claim that such concentration of power should be eliminated. Other ideologies—like fascism—make the empirical claims that concentration of power is widespread and perhaps an inevitable feature of all social groups while also making the normative claim that the resulting leadership is good for society and human progress.

Embassy

A group of diplomats headed by an ambassador, or their establishment located in a foreign state.

Emergency Powers

Authority granted to a government or executive agency that allows normal legislative procedures and/or judicial remedies to be by-passed or suspended during a national emergency. Such emergency powers have been usually strictly controlled by the legislature and permitted only for the duration of the crisis period.

Empire

A nation of great territorial expanse and strong political influence. In its early usage, the term denoted a territory over which a supreme sovereign exercised authority. Later on, however, the term is applied to an amalgam of territories formed by colonization or conquests, provided they remained subject to the control of a hegemonic state. In this last sense, the term empire became equated with imperialism.

End-of-History Thesis

The claim by Francis Fukuyama, a U.S. State Department analyst, that humankind has arrived at the end of history. This claim is based on the idea that democratic and free market countries (the Allied powers) have triumphed over totalitarian and corporatist countries (the Axis powers) at the end of the World War II, and that the liberal democratic and capitalist West has triumphed over the totalitarian command economies of the communist bloc. According to this Hegelian thesis, the big questions about politics have been settled, especially after the fall of Soviet Union, and there can be no further significant historical evolution in political thinking. According to Muslims, Islam is the final and ideal synthesis in terms of the Hegelian dialectic and will be embraced by a majority of mankind until the end of the world.

End-of-Ideology Thesis

The claim that ideological conflict is ending. The claim was first made at the end of the 1950s to suggest that both right-wing and left-wing ideologies were moving toward the center and that a "rough consensus" on big political issues could be reached.

Endo-Colonialism

It refers to the ways in which powerful national institutions (government, the army, bureaucracies) practise overt and covert forms of "colonialist violence" against groups within their country through the use of physical violence and/or by denying them political rights. It is also referred to as internal colonialism.

Enlightenment

An intellectual movement during the eighteenth century in Europe that sought to free humans from ignorance and superstition and to develop understandings of the universe, society, and humans based on reason and scientific applications of reason. Thus, Enlightenment is characterized by, among others: the partial replacement of religion by human values (liberty, equality, fraternity, individualism); the rise of science and scientific methods; a belief in reason, rationality and the civilising effects of culture and technology; and, a belief in progress. These beliefs and values gave rise to new institutions and practices—forms of democracy, educational institutions, political parties and movements, nation-states—which were exported, in time, to all parts of the globe. The extent to which a people could be designated, by the West, as civilized came to depend on whether or not they subscribed to, and developed, the beliefs, values, practices and institutions of "enlightened" modernity.

Environmentalism

An ideology claiming that humans must stop treating the natural environment, including other animals, as a warehouse of resources whose value depends solely on their use to humans. It calls for a deeper appreciation of ecological systems and diversity, and for restraint in the pursuit of economic growth, in order to attain a healthier environment. Green parties and movements have grown rapidly since the 1960s. Moderate environmentalists (light greens) criticize waste and pollution, and stress the need to protect the environment. Fundamental environmentalists (dark greens) completely reject the priority of consumerism and economic growth, and call for a different lifestyle based on conserving non-renewable resources.

Equality

The principle that each individual has intrinsic value as a human being and, as a consequence, deserves a certain similarity of treatment by society and the political system. In its proper practical sense, equality means the absence of special privilege on any grounds such as birth, status, sex, caste or creed. It implies fundamentally a certain levelling process. It means that no person shall be so placed in society that he/she can overreach his/her neighbour to the extent which constitutes a denial of the latter's citizenship. In short, it means such organization of opportunity that no one's personality suffers frustration. The provision of adequate opportunity is one of the basic conditions of equality. Equality may be divided into several aspects including natural, civil, political and economic equality. Some scholars argue that political equality is never real unless it is accompanied by virtual economic equality.

Escalation

Accelerating stages of response to attacks or the threat of attacks. Escalation is a military term and is widely employed by nuclear warfare specialists. The term has been replaced with the notion of flexible response.

Ethnic Cleansing

The harassment, removal, or murder of citizens based solely on their ethnic or racial attributes. A term that emerged in the conflict following the break-up of the former Yugoslavia. Serbs committed widespread ethnic cleansing against Bosnian Muslims.

Ethno-Nationalism

The claim that an ethnic group is and ought to be recognized as a distinct nation, entitled to political self-determination.

Ethnicity

A sense of belonging to or identification with an ethnic group. An ethnic group is usually defined as a group of people who see themselves and/or are seen by others as a distinct cultural community, and who share a language, dialect or idiom, religious beliefs, kinship and social ties, traditions, values, physical characteristics and similar features. In the 1940s, the UNESCO Declaration sought to promote the use of ethnic group to refer to national, cultural, religious and linguistic groups, in an attempt to displace the notion of race with its deeply embedded evolutionist and biological connotations. Despite this attempt, the two concepts are still closely interlinked and are sometimes used interchangeably.

Ethnocentrism

The belief that one's group or nation is of universal importance. Ethnocentrism is considered to be the product of the divisive quality of nationalism. See NATIONALISM.

Euro-Communism

In Western Europe, a modification of traditional Soviet communist theory that renounced violent revolution and dictatorship in favour of control of the existing governmental structure through elections.

European Parliament

One of the political institutions of the European Union. It consists of delegates elected directly by the national electorates of the member states based on the size of population. The European Treaties originally created an "Assembly" which converted itself to a parliament in 1962. This body, however, is weak in passing legislation, and its role is still limited to that of oversight and discussion. The Maastricht Treaty augmented the powers of the Parliament.

European Union

The crowning stage of a long process of European economic and political integration. The term was adopted as a result of the ratification of the Maastricht Treaty in November 1993. The treaty sought to provide a legal basis for developments concerned with European political union and economic and monetary union. One of the objectives of the treaty was to create a single European currency, the Euro which was implemented after January 1999. The Maastricht treaty is a successor to the European Community which resulted from the Treaty of Rome of 1957. The entire process was triggered in 1952 with the establishment of the European Coal and Steel Community to integrate the coal and steel resources of six European nations, eventually evolving into the European

Economic Community with 12 nations. The future broadening of the European Union seems inevitable as the line dividing Europe into East and West no longer exists. The goal of the Union is to achieve four freedoms of movement: of people, of capital, of goods and of services. See INTEGRATION.

Executive

The apex of power in a political system at which policy is formed and through which it is executed. May be headed by a single leader (monarch, prime minister, president, dictator) or a small group (cabinet, junta, politburo). In effect, the executive includes those positions occupying the commanding heights of government. Political executives carry out or enforce laws passed by the legislative branches of government. Implementation consists of rule making, adjudication, and law enforcement. It may also entail the setting of priorities. See LEGISLATURE, GOVERNMENT.

Executive Order

The directive from a chief executive to administrative officials communicating instructions about the implementation of laws. The executive order has the force of law.

Executive Clemency

The power of a chief executive to grant reprieve, pardon, or commutation of sentence. It changes the effects of a punishment but does not touch the judicial pronouncement as such; adding a humane strain to law enforcement and indicating that justice is the concern of all government branches. See PARDON.

Existentialism

Twentieth century philosophical current that stresses personal responsibility and the relation of the individual to the universe or to God. Existentialists emphasize the fear and despair that isolated individuals feel. The major philosopher of existentialism was Jean-Paul Sartre, who argued that there was no God and that human nature was finitely variable: humans were free to make their own destiny and therefore responsible for their own lives.

Expansionism

A strategy by which a nation seeks to enlarge its territory or influence.

Extradition

Handing over by one state to another, at its request or demand, a person who has committed an offence or suspected to have committed an offence for trial or punishment. Extradition in such cases is effected only if a state is bound by the provisions of an appropriate agreement.

F

Fabians

A group of British intellectuals (prominent among them were Sidney Webb, George Bernard Shaw, Graham Wallas and Mrs. Annie Besant) who founded the Fabian Society in 1884 to educate the public about the desirability of moving slowly away from capitalism and towards democratic socialism. The Fabians were not revolutionary Socialists and they did not outright condemn capitalism or identified it with exploitation. They aimed at changing the social structure by a slow and gradual process through the agency of a democratic State and by constitutional means. See DEMOCRATIC SOCIALISM.

Faction

The word faction is derived from the Latin verb *facere* (to do, to act), and *factioI* in Latin was used to indicate a political group bent on a disruptive and harmful act. Faction, at least in common parlance, is a bad name, and factions are an evil. It is always contrasted with a party. Parties are a necessity. Factions are not a necessity; they simply exist. Factions are nothing but the expression of personal conflicts, of ego-regarding and public-desregarding behaviour. In short, factions are organized groups with a reasonably stable membership inside a larger body. See POLITICAL PARTY, INTEREST GROUP.

Faḍīlah (pl. *faḍā'il*)

Moral excellence, virtue, merit and excellent quality. Sometimes, it is used as a title for eminent Islamic scholars as, for instance, *Sahib al-fadilah* Rector and Sheikh of Al Azhar University. Sometimes it precedes the title of Sheikh such as *Fadilat al-Sheikh.*

False consciousness

A term associated with Marxist thought which maintains that individuals and the class to which they belong may well demonstrate a sense of social understanding that is predominantly "false," in that it hides from them or prevents them from recognizing the "real" nature of their position within the social order and the extent to which they are exploited. See MARXISM.

Faqīh (pl. *fuqahā*)

Legist, jurisprudent, an expert of *fiqh*. A person learned in the knowledge of *fiqh*, who by virtue of his knowledge can give a legal judgement. A person who has mastered the science of the application of *shari'ah*. See *FIQH*.

Farḍ 'Ayn

Individual obligation. *Farḍ al-'Ayn* is the obligation whose fulfilment is demanded of each and every legally capable Muslim. No one is free from this obligation until he or she fulfils it himself or herself. It includes such obligations as prayer and fasting, doing good to parents and maintaining good relations with relatives and others. See *FARḌ AL-KIFĀ YAH*

Farḍ Kifāyah

Collective obligation. This is called collective obligation because if a few competent Muslims fulfil the obligation, it is considered to be sufficient for its fulfilment. The rest of the Muslims who do not discharge it are exonerated from it. If no one discharges it, all will be sinners. *Farḍ Kifayah* generally applies to obligations of social and collective life of the Muslims. They are, for example, enjoining the good and prohibiting the evil, specialisation in the sciences of the *Shari'ah* and other social sciences needed by the community such as medicine, engineering, agriculture and other physical sciences. It also covers social works, like helping the oppressed and the needy, educating the unlettered, medical treatment of the patients, administration of justice, and appointment of a ruler to conduct the affairs of the state. See *FARḌ AL-'AYN.*

Fasād

Corruption, decay, decomposition, immorality, weakness. In Islamic law it refers to an imperfect legal transaction. In Qur'anic terminology, it means creating disorder and corruption on earth by following a path other than God's. Islam maintains that true peace and happiness emanate only through the observance of God's commands and through making a conscious effort to see that His laws alone are implemented in every sphere of life. *Fasad* occurs when man violates God's laws and disobeys Him. *Fasād* may therefore be partial as well as total; partial when one disregards God's law in one aspect of life while acknowledging His sovereignty in other spheres. If a society is based on the denial of God, that society is bound to be a corrupt and exploitative society, and full of *fasad*.

Fascism

An ideology most clearly articulated by the Fascist Party of Italy under Mussolini between 1920 and 1945. It is a synthesis of extreme nationalism and anti-Marxist socialism. State and nation become one: as Mussolini put it, "everything in the state: nothing against the state, nothing outside the state." It calls for a totalitarian state to control all aspects of social and individual life in order to achieve state goals and demands the complete obedience of citizens to the dictates of an authoritative central leader. Neo-fascist parties, centred upon hostility to immigrants and ethnic minorities, have been a feature of post-war European politics. See TOTALITARIANISM.

Fāsiq (pl. *fusāq*)

Sinful, dissolute, licentious, and iniquitous. A person not meeting the legal requirements of righteousness of a Muslim. Such a person is a sinner, deviant and profligate, and the testimony of such a person is inadmissible in Islamic courts.

Fatimid

The rulers of North Africa, Egypt and southern Syria between 909 and 1171 (297–567 H) and the culture that flourished under their regime. The Fatimids entered Old Cairo (Fustat) in 969/358 and from there extended their rule into Palestine and Syria. At the time of the First Crusade at the end of the eleventh century, Jerusalem was taken from its Fatimid govenor, but by that time the Fatimid influence in Palestine and Syria had dwindled to essentially just the coastal towns. The Fatimid rulers proclaimed themselves true caliphs. Under Fatimid rule, the society and the arts prospered, and there was considerable commercial contact with non-Muslim Mediterranean regions.

Fatwā

A formal legal opinion given by a *muftī* or canon lawyer of standing, in answer to a question submitted to him either by a judge or by a private individual. On the basis of such an "opinion" a judge may decide a case, or an individual may regulate his personal life. The act of giving the opinion is *futyā* or *iftā'*; the person who gives *fatwā* is a *muftī*, and the one who asks for opinion is a *mustafti*. The classical doctrine requires certain conditions for the exercise of *fatwā*: Islam, integrity, and legal knowledge. Most *fatwās* are given in such matters as marriage, inheritance and divorce. All other legal questions are decided by other codes.

Fauḍāh / Fauḍawī

Disorder, disarray, confusion, chaos, anarchy. The term is used mostly to denote acts that are anarchic and chaotic. It is a state of complete disorder and confusion in a society which does not abide by the law, causing political disorder.

Fawāḥish

Abomination, atrocity, vile deed. Crime, adultery, fornication. The term applies to all those acts whose abominable character is self-evident. In the Qur'an all extra-marital sexual relationships, sodomy, nudity, false accusations of unchastity, and taking as one's wife a woman who had been married to one's father, are specifically reckoned as shameful deeds. In *Hadith*, theft, taking intoxicating drinks and begging have been characterized as *fawaḥish* as have many other brazenly evil and indecent acts.

Fay'

Wealth and property, especially land, of non-Muslims acquired by Muslims either through a treaty or by force. All the income accruing from such arrangement is called fay' and are considered public wealth which should be distributed among Muslims and the local inhabitants under the supervision of the state.

Federalism

Derived from Latin "foedus" which means a treaty, agreement or union. It is a system with constitutionally guaranteed division of power between a central government and a number of regional governments so that the government at each level has some activities on which it makes final decisions. It is characterized by two sets of government; a written, rigid constitution; division of power between two sets of government and judicial review. Examples of the federal system include the United States, Canada, Malaysia and Pakistan.

Feminism

A set of social theories and political practices demanding women's political, social, economic and sexual equality with men. They deplore the dominance of men and under-representation of women in public life. Feminist theorists question such issues as the relationship between sex, sexuality, and power in social, political, and economic relationships. They advocate such issues as women's suffrage, salary equivalency, and control over reproduction. More radical feminists question not only the relationship between men and women, but the very meaning of "man" and "woman." Some argue that gender roles, gender identity, and sexuality are themselves social constructs. For these feminists, feminism is a primary means to human liberation. Feminism has been principally a movement within the Western societies in the twentieth Century. Some limited advances have been made in some non-Western countries; but the movement has been principally Western in origin and effects. See GENDER AND POLITICS.

Feudalism

Feudalism is a political, legal, and military system in which lords exercised rule over fiefs, and the lords' vassals pledged homage, paid a variety of dues, and rendered military service. Classic feudalism flourished in Western Europe from the ninth to about the fifteenth century, but elements of the system have appeared in many other times and places. Some historians insist that the term should be used only in reference to the classic model of medieval Europe. Karl Marx and followers, however, use the term broadly to refer to an economic and social system based on landed privilege and self-sufficient agricultural units in which rural peasants are exploited by a small group of land owners.

Fiqh

Understanding, comprehension, knowledge, intelligence. Technically, it applies to Islamic law which covers all aspects of life, social, political, civil, and religious. In addition to the laws regulating ritual and religious observances *('ibādat)*, *fiqh* includes the whole field of family law, the law of inheritance, of property and of contract, in a word provisions for all the legal questions that arise in social life (*mu'āmalāt*); it also includes criminal law and procedure and finally constitutional law and laws regulating the administration of the state and the conduct of war.

Filibuster

A technique by which a parliamentary minority attempts through continuous talking to defeat or alter a measure favoured by the majority. It is a form of legislative obstruction, a parliamentary tactic almost unique to the U.S. Senate. The U.S. House of Representatives eliminated the practice in 1892.

Firqah (pl. *firāq*)

Part, portion, division, section, unit, party, detachment, troop. In a broader sense, the term refers to detachment of some groups from the origin of the already existing one. A group of people working towards the same objectives could also be called *firqah*.

First-Past-the-Post

An electoral system in which legislative candidates run in single-member districts and the winner is decided by a plurality vote; this system favours broad-based, entrenched political parties and tends toward a two-party configuration. Critics argue that it is undemocratic because it places a huge hurdle in the path of small or new parties and forces voters to decide between voting for a major-party candidate near the center of the political spectrum or wasting their votes on a third-party candidate who cannot possibly win. This system is practised in most of the democracies including US, UK, Canada and Malaysia. See ELECTORAL SYSTEM.

First Strike Capacity

A country's ability to strike first and destroy most of the enemy's nuclear force. Theoretically, the enemy has the ability to retaliate with its remaining forces because it would then suffer nuclear attack on its cities. This situation is contrasted to second strike capability where one side could survive an enemy strike and retaliate.

First World

The industrialised democracies. The term is very much in disrepute because of the related terms "second world" and "third world" referring respectively to the communist and the poor countries. See THIRD WORLD.

Fiscal Crisis of the State

A real or supposed failure of the state to generate tax revenues to implement its public policies. Fiscal crisis of the state was believed to be inevitable as no authority could raise more in tax without jeopardizing democratic rule nor could it cut policies. In response, the neo-conservative leaders like Ronald Reagan in the US and Margaret Thatcher in Britain brought significant tax reforms to avert the crisis. These reforms included broadening the tax base and cutting marginal rates of income tax.

Fiscal Policy

A policy made by the government that affects the economy. Fiscal policies involve decisions on how money is to be raised and spent by the government, and whether the government debt will be increased or decreased. Policymakers must strike a balance among encouraging economic growth, holding down inflation, maintaining solvency (avoiding bankruptcy), keeping programmes adequately funded and other goals. A tax increase to reduce inflation and limit government borrowing is an example of a fiscal policy.

Fitnah

Temptation, trial, enchantment, civil war, strife. Trial, testing. *Fitnah* has two interpretations as used in the Qur'an. It refers, firstly, to persecution, to a situation in which the believers are harassed and intimidated because of their religious convictions. Secondly, it refers to the state of affairs wherein the object of obedience is other than the One True God. In Islamic history, the term is often used to refer to civil war, particularly with reference to the era of conflict between Ali b. Abi Talib and Muawiyah b. Abi Sufyan.

Flexible Response

A military doctrine adopted during the Kennedy administration by the United States. With nuclear parity and the development of new weapons system, Washington shifted its nuclear war strategy from massive retaliation to flexible response. Henceforth, if the Warsaw Pact attacked NATO, Washington would only use nuclear weapons if the Soviets appeared on the verge of winning a conventional war. But rather than launch strategic nuclear warheads against Moscow, the US would use tactical nuclear weapons against Warsaw pact armies in central Europe. See MAD, WMD.

Floating Voters

Voters who are not strongly committed to any political party. They vote on the basis of issues. Surveys carried out in America and Europe indicate that most of these voters are hostile to extreme proposals and tend to favour only marginal changes in the status quo.

Foreign Policy

Foreign policy is the system of activities evolved by communities for changing the behaviour of other states and for adjusting their own activities to the international environment. Foreign policy involves the formulation and implementation of a group of principles which shape the behaviour pattern of a state while negotiating with other states to protect or further the scope of its vital interests. Not all international contacts and relations are associated with foreign policy. Only those matters which originate with or are overtly or tacitly sponsored by the government of state may be considered as belonging to its foreign policy. See PUBLIC POLICY, DIPLOMACY.

Franchise

The right to vote in an election. Another word for the right is suffrage. Obtaining the franchise does not automatically allow one the right to vote in every election. The franchise, or suffrage, can be restricted by other rules, such as a requirement that one must reside in an election district or constituency for a certain stipulated period of time. See UNIVERSAL SUFFRAGE.

Free Trade

International trade free from protective duties and subject only to such tariffs as are needed for revenue. It calls for the elimination of all barriers to international trade. The liberal perspective of the international political economy asserts that free trade benefits all parties to it, and as such it is viewed as a positive-sum-game. This is contrasted to the Mercantilist perspective which views international trade as a zero-sum-game in which there are winners and losers. Free trade proponents call for the elimination of all protectionist policies such as quotas, export subsidies, and tariffs.

Freedom

The idea that individuals should be able to pursue their own interests and maintain their own beliefs without interference from the government. What some may see as freedom, however, may appear to others as deprivation of freedom. Slave owners before the Civil War in America maintained that their freedom included the right to own and use slaves; obviously, the slaves and many others within society shared a different point of view.

Freedom of Expression

Rights that assure an individual freedom of expression which includes: freedom of speech i.e., the right to speak in support of any idea, however unpopular it may be; freedom of petition, that is the right to present written statements criticizing or recommending changes to any public officials; freedom of assembly, i.e,. the right to meet in one's home or other meeting places without interference from the government; freedom of the press assuring journalists the right to report the news as they deem fit; and, freedom of religion, i.e., the right to choose and practice one's religion without interference from others. See CIVIL RIGHTS.

Freedom of Information

The right of the public and of the press to have free access to information especially to government documents. Military security and personal privacy have been recognized as exceptions. In the United States there exists Freedom of Information Act, enacted in 1966 and strengthened in 1974, which provides that agencies must respond to requests for information within 10 working days and appeals to be settled in another 20 days.

French Revolution

An upheaval that began in France in 1789. Its leaders set out to abolish aristocratic and clerical privileges and limit the power of the monarchy. It brought down the Bourbon monarchy in France in the name of liberty, equality and fraternity. For the most part, the revolution was based on liberal and democratic principles, although some radical ideas were pursued. The revolution was marked by terror and bloodshed, and finally ushered in the rule of Napoleon Bonaparte in 1799. See REVOLUTION.

Functional Representation

Representation by economic or social groups. The central idea of functional representation is that citizens in a polity are represented in terms of their membership of social groups. Groups in this context may be organizations that admit of voluntary membership, such as civil associations; or more inclusive entities taken to represent particular sectors in society, for example, minority groupings or occupational interests. Such a method is both ancient and modern. In ancient times representation was based on class and status. In the twentieth century, in fascist Italy, for example, the legislature comprised groups from different economic and social segments of society.

Functionalism

An approach to studying politics which concentrates on the functions which any political system must perform if it is to survive and operate effectively. Conversely, it is argued that a government's failure to perform the functions expected of it results in a revolutionary change. Specifying these functions is extremely difficult. In international relations, it refers to an approach to the building of supra-national community primarily through economic integration.

Fundamental Rights

Certain basic rights which are deemed fundamental to the existence and growth of man, and together with him of society. Without these rights life would be sordid and meaningless. The tendency in a modern democratic State is to incorporate such basic rights in its constitution so as to ensure their full enjoyment by all citizens without discrimination of any kind. See BILL OF RIGHTS.

Fundamentalism

The term originated in America and referred specifically to a movement in American Protestantism whose main objective was to combat modernist or liberalist tendencies. Coined early in the twentieth century, protestant fundamentalism refers to the struggle for the achievement of fundamentals, viz., inerrancy of scripture, the virgin birth of Christ, the substitutionary atonement, the bodily resurrection of Christ, and the authenticity of miracles. The fundamentalists of the 1920s achieved notoriety because of their vigorous campaign against schools of modernist tendencies and against the teaching of Darwinian evolution in public schools. Losing the battle, the fundamentalists retired to a kind of cultural ghetto and resurfaced later in such movements as the Moral Majority. The growth of religious right has been striking in the US politics since the 1970s.

Despite its Protestant origin, the term fundamentalism has been applied to movements in the Muslim world which aim at establishing an Islamic political order in which the Shari'ah will be legally recognized and enforced. The vast majority of regularly labelled fundamentalists seek to promote the goals of Islam not through violence and bloodshed but by peaceful persuasion and through constitutional means. The frequent association of the term, in the Western media, with terrorism, reactionary fanaticism and medieval mentality is to malign Muslims and their attempts at living an Islamic way of life. See ISLAM.

Fusion of Powers

It refers to the concentration of all powers in the parliament. It is an essential feature of the parliamentary system which, by definition, is a government principally organised according to the fusion of powers. The powers are fused in two ways. One, the executive leader and the cabinet ministers selected from among members of parliament, continue to lead their parties in the parliament, and take active part in parliamentary debates. Two, the ministers are directly responsible to the parliament and can remove a particular cabinet or ministry by passing a vote of no confidence in them. In such cases, either the ministry must resign and be replaced by another acceptable to the parliamentary majority or a general election must be held to elect a new parliament which may then either reappoint the old cabinet or replace it with a new one. See PARLIAMENTARY SYSTEM, SEPARATION OF POWERS.

Fath (pl. *futūḥāt*)

Opening, beginning, introduction, commencement. It also means conquest, victory, triumph. The word *fath* is used to denote the rise and expansion of Islam as opening of frontiers to Islamic civilization, culture and values. The orientalist's interpretation of *futūḥāt* to mean conquest is not acceptable to Muslims.

G

Gag order

An order by a court that is directed at media representatives to prohibit the reporting of a court proceeding. A gag order is an injunction intended to prevent prejudicial pre-trial publicity. It is an extreme measure and constitutes a substantive encroachment on freedom of the press.

Ghallabah, al

Victory. The term is used to denote the act of winning or victory over a dispute or fight. Hence, in terms of dispute it is the act of overcoming other's opinion or power. But the term can also be used to mean the most "common" of something or use of something.

GATT (General Agreement on Tariffs and Trade)

An international organization founded in 1947 as part of the Bretton Woods formula. Its headquarter is located in Geneva, Switzerland. Its major mandate is to negotiate reductions in trade barriers among member nations. GATT has ninety-six nations as members, and twenty-nine more nations accept its rules. The member nations periodically meet in a "round" of negotiations, such as the Kennedy, the Tokyo and the Uruguay rounds, to revise the rules. These rounds resulted in reducing trade barriers for manufactured goods and to create freer trade in services and agricultural goods. About 90 percent of the world's international trade is conducted according to GATT rules on such matters as import and export quotas, customs regulations, and, above all, tariff rates on imported goods. GATT uses Conference diplomacy to organize rounds of negotiations and uses panels of experts to handle complaints about violations of its trade rules that cannot be resolved through more routine consultation procedures.

Gaullism

A political movement in France led by Charles de Gaulle (1890–1970). De Gaulle was opposed to the Constitution of the 4th Republic and insisted that a strong executive was needed to ensure stability, independence, and modernization of the French economy. These suggestions were embodied in the new Constitution of the 5th Republic enacted in 1958. Gaullism was devoid of a clear ideology, but many centre-right French political parties mirrored de Gaulle's political career e.g., Union for the Defense of the Republic (UDR) and the Rally for the Republic (RPR). Because of pragmatism and flexibility of the movement, Gaullism has undergone basic changes under subsequent Gaullists, notably Georges Pompidou and Jacques Chirac.

Gender

It refers to the notion that "masculinity" and "femininity" (and the values they come to represent) are always being "renegotiated" as circumstances change. What is understood by the terms "man" and "woman" is in no way universal or ahistorical, but changes depending on cultural and historical circumstances, ideas and values.

Gender and Politics

Political thought contributed by feminists focusing on the exclusion of women's issues, concerns, and participation in public political life. These contributions emphasize the primacy of granting women greater access to politics and the whole reconstitution of the world of politics. Black feminists argue that this exclusion from politics is due to two causes: gender and race. Third World feminists tend to emphasize on the notion of struggle against imperialism and neo-colonialism. See FEMINISM.

General Will

Associated with Jean-Jacques Rousseau, the term expresses the idea that collective bodies such as nations and their governments have a common Will or mind of their own. This Will operates on a level apart from, even superior to, the lives and wills of the individuals who are its building blocks. It reflects the undisputed common good, the highest public interest, what is best for everyone in the society. This General Will is by definition moral and ethical: it is good for each individual and expresses a just balance between the needs of all individuals. It is general because it leads people to think, not of narrow self-interest, but of the happiness of the whole. It is a will, since the choice to obey is a voluntary act. By obeying this Will, people are able to attain true freedom and equality. See POPULAR SOVEREIGNTY, PUBLIC OPINION.

Genocide

From the Greek "genos" (race) and the Latin "cite" (killing), genocide means the killing of a race or tribe. It is premeditated, state-directed, mass murder of racial, ethnic, religious, or national groups, either within or outside of a country. The term was first defined during World War II by Raphael Lemkin, a Polish legal scholar, who was partially responsible for the passage of the United Nations Genocide Convention on December 9, 1948. This convention defined violent organized attacks on national, racial, ethnic, and religious groups, whether carried out in war or peace time, as international crimes. Although genocidal killings have occurred throughout recorded history, the scale of mass murder in the twentieth century is without historical parallel.

Geopolitics

The combination of geographic and political factors influencing or delineating a country or region. Simply defined, geopolitics means the role of geographic factors in international politics. Geopolitics heavily influenced both scholars and practitioners in the early part of the twentieth century. In 1890 Alfred Mahan attributed the rise of British power to the country's island position and its related development of naval power. His writing encouraged President Theodore Roosevelt to develop U. S. naval power. Sir Halford Mackinder retorted in 1904 that history alternates between land and sea power and argued that modern industry and the railroad would favour the great land powers in the twentieth century. Moreover, MacKinder described East Europe and Central Russia as the heartland of the world's greatest land mass, which he called the world island. Scholars and practitioners do not devote as much attention to geopolitics as they did a century ago. This is due to the fact that industrialization and technological advance has reduced the potency of geographic barriers to human movement in commerce or military action.

Gerontocracy

A government or ruling body made up of the oldest people within the social and political system. See DIRECT DEMOCRACY.

Gerrymandering

Drawing of electoral district boundaries to the advantage of a particular political party or interest group. The party in power or the dominant political party will draw the boundaries in such a way as to make the most effective use of its own votes and to waste those of the opposition. The basic technique is to concentrate large blocs of opposition voters in a few districts and distribute large blocs of favourable voters more broadly.

Ghanīmah (pl. *ghanāím*)

Spoils of war, booty. This includes weapons, horses and all other movable possessions taken in battle from unbelievers. 80 per cent of the booty are to be divided among the troops who have been present at the battle. The remaining 20 percent belongs to Allah (s.w.t) i.e., granted to the ruler in God's name to defray the expenses of the state.

Ghāzī

War lord, warrior, champion. One who carries out a military expedition or a foray. It refers to a Muslim warrior returning after participation in *Jihād* (the holy war). The one who dies in Jihad is called *shahid*. See *JIHĀD*.

Gazwah (pl. *gazawāt*)

Military expedition, usually of a limited scope, foray, raid. A *ghazwah* is used particularly with reference to the Prophet's (SAW) expeditions against the infidels. The institution of *gazu* predates Islam which was the practice of the camel-breeding tribes of Northern Arabia. At that time the term was distinguished from warlike activities whose aim was territory, and also punitive raids of retaliation. The aim of *gazu* was the acquisition of camels. Islam prohibits this type of activity.

Ghuluw

To exceed the proper bounds, be excessive, go too far, overdo and even exaggerate something. In economics, it is used in the sense of demanding too high a price or charging too much.

Glasnost

From Russian, literally translates as "openness." Initially referred to the policy introduced by Gorbachev of allowing frank and open discussions of public issues in the Soviet Union. It was argued that only through free discussions can the nation's leaders and citizens discover what is wrong and put it right. The term has now passed into the language of international politics. See PRESTROIKA.

Globalization

The increasing integration of nations which affects a wide range of issues including economic, cultural and political affairs (especially the spread of liberal democratic political values). In a globalized system most countries become economic players in the world market, a largely capitalistic competition where goods, money, and ideas flow easily to wherever there are customers. The few countries that do not want to play the capitalistic game, such as Cuba and North Korea, live in isolation and poverty. The spread of globalization has created resentments especially in the Muslim world of the American and capitalist culture of a globalized system: "McWorld." The Muslim world would like to become modern in their own way and with their culture and values in tact. See MODERNIZATION.

Government

The body of people and institutions that make and enforce laws for a society. It is an agency that has the monopoly of legitimate use of physical force in enforcing its rules within a given territorial area. The rules of government are generally recognised as authoritative; that is, they are generally considered to be binding upon all members of a society. The government makes laws, gives direction by mapping out policies, implements and enforces rules, and settles dispute arising from rules enacted. It is through the government that common rules are framed, common affairs regulated and common interest promoted. There are many classifications of government. Organizationally, governments may be classified into parliamentary or presidential systems, depending on the relationship between executive and legislature. On the basis of the distribution of power at different levels, governments may be unitary—i.e., with the central government controlling local affairs, it may be federated with two sets of government exercising power over their defined jurisdictions, or confederated where the constituent units delegate some power to the central government. See UNITARY AND FEDERAL GOVERNMENT.

Governor

Chief executive of a dependent or component unit in a political system. A person responsible for the political administration of a region or a province or a state. In the United States, a governor is the chief executive of each state and is elected by the people of the state. In the British, French, and Dutch empires, a governor was traditionally appointed to rule over each of the colonies. In some cases, the governor is the supreme executive of the region but in other cases, he acts on the advice of the council of ministers as in India.

Governor-General

The supreme executive representing the British colonial government before the colony became a republic. The Governor-Generals had enormous powers. In addition to the executive power, they could pass laws and promulgate ordinances over the head of legislature. They could appoint judges and grant pardon. Since the Imperial Conference of 1926, the Governor General has become a ceremonial chief. Nowadays, the Governor-General acts on the advice of his government and is independent of the British Crown.

Gradualism

Slow, incremental progress towards a policy objective. Gradualism is a version of socialism which denies the need for revolution, and argues instead that the ordinary and slow means of competitive democratic politics can, in time, produce the needed changes in social and economic organization.

Grassroots Politics

Situations where the average citizen participates in or exerts pressure on government usually at the local level. Grassroots efforts can involve established political groups, such as parties or interest groups, or can occur outside them. They represent communication from the bottom up. This bottom-up approach to involvement includes such activities as petition drives, letter-writing campaigns, marches, referenda, and demonstrations.

Great Conversation

A metaphor for the kinds of analyses that take place in political philosophy. In this metaphor, each viewpoint on a big issue is presented, and these viewpoints are criticized, defended, debated, and modified at great length and in great depth. In the metaphor, these exchanges are conversational; in length and in philosophical practice, they occur largely through books and articles.

Green Revolution

Recent agricultural trends that have greatly increased crop production in some under-developed countries. Based on new varieties of crops and dependent on pesticides and fertilizers, the green revolution's goals of feeding the world's increasing population have been thwarted by high prices and ecological problems.

Greens

Greens are "deep ecologists." The use of "green" as a term was promoted by environmental-issue-based political party activists who called their new organization "green" parties. Green is a name given to policies, politicians, and activists who advocate environmental responsibility in policy decisions.

Ground Zero

Literally, the point on the surface of the earth or water directly below, directly above, or at which an atomic or hydrogen bomb explodes. The term came to the limelight in the wake of the attack and the collapse of the World Trade Centre in New York on September 11, 2001.

Guerrilla War

A low-intensity, unconventional war, usually fought by an insurgency of irregulars, often in an enemy-held territory. Traditionally, this strategy has been waged against larger and better equipped conventional forces, for instance, the Viet Cong forces opposing the U.S. in Vietnam. Guerrillas avoid open battles as much as possible; exploit the mobility gained from lack of equipment and supply lines; and, rely upon popular support. They rely on hit-and-run tactics, ambush, sabotage, and the psychological effects of unpredictable attacks.

Guided Democracy

The system of administration introduced by President Soekarno in Indonesia in 1959 replacing the parliamentary system instituted a decade earlier. Guided democracy, the regime's slogan, was based on three pillars of Indonesian society – nationalism, religion and communism – and aimed at maintaining the loyalty of the army and the communists to the President. General Suharto, who succeeded Soekarno, set up a "New Order" administration in 1968. Suharto regime, in turn, was dismantled in 1998 as the result of financial crisis, popular unrest and demonstrations.

Gulf Co-Operation Council (GCC)

Founded in 1981, the GCC is composed of Bahrain, Kuwait, Oman, Qatar, Saudi Arabia, and the United Arab Emirates. The GCC aims to strengthen economic, cultural and strategic relations among its members. (Established in March 1991 by the Declaration of Damascus, GCC committed Bahrain, Kuwait, Oman, Qatar, Saudi Arabia, the United Arab Emirates, Egypt, and Syria to form a regional peace-keeping force and an aid fund to promote development among member states.)

H

Habeas Corpus

A writ issued to bring a party before a court to prevent unlawful restraint. Habeas corpus is a concept of law, in which a person may not be held by the government without a valid reason for being held. A writ of habeas corpus can be issued by a court upon a government agency (such as a police force or the military). Such a writ compels the agency to produce the individual to the court, and to convince the court that the person is being reasonably held. The suspension of habeas corpus allows an agency to hold a person without a charge. Suspension of habeas corpus is often equated with martial law.

Ḥadd (pl.*hudūd*)

Boundary, limit, prescribed penalty. In the Qur'an, where it is usually found in the plural, it means the "limit" laid down by God i.e., the provisions of the law, whether commands or prohibitions. In Muslim criminal law *hadd* means an unalterable punishment prescribed by the Qur'an and the Sunnah for particular crimes—intoxication, theft, rebellion, adultery and fornication, false accusation of adultery, and apostasy. These crimes involve transgressing the limits of acceptable behaviour.

Politically, *ḥadd* punishments like stoning or scourging for illicit intercourse (*zinā*), and cutting off the hands for theft are meant to be a deterrent so that people may not become complacent and commit crimes simply because they find the punishment trivial as in the West. However, the judge must make sure that the crime was definitely committed, otherwise he must refrain from the use of the '*hadd*' punishment, because it is better for a judge to "err in acquitting the accused rather than erring in awarding punishment."

Ḥadith (pl. *aḥādīth*)

Report, event, news, narrative. Narrative relating deeds and utterances of the Prophet (SAW) and his Companions. Initially, there existed a distinction between the term

Sunnah, referring to the practices of the Prophet (SAW), and the *ḥadīth* denoting his utterances as narrated by his companions. Gradually, however, the entire *Sunnah* was reflected in the *ḥadīth* to such an extent that, by the fifth century AH, the two terms became synonymous. *Ḥadīth*, therefore, refers to all authentic reports of the acts, utterances and silent approvals of the Prophet (SAW). These are mostly recorded in the six *ṣiḥaḥ* (authentic collections). A *ḥadīth* which has a complete chain of transmission from the last narrator all the way back to the Prophet (SAW) is called *ḥadīth muttaṣil*, a continuous *ḥadīth*. The majority of ulama' have divided the continuous *ḥadīth* into the two main varieties of *mutawātir* (continuously recurrent) and *Āḥād* (reported by a single person). A *ḥadīth* whose chain of transmitters is broken and incomplete is known as *ghayr muttaṣil* or discontinuous. See *SUNNAH*.

Hajīb (pl. *ḥujāb*)

Doorman, gatekeeper, chamberlain. The term is used for the person responsible for guarding the door of access to the ruler, so that only approved visitors may approach him. The *ḥajib* or chamberlain introduced not only friends and visitors into the Caliph's presence but also supervised the organization of the solemn audiences. During the Umayyad period, the *ḥājib* figured in the sovereign's entourage on a level equal to that of secretaries (*kuttāb*). The Abbasids elevated the position of the *ḥājib* further so that it rivalled the position of the *wazīr* (minister). See *WAZĪR*.

Ḥājiyyāt

Complementary. The *ḥājiyyāt* are on the whole supplementary to the five essential values of religion, life, intellect, lineage and property. It refers to interests whose neglect leads to hardship in the life of the community although not to its collapse. Thus, the Shari'ah concessions to the sick and the traveller not to fast, and to shorten the prayers, are aimed at preventing hardship. Similarly, the basic permissibility regarding the enjoyment of victuals and hunting is complementary to the main objectives of protecting life and intellect. See *DARŪRIYAT*.

Ḥakam

To pass judgment, express an opinion, judge, arbitrator. An arbitrator appointed by a *Qāḍī* to settle disputes. According to the Qur'an, quarrels, especially domestic ones, should be settled by an arbitrator.

Al-Ḥakām is one of the ninety-nine attributes of God. Thus understood, it means the One Whose word is final in determining what is right and what is wrong, in distinguishing between acts of righteousness and those of sinning. He rewards each soul according to what it earns, Who decides between His servants as He pleases. *Al-Ḥakām* is the precise Arbitrator, the absolutely correct Judge, Whose decision none can overturn, nor can anyone repeal His decree.

Ḥakīm (pl. *ḥukkām*)

Ruling, governing, decisive. The word conveys two meanings. First, it refers to the creator, or originator of law, the one from whom the communication issues. He is God, the Almighty. He originates the law and gives the command. The function of the Prophet (SAW) is to convey the command to the people and to explain it. The function of the jurists, after him, is to derive this command from the sources set up by God for knowing it. The term *Aḥkām al-Ḥakimīn*, "the Most Just of Rulers," is used for God. Second, *ḥakīm* refers to the discoverer or perceiver of law. In the second sense it refers to the Shari'ah. It is not possible to have the knowledge of the divine law without the scriptures and prophets. It is, therefore, said that the lawgiver is God, the Exalted, and the revealer is the *Shari'ah*. See *SHARI'AH*.

Ḥākimiyyah

Domination, dominion, rule, sovereignty, judgeship, jurisdiction. Generally, the term *ḥākimiyah* is used in the sense of sovereignty which is vested in the general public in the West. Islam repudiates the notion of popular sovereignty and rears its polity on the foundations of the sovereignty of God and the vicegerency (*khilāfah*) of man. According to Islam, sovereignty belongs to Allah (SWT). He alone is the law-giver. No one, not even a prophet, has the right to order others in his own right to do or not to do certain things. Allah alone is the real law-giver and the authority of absolute legislation vests in Him. The believers as vicegerents (*khalīfah*) cannot resort to totally independent legislation nor can they modify any law which He has laid down. The believers are to run the state in accordance with the Book of Allah (SWT) and the practice of His Prophet (SAW). See SOVEREIGNTY.

Ḥanafiyyah

Madhhab of *Sunnī* law founded by Abu Hanifah (d. 767 AD) (adj. Hanafi or Hanafite). The *Ḥanafiyyah* school is the first of the four orthodox Sunni schools of law. It was founded by Nu'man Abu Hanifah (d.767) in Kufa in Iraq. It derived from the bulk of the ancient school of Kufa and absorbed the ancient school of Basrah. Abu Hanifah belonged to the period of the successors (*tabi'īn*)of the *Sahabah* (the companions of the Prophet). He was a *Tabī'i* since he had the good fortune to have lived during the period when some of the *Sahabah* were still alive. *Hanafiyyah* places less reliance on mass oral traditions as a source of legal knowledge. It developed the exegesis of the Qur'an through a method of analogical reasoning known as *Qiyās* (see Sunni Islam). It also established the principle that the universal concurrence of the Ummah (community) of Islam on a point of law, as represented by legal and religious scholars, constituted evidence of the will of God. This process is called *ijmā'*, which means the consensus of the scholars. The Hanafi School is predominant in Turkey, Afghanistan, India, Pakistan, Bangladesh and among Chinese Muslims. See *ḤANBALIYAH*.

Ḥanbaliyah

Ḥanbaliyyah is the fourth school of law within Sunni Islam. It derives its decrees from the fundamentals of the religion: strictly the Qur'an and the verifiable tradition of the Prophet (SAW). It rejected both reason and community consensus as the bases of legal rulings. It was established by Ahmad b. Hanbal (d.855), also studied law under different masters, including Imam Shafi'i. He is regarded as more learned in the traditions than in jurisprudence. His status also derives from his collection and exposition of the *ḥadiths*. His major contribution to Islamic scholarship is a collection of fifty-thousand traditions known as *Masnadul al-Imam Ḥanbal*. The Hanbali School is the predominant legal school in Saudi Arabia. See *SHĀFI'ĪYYAH*.

Hansard

An official record of the daily proceedings of the parliament, which is edited, translated, and printed. Hansard is the name of the printer in England who began preparing reports of parliamentary debates in the eighteenth century.

Ḥaq (pl. *Huqūq*)

Truth, justice. Legal rights, title, legal claims and corresponding obligations. In theology, it is used for that which is true e.g., the word of God. In law, it implies that which is due. A thing decreed; a claim. *Ḥaq* means an interest of an individual or society or of both together established by the Lawgiver, the Wise. *Al-ḥaq* is an attribute of Allah (SWT).

Ḥaq al 'Abd

The right of man in a state or community. The rights of man correspond to private rights. This class of rights comprise matters which are entirely the right of individual men, such as the right to the enforcement of contracts, protection of property and the like. The enforcement of the rights of men is at the discretion of the person whose private right is infringed. It is, however, at the discretion of man whose right is affected whether to pardon the wrongdoer or to demand its redress. See *ḤAQ ALLĀH*.

Ḥaq Allāh

The right of God, Allah (the creator) on all His creatures, or on any particular judicature or jurisdiction or issue and matter. These rights cannot be extinguished or forgone by any person except God. These rights correspond to public rights and involve the benefits of the whole Muslim society. These rights comprehend, in the main, obligatory devotional acts (*ibādat*) and prescribed punishments (*ḥudūd*). They are beneficial to the whole society. The enforcement of these rights is a duty of the state.

Ḥarakah (pl. *ḥarakāt*)

Movement, motion, military operation. Used in conjunction with Islam, *al-ḥarakāt al-Islāmiyah* refers to the organized and collective work undertaken by the people, to implement the Shari'ah, unify the Muslim ummah and restore the lost glory of Islam.

Ḥarb (Pl. *ḥurūb*)

War, fight, combat, battle. In legal terms, *ḥarb* may mean either fighting (*Qitāl*) in the physical sense or "state of war" between two or more groups.

Hare System

An electoral system in which the voter ranks his or her choices of candidates as first, second, third, and so on. When a candidate achieves a quota of votes set on the basis of law or calculated from a formula of seats in that constituency, that candidate is elected. The surplus votes are given to the candidate who scored the second in terms of preference. The idea of the system is to transfer votes until the number of seats is filled.

Hawā (pl. *ahwā'*).

Vain or egotistical desire; individual passion; impulsiveness. Following one's own desires is described in the Qur'an as taking these desires as your 'god' or object of worship. Following *hawāa* leads to arrogance and destruction and is contrasted with following the Shari'ah which is designed to discipline and lead man to fulfillment and happiness.

Head of Government

(also known as chief executive). The leader of the government who is responsible for formulating and administering public policy. In a parliamentary system, the head of government is known as a premier, a prime minister or a chancellor. In presidential systems, the head of government is usually the same person as the head of state which is usually titled president in a republic. In some semi-presidential systems, the head of government is a separate premier or prime minister who is answerable to the president or an absolute or semi-absolute monarch rather than to parliament. In others, the prime minister may be answerable to both the head of state and parliament. Such is the case in the French Fifth Republic (1958-present). See HEAD OF STATE.

Head of State

The chief public representative of a nation-state, federation or commonwealth performing largely ceremonial functions. In a monarchy, the monarch is the head of state. In a republic, the head of state is usually called president. In Presidential systems or in absolute monarchies, a head of state is also the active chief executive officer of the government. In parliamentary systems, the head of state is the nominal chief executive officer of the state, in reality powers are usually exercised by the Prime Minister and a cabinet. The Head of State represents the country in such activities as receiving ambassadors, greeting foreign dignitaries or awarding honours. Occasionally, however, the head of state may play some role. In Spain, Great Britain, Holland, and India, the King, the Queen and the President respectively is the head of state. See HEAD OF GOVERNMENT.

Hegemony

The predominance of one group, class or nation over others, usually by means other than brute force. This is accomplished by the diffusion through society of the value and knowledge systems of a ruling group. A state exercising hegemony is referred to as a hegemon. An alternative characterization reflecting pre-eminent position for a state, but not necessarily implying dominance, is to refer to it as a leader exercising leadership of other states within its sphere. The difference between hegemony and leadership is a subtle distinction and perhaps more a matter of nuance or connotation intended by the user of the term.

High Commission

A diplomatic mission of a state that is a member of the British Commonwealth of Nations. See EMBASSY.

High Politics

Refers to matters of security, particularly the strategic interests of states. Realists have tended traditionally to draw a distinction between such high political concerns and those dealing with socio-economic or welfare issues of lesser interest to statesmen; the so-called low politics. See LOW POLITICS.

Hijrah

Migration. The act of leaving a place to seek sanctuary of freedom or worship in another or for any other purpose. Also the act of leaving a bad practice in order to adopt a righteous way of life. Specifically, *hijrah* refers to the Prophet's journey from Makkah to Madinah in the month of Rabiʿ al Auwal in the twelfth year of his mission, corresponding to June 622 AC. The Islamic calendar begins from this event (AH) The word *hijrah* implies not only change of residence but also the ending of ties of kinship and the replacement of these by new relationships. In Indo-Pakistan sub-continent, the term is used to refer to millions of Muslims who made their way to the new state of Pakistan in 1947, afraid of what the future might hold for them in an independent India dominated by Hindu majority.

Ḥilf (pl. *aḥlāf*)

Sworn alliance, confederacy, league; federation. It refers to a compact, covenant or oath entered into between different parties or tribes. The term is used sometimes to mean an agreement between the clans within one tribe to settle their problems. See ALLIANCE.

Ḥisbah

The *ḥisbah* is an institution unique to Islam. It is essentially organized around safeguarding the limits of Allah from being violated, protecting the honor of the people, and ensuring public safety. It also includes monitoring the marketplace, craftsmanship, and manufacturing concerns to make sure that the laws of Islam are upheld by these entities. It must also ensure that quality standards are maintained. The *Ḥisbah* carries out these responsibilities in conjunction with the appropriate government agencies and other relevant establishments. The person entrusted with the work of *ḥisbah* is called *Muḥtasib.* See OMBUDSMAN.

Ḥizb (Pl. *aḥzāb*)

Group, troop, party, faction. It refers to a group of people brought together by either *āqīdah* (faith), an ideology or common interests. Every *ḥizb* has its own objectives, its own internal by-laws. Whosoever agrees to abide by these rules becomes a member of that *ḥizb*. Earlier Muslim scholars argued that there are only two parties: *the ḥizb Allāh* (God's Party) and the *ḥizb al-Shayṭān* (Devil's Party). All Muslims belong to the former. Thus, there could only be one *ḥizb*. Given Islam's emphasis upon equality, freedom and justice, it is argued that Islam approves of the multiplicity of groups but it prohibits all groupings that are anti-thetical to people's interests or operate outside the framework of the Shari'ah. See POLITICAL PARTY.

Holocaust

A great or complete devastation or destruction especially by fire. The term is used to refer, in particular, to the systematic mass extermination of European Jews and non-Jews in Nazi concentration camps prior to and during World War II. The victims were both Jews and non-Jews. Unfortunately, the non-Jewish victims are forgotten from Holocaust remembrance. The Zionist killings of hundreds of Palestinians in Dir Yassein and other places in Palestine are also examples of holocaust.

Home rule

The break-up of a nation into a number of units, each exercising total control over its internal and external affairs. This demand is usually based on the existence of a national identity.

Hudnah

Peace, tranquillity, truce, armistice. An abstract noun from the root "h.d.n." with the sense of "to be or become quiet, to calm down, to conclude a truce with someone. Hence, *hudnah* is referred to as peace agreement. The related term *Muhādanah* means peace negotiations or a process of entering into peace agreement with the enemy in which the term *hudnah* serves as the instrument.

Ḥujjat al Islam

Literally, "the proof of Islam." In Iran, it refers to a rank of a would be *Mujtahid* below that of *Āyatullāh.* The term is often used by shi'ite Imams and Sunnis to refer to great scholars. See *ĀYATULLĀH.*

Ḥukm (pl. *aḥkām*)

Statutes, regulations, stipulations; judgement, legal effect, juridical norm. The word *ḥukm* in its absolute sense means to judge the position of a thing to another thing in the relation of an attribute to its subject, affirmatively or negatively. If the method of affirming or negating it is reason, it is called *ḥukm aqli* (rational judgement), if the method is based upon habit, it is called *ḥukm 'adi* (habitual judgement). If the method affirming or negating it is the *Shari'ah* (divine law), it is called *ḥukm sharī'ī* (legal judgement). Technically, it is called the command or ruling of the *Shari'ah*. For example, prayer is obligatory; drinking alcohol is forbidden. It is a juridical norm or value determined by the Shari'ah. *Ḥukm shara'ī* is divided into two main varieties of *al-ḥukm al-taklīfī* (defining law) and *al-ḥukm al-waḍ'ī* (declaratory law). See *ḌAḌA*.

Human Rights

Rights to which all human beings are entitled because of their humanity and not because of their social status or individual merit. Such rights are believed, by proponents, to be necessary for freedom and the maintenance of a reasonable quality of life. Inalienable rights cannot be granted or limited but can only be secured or violated. Human rights are divided into three generations. First-generation human rights deal essentially with liberty. They are fundamentally civil and political in nature and include freedom of speech, the right to a fair trial, and freedom of religion. Second-generation human rights are related to equality. They are fundamentally social, economic, and cultural in nature and include, among others, equal conditions and treatment to all and the right to work and to be employed, thus securing the ability of the individual to support a family. Third-generation human rights focus essentially on fraternity and, in generic terms, can be seen as rights of solidarity. They cover group and collective rights: the right to self-determination, to economic and social development, and to participate in the common heritage of mankind. Many of these rights have been codified in treaties and conventions, the most important of which is the U.N.'s Universal Declaration of Human Rights of 1948. See CIVIL RIGHTS, CIVIL LIBERTIES.

Humanism

A philosophy centered on humankind and human values, exalting human free will and superiority to the rest of nature. Renaissance thinkers such as Petrarch began a trend toward humanism that embraced such figures as Machiavelli, Thomas More, and Erasmus and that led to much subsequent secular thought and literature, as well as to the Reformation.

Hung parliament

A parliament where no party has a clear majority and thus unable to form a government. The only way government could be formed is through coalition which is generally considered unstable. Hung parliament is a British term but is used greatly in Anglophone countries. See PARLIAMENT.

Ḥurriyah

An abstract noun derived from *ḥur* meaning free. Islam accords freedom to act according to one's own moral convictions and choices. The Qur'anic dictum *lā ikrāha fī al-dīn* (2:256), meaning there is no coercion in *al-dīn*, refers not merely to matters of faith but to every conceivable area of human life and negates all attempts at regimentation of individual life. The freedom espoused by Islam is not confined to believers but extends to minorities and non-Muslim citizens of the Islamic polity. This freedom, it should be noted, is not absolute but relative and proportionate to man's capacity and responsibility. Advocating absolute freedom is irresponsible as its complete denial is erroneous. See FREEDOM, LIBERTY.

I

'Ibādah (pl. *'Ibādāt*)

Worship, devotional service, religious observance. The term is derived from Arabic word *'Abd'* meaning servant. *'Ibādah* therefore refers to the performance of duties and obligations laid upon Muslims by Allah (SWT), including ritual practices, and abiding by the order of Allah (SWT) in each and every step of life, in action, and thought. Ibadah, therefore, refers to a life of continuous worship, of doing everything which Allah (SWT) loves and is pleased with. As used in the Qur'an, *'ibadah* refers to humility, obedience and devotion in carrying out the Will of Allah (SWT).

Ibāḥah

Divulgence, disclosure, permission. *Ibāḥah* has been used in the sense of option, lawfulness, permissibility and absoluteness. It has been defined as the antonym of prohibition. It means non-existence of harm either in the commission of an act or in its omission. According to the jurists, if the law provides no ruling to specify the value of a certain conduct, then permissibility (*ibāḥah*) remains to be the original state which is presumed to continue. The authority for this presumption is found in the Qur'an which says that Allah (SWT) "has created everything in the earth for your (mankind) benefit" (2:29). There is the proviso that the act should not have been forbidden or should bring no harm to oneself or to others.

Idealism

A theoretical perspective of international relations that takes an optimistic view of possibilities for cooperation in the international system. Idealists acknowledge the absence of a global authority to impose order on international relations, but they believe that global anarchy and war are not givens. Many idealists look to international organizations such as the United Nations as nascent world governments, with some anticipating the eventual development of a world federation. Idealists therefore focus on the commonality of human interests rather than competition over finite resources. They tend to see states as an obstacle to global cooperation, so idealists question the legitimacy of state interests. It follows that policies made on behalf of a state must be held to a moral standard. The most optimistic idealists believe that if decision makers world wide abide by an understood universal morality, conflict could be eliminated. See REALPOLITIK.

Ideologue

A person who tends to interpret the world strictly in ideological terms. The ideologue is a true believer so strongly influenced by ideology that his beliefs are little influenced by what is happening in the world. Ideologues have at times been powerful actors on the world political scene. For instance, Adolf Hitler was an advocate of NAZISM.

Ideologues

(1) A group of French philosophers who were most active between 1795 and 1815, who sought to develop a "science of ideas," and who coined the term "ideology." They sought to reveal the biases and inadequacies of traditional ideas and replace these ideas with the new, "more rational" ideas that became known as classical liberalism. (2) According to Philip Converse, those few people who have the most sophisticated intellectual understanding of politics, because they understand and effectively apply concepts drawn from ideologies.

Ideology

Interrelated social, economic, and political ideas constituting a comprehensive worldview. The logically-connected ideas within such worldviews provide descriptions and explanations about political life and prescriptions for how political communities should be structured and perform in the near future. The ideas within these worldviews often have deep philosophical foundations and are expressed as abstract generalizations, but these ideas nevertheless provide a basis for understanding and evaluating concrete political events and conditions and for acting in the everyday world of politics. Because the ideas of ideologies serve political purposes, their validity is problematic.

Iḥsān

Beneficence, charity, almsgiving, performance of good deeds. Literally, *iḥsan* has two meanings: one doing something well and perfectly, the other doing someone good and a favour. According to Muslim scholars, *iḥsān* is an act of heart which means thinking according to the standards of truth, forming the intention to do good, useful things and doing them and performing acts of worship in consciousness of presenting them to the view of God. In order to attain *iḥsān*, it is necessary to establish one's thoughts, feelings and conceptions on a firm belief and deepen in it by practicing the essentials of Islam. Only then can one really do good to others just for God's sake and without expecting any return. According to the Prophet (SAW), *iḥsan* is that you worship God as if seeing Him; even if you do not see Him, He certainly sees you. A person with such degree of awareness of God's constant supervision of him and therefore tries his utmost to do whatever he does in the best way possible cannot help but do others good.

Ijmā'

Consensus. Agreement, unanimity, consensus of authorities in a legal question. *Ijmā'* is the third source of Shar'iah. It is the verbal noun of the Arabic word *ajma'a* which has two meanings, to determine and to agree upon something. *Ijmā'* is defined as the unanimous agreement of the Muslim jurists (*mujtahidūn*) of the Muslim community of any period following the demise of Prophet Muhammad (SAW) on any matter. *Ijmā'* applies to all juridicl, intellectual, customary and linguistic matters. *Ijmā'* plays a crucial role in the development of Islamic law. The existing body of *fiqh* is the product of a long process of *ijtihād* and *Ijmā'*. It ensures the correct interpretation of the Qur'an, the faithful understanding and transmission of the Sunnah and the legitimate use of *ijtihād*. From the viewpoint of the manner of its occurrence, *Ijmā* is divided into two types: (1) Explicit *Ijmā'* in which every *mujtahid* expresses his opinion either verbally or by action; and (2) Tacit *ijmā'* wherein some of the *mujtahidūn* of a particular age give an expressed opinion concerning an incident but the rest remain silent.

Ijtihād

Literally, "effort, exertion or endeavour" but technically it signifies exerting the utmost effort to ascertain the injunctions of Islam and its intent through the efficient use of jurisprudential evidences and principles. *ijtihād* has been defined as exerting one's self with a view to form an independent judgement on a legal question. The decisions arrived at through *ijtihād* should neither contravene the Shari'ah nor distort its brilliant clarity and it should be resorted to only in the absence of an applicable text of the Qur'an or the Sunnah. Epistemologically, *ijtihād* involves both induction and deduction to the extent that it uses the existing body of knowledge and pure logical reasoning. It presupposes an ultimate agreement between reason and revelation with the provision that the former is subservient to the latter. *Ijtihād* is the most important source of Islamic law next to the Qur'an and the Sunnah. The various roots of jurisprudence that feature next to the two revealed sources are all manifestations of *ijtihād*, albeit with differences that are largely procedural in character. In this way, consensus of opinion, analogy, juristic preference, considerations of public interest (*maslaḥah*) etc., all interrelated not only under the main heading of *ijtihād*, but through it to the Qur'an and the Sunnah.

Ikhtilāf

Difference of opinion, disagreement, dispute, controversy. *Ikhtilāf* has generally been used in the negative sense of disagreement and dispute. However, *ikhtilāf* has a positive meaning as well. Positive *ikhtilāf* is part of the human nature. The difference (*ikhtilāf*) of the night and the day, the differences of the languages and colors, the difference of human beings, the difference of personalities, the difference of opinion and, indeed, the difference of views among the Muslim jurists that do not affect great principles (*ikhtilāf al-madhāhib*) are positive differences. These differences are necessary to promote healthy competition and development of the civilization. This positive *ikhtilāf* is considered by the Prophet (SAW) "as a mercy for people." The negative meaning of *ikhtilāf* is conflict which causes divisions in the whole and divides the ummah into various factions.

Ikhwān

Brethren or members of an order. Human brotherhood is one of the fundamental elements in the value system of Islam. This value is based on an unshakable belief in the Oneness and Universality of God. The Muslims believe in the unity of mankind with regard to the source of creation, the God the Almighty, the original common parentage of Adam and Eve, and the final destiny of returning to God, the Creator. When these concepts are properly interpreted and applied in one's life, there will be no room for pretended supremacy or presumptuous exclusivity and man will be provided with a clear concept and a solid basis of human brotherhood. See *UKHUWWAH*.

'Ilm (pl. *'ulum*)

Knowledge, learning, intellection, science. Generally translated as knowledge, the concept of *'ilm* in Islam is very vast. It ranges in its meaning from the Sufi understanding of the term *ma'rifah* (gnosis) to the interpretation of knowledge as it concerns every day activities of the individual. *'Ilm* in general is divided into two categories: revealed knowledge, which basically includes the Qur'an and the Sunnah, and science-derived knowledge, which is acquired through experience, observation, and research. The former category is further sub-divided into *farḍ al-ayn*, which is binding upon every individual Muslim, and *farḍ al-kifāyah*, which is binding upon the community as a whole but which can be discharged on its behalf by some members of the community. *'Ilm* is mentioned in the Qur'an with unusual frequency and its pursuit according to a *hadith*, is incumbent upon every Muslim even if it entails travelling to China. However, *'ilm* becomes a value only if it is pursued within the value-framework of Islam and only when it is pursued for the benefit of the individual or the community and ultimately for gaining the pleasure of Allah (SWT).

Imām (pl. *a'immah*)

Prayer leader, master, leader. The term *imām* is used in four different senses. First, it is used to refer to the one who stands before the congregation to lead the prayer. Any respected Muslim who is well-trained in prayers can be an *imām*. In general, it is the most learned and most respected person in the assembly who is offered the honour of being the *imām*. In modern times, many mosques have an employed leader of the congregation. Second, the term has been applied to caliphs because they were the supreme leaders of the community. With the abolition of the caliphate, this usage of the term has disappeared. Third, eminent religious scholars are also called *imām*. Usually the term is added before the names of learned men e.g., Imam al-Ghazali, Imam Abu Hanifah. Fourth, it is used by the Shi'i to refer to the person who is supposed to be the guidance of the human race, in both religious as well as secular issues. See *SULTAN.*

Imāmah

Political or religious leadership, the office of the *Imām*, imamate. The term is of great significance in the *Shi'ī* school of jurisprudence. The ideas around the *imām* are the very foundations upon which the *Shi'i* theology rests. *Imāmah* is continuation of the work of Muhammad (SAW). Shi'is divide the historical epoch of the universe into two cycles: the cycle of prophecy (*nubuwwah*) and the cycle of interpretation, known as *wilāyah*, meaning "sainthood," specifically of one who is a close associate or friend of God. Muhammad (SAW) was the last in the cycle of prophecy, whereas Ali began the cycle of *wilāyah*, which continues until the day of judgment. During the cycle of *wilāyah*, the imams dominate and guide. The imam is supposed to have a special closeness to God, and a descendant of the Prophet (SAW), and has something that comes close to divine powers. The imam is the only one who fully understands all aspects of Islam, he is infallible and the only one who can give interpretations of the Qur'an and the Sunnah. The *imams* are uniquely qualified by means of a divine light, known as the "*nūr muhammadī*," the Muhammadan light, to serve as authoritative teachers for the Muslims during this historical phase of the cosmos's existence. *See KHALĪFAH.*

Īmān

Faith, surrender. The term is derived from the Arabic root *amana* meaning to behave and *amina* to be tranquil at heart and mind. Faith in Islam is not simply a confession of belief in the Oneness of Allah (SWT), His messengers and the books but a state of happiness acquired by virtue of positive action and constructive conceptions as well as dynamic and effective measures. It is a principle of Islamic law that the *Īmān* is adhering to a certain set of doctrines and anyone who accepts these doctrines becomes a *Mu'mīn*. However, *Īmān* in its true sense is valid only when it entails complete surrender of one's will and freedom of choice to the will of Allah (SWT), renouncing all claims to his own supremacy. A Muslim, who has real faith in Allah (SWT), makes his entire life one of obedience and surrender to His will. He never behaves arrogantly or selfishly or as if he were master of his own destiny. His political, social, economic and cultural outlook must all be in tune with the code of guidance revealed by Allah(SWT). See *SHI'ISM.*

Imārah

Position or rank of an emir, princely bearing or manners, principality, emirate, authority, power.

Impeachment

The power of the Assembly to indict a public official (a president, or members of the cabinet and judiciary) charged with misconduct in office. Impeachment comprises both the act of formulating the accusation and the resulting trial of the charges; it is frequently but erroneously taken to mean only the removal from office of an accused public official. An impeachment trial may result in either an acquittal or in a verdict of guilty. In the latter case the impeached official is removed from office; if the charges warrant such action, the official is also remanded to the proper authorities for trial before a court. In the U.S., Congress can indict a public authority by a simple majority in the House of Representatives, followed by a trial in the Senate, where a two-thirds vote of members present can convict and remove the president from office. See ACCOUNTABILITY.

Imperialism

Political dominance by a metropolitan power of territories and peoples beyond its borders. Imperialism is an imposition of the stronger nation's will or rule over the weaker nations by means of force, with territorial, political, economic, social, religious and cultural implications. The motives of imperialism include conquest for the sake of loot, the search for competition-free markets, the quest for fresh fields of investment, and the urge to secure certain strategic raw materials. Imperialism also satisfies certain psychological urges not only of the leaders but also of the people, such as the lust for adventure, for power, prestige and glory accruing from a vast colonial empire. It also satisfies the sense of vanity and superiority. English men glorified in the boast that the sun never sets in the British Empire. American empire builders developed a concept of "manifest destiny" to rationalize their settling and exploitation of the North American continent. They established a religious conviction that they were ordained by God to settle and govern the New World. V. I. Lenin saw imperialism as a consequence of monopoly capitalism and as a means of extending the life of capitalism, which, he thought, would otherwise have already been doomed by its internal contradictions.

Implementation

The process of carrying out a policy. Policy implementation was the exclusive jurisdiction of the administrators and hence there existed a dichotomy between politics and administration. This distinction has now been done away with. Implementation is now considered to be an interrelated activity which is hoped to arrest the problem of implementation failure. See EXECUTIVE.

Independence

State or quality of being independent. A territory not under the control of any other power. Independence is one of the characteristics of modern states. A state is a political unit that has ultimate responsibility for the conduct of its own affairs. In political science terminology, this characteristic is called sovereignty. The term independence is also associated with the concept of nationalism. With the modern importance of nationalism, it is common to think that it is the right of people, if they feel they have a common nationality, to have a state with the ultimate responsibility for the conduct of their own affairs. See SOVEREIGNTY, STATE.

Indirect Election

A two-stage election in which the first election chooses electors who then vote for the person or assembly they prefer. The U.S. presidential election is the best known example of an indirect election. The U.S. president is elected by an electoral college of 538 electors. See ELECTION.

Indirect Rule

The practice of a power ruling a colonial territory by utilising existing indigenous government institutions and elites. This was a characteristic of British colonial administration as opposed to French direct rule. See COLONIALISM.

Individualism

The belief that the individual should be at the center of any conception of society or politics. It is the idea that people should be able to go their own way, "do their own thing," advance within the society as far as their own talents, ability, and efforts will allow. Society and government exist, not to control, but to facilitate individual opportunity. Individualism has played a long and complex role in the development of capitalism and democracy in the West. Democracy takes the individual as its core value. Islamic conception of participatory political system, in contrast, gives equal importance to both the individual and the group. The opposite doctrine to individualism is collectivism, in a social sense, and holism, in a logical sense.

Industrial Democracy

The control of a workplace by its workers. It refers to the popular administration and control of each industry or service by those who work there. This idea of industrial democracy is generally associated with socialists but some liberals have also argued that people should have as much power to decide in the workplace as in the political arena.

Industrial Revolution

The name given to the rapid transformation in economic life brought about by the application of science and technology to the production of goods. The industrial revolution involved methods of production based on the use of new scientific inventions driven steam engine. The revolution started in England during the period from approximately 1760 to 1840. This period is sometimes called the "first industrial revolution" to distinguish it from the "second industrial revolution" (approximately 1880 to 1910). The first revolution relied on mechanical innovations, while the second revolution was based on chemical and electrical innovations.

Industrial Society

A society characterized by economies of scale and the extensive use of machinery. The term refers to those market societies which emphasize widespread participation in the labour market. Lately, some writers are championing the emergence of the post-industrial society characterized by a more loose division of labour than under the industrial society. See FIRST WORLD.

Initiative

A procedure in which citizens can put an issue on the ballot. Voters can accept or reject the issue. For an issue to get on the ballot, a small percentage of the citizens must sign a petition. In Switzerland and several American states, ordinary voters are allowed to file such a petition. See REFERENDUM, PLEBISCITE.

Inqilāb

The term refers to upheaval, revolution, and overthrow of government. It may sometimes be used for alteration of action, transformation and change of administration. In contemporary Arab jargon, *inqilāb* denotes a coup d'etat. See REVOLUTION.

Insurgency

A form of unlawful political behaviour, involving violence or threat of violence, with the goal of overturning the existing government or political leadership, or undermining it to the point where it will acquiesce to its opponents' desires. An insurgency usually involves a prolonged struggle that may last years without resolution. See VIOLENCE.

Institutions

Habitual practices of society but generally to specific associations or organizations which are formed for the purpose of co-ordinating the achievement of a known set of goals. Society is organized into numerous institutions, each pursuing its set of goals and in the process interacting with other institutions of society. Social institutions refer to well-defined and formal organizations of society that govern the way that society operates – e.g., class system, family system, educational system. Political institutions refer to the systems that govern the operations of the government of a particular society – e.g., formal power structures, political parties, mechanism of getting into power.

Intelligence Service

Institutions of a national government that gather information, particularly about clandestine activities of other countries or enemies for the purpose of protecting national security. Such functions were once performed chiefly by foreign ambassadors. Now, all the governments have their own intelligence branches. In the United State, the CIA coordinates the intelligence functions of all government departments and agencies. See CIA, KGB.

Interest Aggregation

The process of combining demands on government and turning them into manageable alternatives. Interest aggregation is achieved by formulation of the general policies that combine interests, or recruitment of personnel committed to a particular pattern of society. Political parties constitute the main instrument of interest aggregation. Government agencies and interest groups also perform a similar function. See POLITICAL PARTY.

Interest Articulation

The process of forming and expressing demands by political interest groups and transmitting demands to government authorities. Some of the principal devices used for interest articulation include: lobbying, propaganda, protest, mass communication, public opinion polls, and campaigns and elections. See INTEREST GROUPS.

Interest Group

An organized association which engages in activity relative to governmental decisions. The interest group aims to influence government policy in a direction favourable to its interest. In order to achieve their goals, interest groups may lobby government officials, donate money to political candidates, organize political marches, or engage in many other forms of political activity. Interest groups are of four types: associational, non-associational, institutional, and anomic interest groups. Other terms often used, generally synonymously with interest groups, include pressure group, organized interest and lobby. See CIVIL SOCIETY, LOBBYING.

Inter-Governmental Organizations (IGOs)

Voluntary associations of two or more independent states that meet regularly and have full-time staffs. They have some common purpose of cooperating with one another. IGOs may be described according to their size of membership or the scope of their goals. Only one organization, the United Nations, approaches global membership, with over 192 states. Regional organizations, such as the Organization of American States (OAS), the Organization of African Unity (OAU), and the Association of Southeast Asian Nations (ASEAN), are multi-purpose IGOs that have limited memberships based on the geographical proximity of states sharing common interests. The IGOs have mushroomed especially in the post-World War II era and currently there are over 400 IGOs all over the world. See NGOs.

Inter-governmental relations

All executive, legislative, judicial, administrative, and political interactions among all elected and appointed officials working in national, state, and local government organizations.

Government policies, that is, intentions and plans for action, and policy implementation are often developed through interactions between public officials.

Inter-Governmentalism

The view which argues that the development of international institutions and regimes tends to be shaped by the actions of and convergence among nation-state actors. See IGOs.

Internal Colonialism

An idea and reality in sociology and society largely associated with the sociologist Richard Blauner. It refers essentially to the experience and social position of certain minority segments in society as analogous to the traditional colonial situation. Furthermore, the dominant nation-state power extracts the material and human resources from the weaker nation (usually third world) while exercising political and economic control. The only and crucial difference, of course, is that with the "internal colonial" situation both the expropriators and the colonialized are within the same national political and economic system. Along these lines, the position of native Americans, Chicanos, blacks, Puerto Ricans, etc., in American society may be seen as a "colonial" one. See COLONIALISM.

International Bank for Reconstruction and Development (IBRD)

(also known as World Bank) An international financial institution forming part of the United Nations and based in Washington, D.C. One of its main objectives is to provide development funds to needy third world countries (especially the poorest countries) in the form of interest-bearing loans and technical assistance. The World Bank operates with funds borrowed primarily from rich nations but increasingly from OPEC countries as well.

International Court of Justice

One of the six major organs of the United Nations Organization established in 1946 to serve as the judicial arm of the international organization. The fifteen judges of the court are appointed jointly by the General Assembly and the Security Council. The court adjudicates conflicts among states only when the countries in conflict consent to take the case to the court and abide by its decision. The court uses international law in its deliberations. See UNITED NATIONS.

International Development Association (IDA)

An international body set up in 1960 to assist the World Bank (IBRD) in its efforts to promote economic development of the underdeveloped countries by providing additional capital on a low interest basis (i.e., through "soft" loans) especially to the poorest of the poor developing countries. See WORLD BANK.

International Labour Organization (ILO)

One of the United Nations functional organizations based in Geneva whose central task is to look into problems of world manpower supply, its training, utilization, domestic and international distribution, etc. Its aim in this endeavour is to increase "world output" through maximum utilization of available human resources and thus improve levels of living for working people.

International Law

A body of rules routinely observed by the vast majority of governments throughout the world, despite the lack of effective centralized mechanisms for its legislation, execution, and adjudication. International law is primarily a coordinative process of interaction between states rather than a subordinate process of governmental adherence to centralized institutional authority, which is weakly developed at the international level. Nevertheless, international law helps to bring a degree of order to interstate relations as governments pursue their interests over and above them. States are generally considered the main subjects of international law. Normally, individual persons cannot bring suit in international courts; only the government of their citizenship or nationality may sue foreign governments. Sources of international law include treaties or covenants made by states, customary practices, generally accepted principles, judicial decisions, and the writings of jurists. International courts such as the International Court of Justice interpret international law and apply it to individual cases brought by states. International law may have precedence over domestic laws that conflict with international obligations. See LAW.

International Monetary Fund (IMF)

A specialized agency of the United Nations, established in 1944 by the Bretton Woods agreement. The IMF is to promote international monetary cooperation, to stabilize exchange rate fluctuations as a means of improving convertibility, to provide an international forum for monetary issues, and to maintain a monetary pool from which member nations can draw in order to correct a deficit in their balance of payments. Countries suffering from economic crises have borrowed from the IMF, but these countries have been subjected to increasing levels of IMF supervision and policy constraints that did not help the borrowing economies develop as desired. See WORLD BANK.

International Relations

A branch of political science which studies how countries interact with one another. These interactions occur in the realms of economics, politics, diplomacy, and warfare. The study of international political interaction has more recently begun to include the analysis of non-state as well as state actors and forces. International relations now claims autonomy as a subject. It has developed numerous sub-disciplines such as international political economy, foreign policy analysis, strategic studies, and the study of international organizations. See POLITICAL SCIENCE.

International Socialism

The socialist doctrine proclaiming the idea of the international brotherhood of the working classes, in part because the nation state has been seen as the prop used by exploiting capitalists. International socialism therefore rejects the idea of nationalism since workers have no fatherland. The Communist Manifesto of Marx and Engels called for workers of all countries to unite. See COMMUNISM, COMMUNIST MANIFESTO.

Internationalism

The belief that the greatest possible cooperation between nations in trade, culture, education, government, etc. is the best way to build peace. This is the opposite of isolationism and nationalism. In the twentieth century the founding of the League of Nations (1919) and the United Nations (1945) were great steps forward for internationalism. See ISOLATIONISM; NATIONALISM.

Intifāḍah al-Ḥijarah

Literally in Arabic, "the stone's uprising." Refers to the uprising led and implemented by the "stone-throwing" Palestinians that shook the very foundation of the Zionist imperialist presence in the West Bank and Gaza Strip. The *intifaḍah* lasted for about six years from 1987 to 1993 during which time about 1,540 Palestinians were martyred, about 130,000 wounded, and about 116,000 arrested by the Israeli government. *Intifaḍah* is widely credited with forcing the Israelis to re-think their occupation strategy, and to enter negotiations with PLO. Following the 1993 Oslo peace treaty, the PLO and other organizations declared the end of the *intifāḍah*, but Islamic-oriented Palestinian organizations like al-jihad and Hamas continued the struggle which erupted once again in 2001. See ROAD MAP.

Iqāmat al ḥudūd

This refers to the enforcement of the prescribed penalties of Shar'iah. *Hadd* penalty is specific in reference to both the quantity of punishment and the type of conduct which it penalises. Under *Hudud* law, theft, robbery, illicit sex, alcohol consumption and apostasy are considered offences. Punishment for these offences are corporal in nature, involving whipping, stoning to death and amputation of limbs. Every offence must be proven as prescribed. In the event there is insufficient evidence, then *hudud* punishments should not be carried out. The court may punish the offender with non-hudud punishments known as *ta'zir* punishment. See *HUDUD, TA'ZIR*.

Iran-Contra Affair

A secret initiative signed by President Reagan that authorized the sale of U.S. arms to Iran in exchange for the release of hostages held by pro-Iranian groups. The initiative went against the government's public policy of not trading with Iran or Iraq.

Iron Curtain

Term used by Winston Churchill in a speech at Fulton, Missouri, in March 1946, to describe the line of demarcation between Western Europe and the Russian zone of influence. It refers to a barrier to the exchange of information and ideas created by ideological, political, and military hostility of one country toward another or others, especially between Soviet Russia and its Eastern European satellite states and other countries.

Iron Law of Oligarchy

The principle stating that all associations eventually become dominated by a minority of their members. This law is associated with French Political sociologist Robert Michels who said: "He who says organization, says oligarchy."

Iron Triangle

The interrelationships that develop among members of Congress, interest groups, and bureaucratic agencies in the United States on particular issues or policy areas. They provide numerous benefits for the political actors in the triangle, but may not be the best way to make policy.

Irredentism

Taken from the Italian expression "Terra irredenta" meaning "unredeemed land," this refers to an attempt, or a desire, or a policy which is directed towards the restoration of a territory (or territories) which is claimed, as historically related to a given political unit (usually a nation-state) by reason of linguistic, ethnic or cultural belonging or some other national attachment. Put more simply, it refers to any attempt made by an existing nation-state, or group within it, to recover or redeem land and peoples that are considered to belong to it, and not to the state in which they are currently situated. Irredentism emerges therefore as a questioning of, and a challenge to, the established boundaries between existing nation-states. It emerges with the birth of the modern nation and the modern nation-state. Adolf Hitler used the irredentist claims of the Sudetenland Germans, who had been included in the new state of Czechoslovakia, as justification for his forcible entry into Czechoslovakia in 1938, one of the major steps on the road to World War II. Iraq's invasion of Kuwait in 1990 is a recent example of irredentism. Indeed, Iraq has been punished severely and was forced to restore Kuwait's sovereignty. Irredentism is used also to refer to national agitation by an ethnic group opposed to foreign rule and demanding incorporation into a country with a similar ethnic composition. See NATIONALISM, SOVEREIGNTY.

Iṣlāḥ

Improvement, correction, reform, prevention, repair and re-establishment of peace and order. It refers to the reform and repair of personal, familial, societal, political and economic affairs. Specifically, *Islaḥ* refers to movements which, concerned by the corrupt state of Islamic life in the society, call upon the people to bring their practices more in accord with the message of the Qur'an and the Sunnah. The well-known reform movements are known generally as *Salafiyyah* movements of the eighteenth and nineteenth century. Its variants include the *Wahhabi* movement of the Arabian peninsula, the Shawkani movement of Yemen, the *Sanusi* movement of Libya, and the *Mahdī* movement of the Sudan. These movements had arisen as a religious reaction within Islam to a perceived corruption of the Islamic faith. This corruption was, quite often, seen to be primarily internal in nature, the result of Ottoman decadence and the declining zeal of the *Ulamā'*. See ISLAMIC REVIVAL.

Islam

Submission, resignation, and reconciliation to the will of God, the religion of Islam. The essence of the meaning of Islam is the procurement of "peace" by submission to the Divine will. The goal is obtained by the belief in one Allah (SWT) and the Messengership of Muhammad (SAW). The declaration of this belief, *shahādah*, requires the followers of Islam, the Muslims, to believe in the revelations of Allah (SWT), His angels, His Messengers, His books, and in the accountability on the day of judgement. The ritual aspects of this belief are encapsulated in the essential rituals; the five daily prayers (*ṣalāh*), fasting (*ṣawm*), the purification tax (*zakāh*), and the pilgrimage to Makkah once in a lifetime (*ḥaj*). However, Islam is not simply a religion with a set of beliefs and rituals. It is a total system of thought and behaviour, a system that manifests its own culture, has produced its own distinctive civilization, and shapes the outlook of its followers on every aspect of human endeavour. Islam requires its followers to shape their lives and societies, their thought and action, according to the principles and precepts of Islam. With more than a billion adherents worldwide, Islam is a major force in world politics. See *DĪN, SHARI'AH.*

Islamic Revolution in Iran

The 1979 revolution in Iran which replaced the most powerful monarchy with a nascent Islamic polity. The leadership of the revolution was provided by a revered leader Ayatollah Ruhullah Musavi al-Khomeini (1321–1409AH/1902-1989CE). Khomeini mobilized the masses against the Iranian monarchy for social injustices, political oppression, economic exploitation and foreign servitude. The purpose of the revolution was the establishment of a just social order: a just society that will morally and spiritually nourish refined human beings. The revolution, in the face of opposition from all major super powers and their clients, is the most significant and profound event in the entirety of contemporary Islamic history.

Islamic Revival

The renewal of heightened interest in Islamic symbols, ideas and ideals subsequent to the period of relative dormancy of interest in Islamic way of life. See ISLAH, NAHDAH, TAJDID.

Islamic State

A variedly-defined concept. Some define it vaguely as a "group of people working to realise the Will of Allah (SWT)." Others define it as a state in which *shari'ah* rules supreme. At the barest minimum, a state is defined as Islamic in which Islam is expressly or implicitly declared to be the religion of the State. Some scholars suggest taking the distribution of population according to religious confessions, as a basic criterion for describing state as Islamic. Majority of Muslim scholars, however, agreed that an Islamic state be defined in terms of important principles provided in the Qur'an. These principles include: *tawhîd* (unity and sovereignty of Allah (SWT)); *shari'ah*, the Islamic legal system; *shura,* decision-making by consultation; *'adalah*, justice in its comprehensive sense; *ḥurriyyah*, freedom; and *musāwah*, equal opportunity for each individual to articulate his/her potential to the maximum limit. See *DAWLAH, KHILĀFAH.*

Islamist

The word is widely used by academics to identify radical political movements, individuals and ideas that are Islamically inspired. The word is distinguished from "Islamic," which is a broader term and refers to something associated with the religion of Islam.

Islamization of Political Science

A process of recasting the discipline of political science so as to embody the principles of Islam in its methodology, in its strategy, in what it regards as its data, its problems, its objectives, its aspirations. It is a part of the larger Islamization of Knowledge movement which aims at developing or generating and promoting human knowledge which is in harmony with the will of Allah s.w.t. The aim is to critique, analyze and reformulate Western disciplines in a form that deals with revelation as a source of knowledge. The International Islamic University Malaysia is in the forefront of this movement.

Isolationism

A policy of abstention from international commitments in the belief that a country's security and well-being are best served by isolating it from the vicissitudes of the larger world. A conservative doctrine, it counsels against reliance on other states for security, against intervention in foreign conflicts, against offering foreign aid to needy countries (especially if no direct national interest is apparent), against participation in global institutions, and against joining international legal frameworks. It is not only the right, but also the duty, of government leaders to direct their efforts primarily to the promotion of their own country's interests. The United States has traditionally been an isolationist country. In 1823, the Monroe Doctrine tried to exclude European powers from America which stayed out of the League of Nations; and entered World War II only when attacked. Thereafter, it played an active role in international affairs. British policy was essentially isolationist in the inter-war period. See INTERNATIONALISM.

Istiḥsān

Literally, to approve or to deem something preferable. It is a derivation of *ḥasunā* which means being good or beautiful. In its juristic sense, *istiḥsān* is a method of exercising personal opinion in order to avoid rigidity and unfairness that might result from the literal enforcement of the existing law. It may fittingly be described as juristic preference as it involves setting aside an established analogy in favour of an alternative ruling which serves the ideals of justice and public interest in a better way. The theory of *Istiḥsān* was enunciated by Imam Abu Hanifah who represents the school of the people of *ra'y* or opinion.

Istiqāmah

Straightness, sincerity, uprightness, rectitude. Integrity, probity, honesty. Muslim scholars have interpreted *istiqamah* as avoidance of all kinds of deviations and extremes, and following in the footsteps of the Prophet (SAW) in one's beliefs and religious deeds and daily practical life. A man can be straightforward in his conduct by performing his religious duties, in his ego or inner self by following the truth of *Shari'ah*, in his spirit by acting in accordance with knowing God, and in his innermost senses or faculties by complying with the spirit of *Shari'ah*.

Ithnā 'Ashariya

The Twelver Shi'is, the major Shi'ah school of law also known as *Ja'fariyyah*. They believe that, after the death of the Prophet (SAW), the *Imamate* (the political and religious leadership of the Muslim community) should have gone to 'Ali—the cousin and son-in-law of the Prophet—and his descendants as a divine right. According to mainstream *Shī'a*, there have been twelve *Imams* as follows: 1) Ali, the cousin and son-in-law of Muhammad (SAW) (d.661); 2) al-Hasan (d.670); 3) al-Husayn (d.680); 4) Ali Zayn al-'Abidin (d.713); 5) Muhammad al-Baqir (d.733); 6) Ja'far al-Sadiq (d.765); 7) Musa al-Kazim (d.799); 8) 'Ali al-Rida (d.818); 9) Muhammad al-Jawad (d.835); 10) 'ali al-Hadi (d.868); 11) al-Hasan al-'Askari (d.874); 12) Muhammad al-Mahdi. The last Imam, the Mahdi, is believed not to have died but to be in hiding and will appear at the end of time in order to bring about the victory of the Shi'a faith. The twelver Shii's are the dominant religious group in Iran and Iraq. See *SHĪ'AH, IMĀMAH.*

I'tiqād

Belief, faith, trust, confidence, conviction. The term is derived linguistically from *'aqada* which means tying, joining, and contracting (a sale). If one says, "*aqadtu* such and such," it means his heart is firm upon such and such. Therefore, *i'tiqād*, according to Muslim scholars, is the firm creed that one's heart is fixed upon without any wavering or doubt. It excludes any supposition, doubt or suspicion. *I'tiqād* is different from *īmān* (faith) because *Īmān* does cover works (*'amal*) and confession. The terms *'aqīdah* and *I'tiqād* are synonymous and interchangeable. See *'AQIDAH, IMAN.*

J

Jahiliyah

State of ignorance, pre-Islamic paganism. *Jahiliyyah* is the time of barbarism, lawlessness, and ignorance. It refers to pre-Islamic desert culture (bedouin) based on ranching, clan solidarity, primitive fatalistic paganism, female infanticide, promiscuity and the like. It is this Arab culture which Islam condemned as *jahiliyyah* and which it replaced with a culture based on true moral values. Islam, thus, marks an evolution and a departure from that primitive state of affairs. In its modern context, *jahiliyyah* was first used by Abul A'la Mawdudi and was popularised by Syed Qutb. They used it to mean any behaviour that deviates from Islamic norms. The deviation from Islam is of two sorts. First, there are those who never entered Islam, chose to fight it, and built for themselves a civilization and culture of *kufr* and *jahiliyah*. Today, this civilization is represented by the western civilization. Like *Jahiliyah*, the women in the West, mix freely with men, dress barely and sometimes even go in the nude. The entire civilization is based upon materialism, secularism and hedonism. This civilization is global. Second, there are those Muslims who have, under the influence of colonial domination, accepted the validity of secularism as a way of life. Islamic movements aim at reforming the Muslims and of reconstructing the civilization based upon Islamic universal value system.

Jamā'ah (pl. *Jamā'at*).

Group of people, party, troop, community. A synonym for the ummah, but it has more restricted meanings too. It may refer to a gathering of people or congregation of people. It may also mean group prayer as well as performing certain obligation collectively.

Jamā'at-e-Islami

An Islamic movement founded in 1941 by Sayyid Abul A'la Mawdudi (1903–1979). The tightly organized, highly disciplined and revolutionary Jama'at was founded to oppose British rule of India, to protect Muslims in India from the Hindu majority and to transform India into the *dar al Islam* (abode of Islam). Following the partition of India and the creation of Pakistan in 1947, the Jama'at dedicated itself to transforming Pakistan into an Islamic state. The Jama'at serves not just as a political entity but also as an educational and social welfare organization.

Jerusalem

A holy Place for three major world religions which have fought over it for centuries: Judaism, Christianity, and Islam. Palestinians demand access to Jerusalem as their inalienable right and Muslims all over the world demand the Liberation of the Holy City from "Zionist hands." Israel, of course, vows that the whole city of Jerusalem shall remain forever the capital of the Jewish state despite the fact that the eastern half was under Jordanian Arab control for the first 20 years of Israel's existence. It was in the Six Day War of 1967 that Israel conquered east Jerusalem along with the West Bank. In the three decades since, about 150,000 Israelis have settled in the eastern half of Jerusalem and now outnumber the Arabs there. They've been encouraged to do so by Israeli governments keen to establish their claim to the whole city by creating facts on the ground. Huge estates have been built on what most neutral outside observers agree to be Arab land.

Jihād

Striving, utmost exertion in the way of Allah (SWT) to fulfil one's responsibilities, both in outward actions and in inward correction of one's own mistakes, military action to defend Islam. *Jihād* is from the root *Jahada*, which means to strive for a better way of life. It may also be defined as a directed and perpetual struggle, of the Muslim as an individual and Muslims as a community, towards betterment, development and refinement in harmony with the values and ideals of Islam. *Jihād* refers to any earnest striving in the way of God, involving personal effort, material resources, or arms for righteousness and against evil, wrongdoing and oppression. Where it involves armed struggle, it must be for the defense of the Muslim community or a just war to protect even non-Muslims from evil, oppression, and tyranny. One who is actively engaged in jihad is a *mujāhid*. The term is erroneously associated with "holy war". Jihād is not a war to force the faith on others. The Qur'ān is categorical in this respect: "There is no compulsion in religion." See JUST WAR.

Jingoism

An enthusiastic and unreasonable belief in the superiority of one's country, especially when it involves support for a war against another country. This boastful nationalism characterized a section of the British press and public opinion in the nineteenth century. It was weakened by the Boer War (1899–1902) and disappeared as an important force in World War I. See IRREDENTISM, NATIONALISM.

Jizyah

Tax, tribute, poll tax. It is a tax paid by non-Muslims living in an Islamic State. Since the non-Muslims are exempt from military service and taxes are imposed on Muslims, they pay this tax to compensate. It guarantees them security and protection. If the State cannot protect those who paid *jizyah*, then the amount paid should be returned to them. There is no amount permanently fixed for it. Imam Shafi'i suggested one *dinar* per year. The tax varied in amount, and there were exemptions for the poor, for females and children (according to Abu Hanifah), for slaves, and for monks and hermits. See *KHARĀJ, AHL-AL-DHIMMAH.*

Judge

A person in a court of law who has the authority to make decisions about how the law is to be applied to a person. See QADI.

Judicial Review

The power of a court to determine whether actions of government officials are in accord with the constitution. It is the power given to a court to declare laws and executive actions unconstitutional. Since Chief Justice John Marshall formally asserted this right in Marbury v. Madison in 1803, the court has played an important role in the American legislative process. Although any court can decide whether a law is constitutional or not, the most important uses of judicial review have involved the Supreme Court. Judicial review is considered to be an essential feature of a federation. However, any constitutionally-mandated distribution of powers to separate bodies requires the equivalent of judicial review. Also see FEDERALISM.

Judiciary

A branch of government that is concerned with the administration of justice. It is composed of a body of judges in a constitutional system and is always separated from the other two branches of government to guarantee the judicial qualities of objectivity and detachment. In democratic as well as Islamic political systems, the independence of the judiciary is regarded as an essential prerequisite of a just and free society. See LAW.

Jund

Soldiers, army. Used in the Qur'an to refer to an armed troop. Under the Umayyads, the term applied to military settlements and districts in which soldiers could be mobilized for seasonal campaigns or for more protracted expeditions. The term also denotes army corps who drew regular pay. The Abbasids established the *diwan al-Jund* and by then the term had come to take a wider meaning, namely the armed forces. See MILITARY.

Junta

A revolutionary government, generally of military nature, that has taken power by force, and not through elections. Commonly associated with countries of South America and Africa. Junta is a pejorative term.

Jurisdiction

(1)The legal authority of a court to hear and decide a case. Concurrent jurisdiction exists when two courts have simultaneous responsibility for the same case. (2) The geographic area over which the court has authority to decide cases.

Jurisprudence

From Latin juris prudentia (by the activity of *prudentes*; advisors, experts), jurisprudence is the philosophy, science and the study of law and structure of the legal system. Jurisprudence refers to two different things. First, in common law jurisdictions, it means simply "case law," i.e., the law that is established through the decisions of the courts and other officials. Second, it means the philosophy of law, or legal theory, which studies not what the law is in a particular jurisdiction (say, Malaysia or the United States) but law in general—i.e., those attributes common to all legal systems. See FIQH.

Jury

A group of people in an American court of law who have been chosen to listen to the facts about a crime and to decide whether the person accused is guilty or not. In the deliberations of the jury, the judge takes no part, and judicial operations are systematically divided between fact finding and law finding.

Jus Sanguinis

"The law of blood ties," whereby individuals receive at birth the citizenship of their parents.

Jus Soli

"The law of soil," whereby individuals acquire the citizenship of the country in whose territory they are born.

Just War

Doctrine concerned with the question of when it is morally just to fight a war and how and against whom it should be conducted. This doctrine is based on such principles as: there must be a just cause i.e., war must be waged as self-defense against an aggressor; a legitimate authority must make the decision to go to war; the warring nations must observe proportionality between means and ends; war can happen only when all other means of achieving peace have been exhausted; and participants must not use immoral weapons i.e., weapons that are indiscriminate or that cause needless suffering. The doctrine comes from Medieval Christian thought and from the development of international law that followed. Public interest in just war theory declined considerably in this century with a growing realization of the horror of total war and the pre-occupation of the combatants with national interest rather than moral justification. See *JIHAD*.

Justice

The quality of being just; righteousness, equitableness or moral rightness. There are two main categories: procedural justice and social justice. Procedural justice is about the due process of law. This involves fair trials, and proper legal procedures. Social justice or substantive justice is concerned with a just, fair, or equitable society. The term is much more comprehensive in Islam. Justice in Islam is not simply legal but pervades every matter in life including oneself. Doing a thing which one ought to do is justice to oneself or to others. See *'ADL*.

K

Keynesianism

Economic theories and associated government policies advocated by John Maynard Keynes (1883–1946) whose economic ideas represented a major aspect of the Bretton Woods system. Based on that, nations retain the ability to intervene into their domestic economies but are limited in this by their agreement to leave international economic markets. This is usually referred to as "Keynesian compromise." As an economic doctrine, Keynesianism describes a particular mix of economic and social policies to be adopted by the state to avoid the worst of slumps and inflationary boom. Keyne's views were influenced by World War I and the chaos of the interwar period.

KGB (Committee for State Security)

Government organization in the former Soviet Union functioning as a secret police force. It was one of the state bodies exercising control over Soviet oppositionists. Its intelligence network kept track of political and military activities as well. It was given that name in 1953 succeeding the earlier state security groups, the Cheka and the NKVD. See CIA.

Khalīfah (pl. *khulafā'*)

Vicegerent; steward, one who comes after, deputy, successor. Man is referred to as the *khalīfah* or vicegerent of God on earth. Man, first, is a moral being and as such, he is a sort of cosmic bridge through which the divine will, in its totality and especially its higher ethical part can enter space-time and become concrete. Second, he is gifted with *'Aql*, discursive intellect, and the power of conceptualization. Third, he has been given divine guidance in terms of moral imperatives —the revelation of God's will in a prescriptive form. In short, he is the highest of God's creation, a theomorphic being, who bears God's trust and stewardship. Notwithstanding this exalted status, Man is but the deputy of God, possessing no authority save that of a steward. As befits his position, Man cannot be the arbiter of his conduct: he must defer it to the judgment of his sovereign. Denial of absolute sovereignty to Man is tantamount to loading him with moral responsibility. It is a natural corollary of man's acceptance of trust that he be born free and innocent. See *IMAM.*

Khilāfah

Succession, caliphate; the institution of vicegerency and custodianship on earth, equivalent of *imām*. It is the political system of Islam. It is defined as succession to the prophethood aimed at protecting the *Dīn* and ruling the world. Under the *khilāfah*, the entire breadth of the Islamic system (be it social, economic, educational, foreign policy, etc.) is implemented. The *khilāfah* is also responsible for spreading the message of Islam to the world. The Islamic political system, which the Prophet (SAW) established in Medinah, serves as the first model of the *khilāfah*. *Khilāfah* exists only when the *Sharī'ah* is the sole source of legislation in a state and its security is controlled by Muslims. See *SHARI'AH, KHALĪFAH, IMĀMAH.*

Kharāj

Tax, land tax. *Kharāj* was used for levies in return for leasing a land. The Arabs used to call land rent or house rent as *Kharāj*. 'Umar, the second caliph, introduced the system of *kharāj*, a custom borrowed from the Persians and the Romans. 'Umar allowed the inhabitants of the conquered lands to live in their own territories and to conduct their affairs according to their own faith and traditions in return for a fixed levy called *kharāj*. The head of state has the right to determine the rate of *kharāj* in the best interest of the state. This flexibility makes *kharāj* an important fiscal tool and a main source of revenue used to provide public goods and distributive expenditures. *Kharāj* was collected after a harvest and its rates varied according to difficulties of irrigation and vicinity to markets. See *JIZYAH.*

Khawārij

Kharijites, the strict religious sect of early Islamic history; dissenters, backsliders, rebels. It refers to those people who dissented to caliph 'Ali's agreement to settle his dispute with Muawiyah, the governor of Syria, through arbitration. They left 'Ali's camp and became the *khawārij*, an often-extremist sect that in different forms continued for some years after. Their name in Arabic means "those who go out" or "split off." They were a rigorously Qur'anically-based movement, fiercely egalitarian and dedicated to divine justice. They had wanted 'Ali to rectify the errors and misdeeds of "Uthman's administration," considering the matter of punishing his killers already resolved. 'Ali was finally able to neutralize most of these *khawarij* in a battle, but the remainder went their own ways and even set up a rival caliph, who never had any power beyond their circles. Sometimes, the term is used to refer to those people who disagree with the rest of the Muslims and cause disunity in the ummah.

Khulafā al- Rāshidūn

"Righteous caliphs"; refers to the first four caliphs (Abu Bakr, 'Umar, 'Uthman and 'Ali) who succeeded Prophet Muhammad (SAW); or their period of caliphate. There is general consensus that the *Khulafā al-rāshidūn* did adhere strictly to the normative standard found in the Qur'an and the Sunnah. This era of "righteous excellence" (632-661) was characterized by legitimacy and justice. None laid the foundation of a hereditary government nor assumed power by force or trickery. The period of *khulafā al-rāshidūn* formed an ideal source from which thinkers could draw the blueprint of an Islamic political order. This ideal appears in the writings of Muslim jurists and thinkers from al-Mawardi to Mawdudi. See *KHILĀFAH*.

Kitchen Cabinet

.A group of unofficial advisers and their support staff on whom the chief executive (the President or the Prime Minister) appears to rely heavily. The term originated with President Jackson's (1829–1837) meeting with such a group in the White House kitchen. See SHADOW CABINET.

Kleptocracy

Rule by thieves. A label sometimes applied to authoritarian regimes in which corruption reaches extraordinary levels and enormous amounts in public funds are siphoned off by top officials for their own enrichment.

Kremlin

Fortified portion of medieval Russian cities, originally a place of refuge to nearby inhabitants. Under Communist rule, the Kremlin became the political and administrative centre of the Soviet Union. The great part of the Moscow Kremlin dates from the fifteenth and sixteenth centuries. Western experts on Soviet affairs came to be known as Kremlinologists.

L

Laissez faire, laissez passer

"Let it alone, leave it be". A slogan developed by classical liberals calling for an unregulated economy. The state is expected to leave the individual alone to determine his/her own destiny and the fullest and free development of his own capacities and interests. The principle of laissez faire meant the free playoff competition which was the law of nature. Most people felt that it was natural and inevitable for some to be rich and privileged and others to be poor and miserable, and that the state ought not to interfere, except to ensure conformity with some rudimentary rules of social life. See CAPITALISM.

Law

That portion of the established thought and habit which has gained distinct and formal recognition in the shape of uniform rules backed by the authority and power of government. It refers to those rules of conduct that officially emanate from any authorized government agency. It includes statutes enacted by legislatures, common law, rules of equity made by the courts as well as the more significant executive and administrative decrees and regulations. There are six sources through which law originates and develops. These are: custom, religion, adjudication, equity and legislation, and scientific commentaries.

Law of Nature

In John Locke's version, basic morally binding rules decreed by God but discoverable by natural human reason. Decrees that no one shall violate any person's inalienable rights to life, liberty, and property.

Leadership

The qualities that make someone a good leader, for example, the ability to make decisions, give orders, and gain people's respect and trust. It also refers to a particular method a leader chooses to use in doing his or her job. In politics, strong leadership is most frequently required and evident during periods of acute crisis. Politics, in essence, is leadership or attempted leadership of whatever is the prevailing form of political community. Many leaders, probably the majority, are not very influential and can affect only marginally the course of events; on the other hand, a few "stars" seem to shape the destiny of humanity. Some leaders, like caliphs Abu Bakr and Umar, transform society while others merely transact matters by making compromises.

League of Nations

The first major international association of nations, set up after World War I. The Charter known as "covenant" was incorporated into the Treaty of Versailles by the war victors. There were three main organs of the League: The Assembly consisted of the representatives of the various member-states; the Council composed of four permanent members and four non-permanent members elected by the Assembly; and the Secretariat headed by the Secretary General. Although American President Woodrow Wilson was the driving force behind the formation of the League, America eventually decided not to join the League. The main objective of the League was to check all future possibilities of war and to evolve a scheme for the settlement of international disputes. However, the League was never effective in settling disputes involving major powers. After World War II proved its failure, the League was dissolved in 1946 and was succeeded by the UNITED NATIONS.

Left and Right

Concepts that provide a rough guide to the political orientation of a person or group. The term "Left" refers to a more liberal orientation, and "Right" to a more conservative position. In one sense, left and right can mean the ends of a continuum along which individuals or positions on a given issue can be placed. Left and right are also used as an identification of extremes: left as "beyond liberal" and right as "beyond conservative", whether as a general orientation or as a position on a particular issue.

Legislation

It has two meanings: the act of making or enacting laws and, a law or body of laws enacted. Legislation is the term used to describe the laws made by the legislature.

These laws can be divided into 3 main categories: Act of parliament, Bills and Delegated legislation. Legislation is also sometimes referred to as statutory law. In terms of legislative procedure, after a bill is introduced, it is sent to a committee which, after screening, reports back to the whole house and are given second readings. After general debate and proposed amendments, the bill is given its third reading and voted upon. After the legislature has enacted a bill, it is submitted to the executive for official approval and inclusion in the collection of statutes in force. See LEGISLATURE.

Legislative Committees

Small groups of legislative experts appointed by the legislature for drafting laws. These committees are created to cope with the complex law—making process. Currently, committees and subcommittees conduct a decisive amount of legislative work. Policies are shaped, interest groups heard, and legislation are hammered out in legislative committees. Although committees usually process legislation, they perform other tasks, such as educating the public on important issues by means of hearings and investigations. In the United States and most European democracies, most of the weeding out is accomplished by legislative committees.

Legislative Institutions

Principal official institutions of modern governments that have the function of making statutes. These institutions include the houses of legislatures and their committees. These are official because these institutions are formally established by constitutions and laws and generally regarded as part of the government.

Legislative Veto

It is a legal device adopted by the US Congress to give itself the power to control the behaviour of the vitally important regulatory agencies which govern many areas of American policy making. Many critics see legislative veto as a way to get round the constitutional separation of powers which forbid the legislative branch to exercise direct control over the execution and application of laws. Others, however, feel that legislative veto actually ensures the effectiveness of separation of powers and checks and balances.

Legislature

Legislatures are elected, multi-membered, official government agencies that enact laws. This is likely to be the national assembly, for example Parliament in the UK or Congress in the USA. They arrive at their decisions by deliberating on alternatives and they register decisions by counting the votes of their members. Legislatures are either unicameral (one chamber), as in Finland, Sweden, and Norway; or bicameral (two chambers) as in the United States, Great Britain, and Malaysia. See *MAJLIS AL-SHŪRĀ*.

Legitimacy

Acceptance by the general population of the right of political institutions or authorities to act. Legitimacy exists if it can be shown that the power is (1) acquired and exercised in accordance with established rules; (2) it is derived from a valid source of authority, and fulfils rightful ends or purposes of government; and, (3) it is publicly acknowledged by relevant subordinates through actions which confirm their acceptance of it. Legitimacy creates or enhances authority because it indicates citizen support for a political body's right to take action, even in cases where popular support might not exist for a particular action. Legitimacy is determined by citizen perception of institutions or authorities, not by the power authorities may exercise over its citizenry. See AUTHORITY.

Leninism

The variant of Marxism that led to the establishment of the Soviet Union. Vladimir Lenin (1870-1924), who furthered the revolutionary cause and teachings of Karl Marx and Frederick Engels, saw the Communist Party as the principal organizing component of the ongoing revolution. He asserted that imperialism is the highest stage of capitalism. He had the greatest influence on communism than anyone else except Marx. After his death in 1924, the theory of communism came to be called Marxism-Leninism. See MARXISM-LENINISM.

Less Developed Country (LDC)

A country that is in the early stages of industrialization or that has not yet industrialized to the extent that Japan and most of the countries in Europe and North America have. In such a country, the major mode of economic activity is agriculture and exports are based on primary goods. Such countries are usually located in Latin America, Africa, Asia and the Pacific. See THIRD WORLD.

Liberal Feminism

An outlook that accepts liberals like values, practices, and institutions, but claims that women have been excluded from public life. Proponents seek reforms that will make women equal citizens in liberal societies.

Liberalism

Used in the late eighteenth and nineteenth century, and until the mid-1930s, liberalism meant the ideology of advocating maximum freedom for individuals from regulation by governments. Liberalism was linked with the doctrine of *laissez-faire*: the maximum of individual liberty and the minimum of state intervention in society and the economy. However, since the mid-1930s, many people have converted the term to mean an ideology that favours not only personal freedom but also strict government regulation of business and government guarantees of minimum standards of living, health, and employment for all. See WELFARE STATE, CAPITALISM.

Liberation Theology

A movement among Roman Catholic theologians that emerged in Latin America during the 1950s. It expresses the traditional Christian concern for the poor and disenfranchised in recognizably Marxist terms, and advocates political (and sometimes revolutionary) action on their behalf.

Libertarianism

A contemporary antistatist viewpoint that draws heavily on classical liberalism. Libertarians seek extensive economic and social freedoms for individuals, an unregulated free market, and the decriminalization of individual behaviours that offend dominant moral sensibilities but do not cause significant injuries to others.

Liberty

From the latin word "*liber*" meaning free. Therefore, literally speaking, liberty means freedom to do as one likes. However, unrestricted freedom means license which is opposite to liberty. Liberty therefore means absence of restraints with some "justified" and "reasonable" restrictions to promote and ensure greatest possible extent of liberty to all. Liberty, however, has a positive aspect. Liberty can exist only when the state maintains conditions and opportunities which help the citizen to grow to be the best of him, to develop his faculties, and to plan his life as he deems best. The true test of liberty lies in the laws of the state and the extent to which they help a citizen to develop all that is good in him. Liberty is, thus, a product of rights. It thrives best where rights are guaranteed to all without any distinction of sex, creed, colour or status in society. See HUMAN RIGHTS.

Limited Government

Government in which the sovereign or executive power is limited by law. It means that there are clear restrictions on majority rule. These limitations take many forms. Government may be restricted by specifying how it can make laws or punish citizens accused of breaking laws. The governmental powers can also be limited by guaranteeing the citizens freedom of speech, press, assembly, and privacy, and guaranteeing the accused a fair trial. Limited government is closely tied to beliefs in citizens' rights—that is, the actions of government are limited by the rights and privileges of its citizens. Limited government is an important characteristic of an Islamic political system. See CONSTITUTIONALISM.

Limited War

As opposed to total war, participants in the limited war deliberately decide not to use their full range of weapons or to attack any and all enemy targets. The immediate military goal of the participants in the limited war is something less than the destruction or unconditional surrender of its opponents. Opposite of total war. The implication is always that limited war could be transformed into total war. Since World War II, limited wars generally took place within the context of the cold war rivalry between the two superpowers. See COLD WAR.

List system

A variant of proportional representation in which each political party nominates as many candidates as there are seats to be filled in that constituency. The voters vote for a party. When all the votes are counted, each party receives the percentage of parliamentary seats equal to the percentage of votes that it has secured at the polls. National list systems operate in Guyana, Israel, and Turkey. See ELECTION.

Lobbying

Direct efforts by representatives of organized interest groups, unions, associations, or private corporations, to influence public officials to act as the groups wish. Legislators usually are the main targets of lobbying, but executives and administrators are also frequently approached depending upon their accessibility. Lobbying is one of the ways that citizens can communicate their policy needs to government officials. The lobbyists can use various techniques of persuasion. They can make a formal presentation of their groups position, they can threaten an elected official with defeat at the next election, and can even offer bribes in cash or kind. See INTEREST GROUP.

Local Government

The administration of the local affairs of a town or district. In a unitary state, local government forms a tier below central government. In a federation, local governments form the third tier below the regional or state governments. In either case, local governments derive their power from the centre. In some cases, local authorities are governed by elected council and their committees. In others, the Mayor is the local executive who is sometimes elected locally and sometimes appointed by the council.

Logrolling

The exchange of backing and favours by legislators for mutual political gain. Logrolling may be regarded as legislative vote trading or back scratching. It takes place when those who represent particular interests are unable on their own to ensure passage of legislation favourable to their interest; they therefore enter into a coalition so that they possess sufficient votes to enact two or more bills. Logrolling is the technique by which appropriations are voted for local projects or programmes. See LOBBYING, INTEREST GROUP.

M

Machiavellism

Denotes a policy of deception. Associated with the Italian political thinker, Machiavelli, who prescribed the double standard of conduct for the statesman and private citizens. According to Machiavelli, it is always wrong for an individual to tell a lie, but often necessary and good for the ruler to do so in the interest of the state. To him, the ruler is not only outside the law, he is outside morality as well. There is no standard to judge his actions except the success of his political expediency. He openly sanctioned the use of cruelty, perfidy, murder or any other means to reach the end. "End justifies the means" was his theory in political activities. Machiavelli's advice does not conform to standards of ethical conduct which is one of the reasons for the evil reputation he earned in politics: Machiavellism.

Madh'hab (pl. *madhāhib*)

"Way" of acting; "procedure." School of Islamic law. The term refers to four Sunni schools of Islamic jurisprudence. The oldest was founded in Iraq in early Abbasid times by Abu Hanifah. The Hanafi school is the most liberal and flexible of the four *Sunnī madhāhib.* The second surviving school is that founded in Madinah and the Hejaz by Malik ibn Anas. He was a great collector of *ḥadīth* and a supporter of the "living tradition." The third school is that of the Shafi'is, founded by Muhammad ibn Idris al-Shafi'i who developed the main principles of Islamic jurisprudence (*usūl al-fiqh*) and the last school was founded by Ahmad ibn Hanbal who carried al-Shafii's enthusiasm for and trust in *Ḥadīth* farther than any other legist had. These schools are regarded by one another as fully orthodox and in practice there is no fundamental difference among them. The Shi'is have also developed, prominently three schools of law: Zaidis, Ismailis, and ithna 'asharis. See *ḤANAFIYYAH, MĀLIKIYYAH, SHAFI'IYYAH, ḤANBALIYYAH* and *ṢHĪ'AH.*

Madrasah (pl. *madāris*)

A religious school associated with a mosque. It was where young and adult Muslims dedicated their lives to the study of the Islamic sciences: Qur'an, *Ḥadīth*; criticism and exegesis; every branch of the *shari'ah*; history, astronomy and geography; Arabic grammar and letters. The *madāris* were autonomous, each with a constitution of its own and was internally governed and regulated. Nobody exercised authority over the internal affairs of the *madrasah* but its own *shaykh* or dean in consultation with his faculty. Muslims regard it as an inviolable institution, worth their greatest respect and material and moral support. In modern usage, the term refers to institution of learning where the Islamic civilization and sciences are being studied. See 'ILM.

Mafsadah (pl. *mafāsid*)

Cause of corruption or evil; scandalous deed, heinous act. Anything that turns justice into injustice, mercy to cruelty, benefit to harm, and wisdom to foolishness and meaninglessness is considered *mafsadah*. According to al-Ghazali, any which violates the five essential values of religion, life, intellect, lineage and property is *mafsadah*. A pernicious person is referred to as *Mufsid*. The acts which prevent *mafsadah* is considered *maṣlaḥah*. See *DARŪRIYYĀT, MAṢLAḤAH*.

Magistrate

A minor judicial officer, as a justice of the peace, or a police justice, having jurisdiction to try minor criminal cases and to conduct preliminary examinations of persons charged with serious crimes. See JUDICIARY.

Magna Carta

A feudal document which recognized the privileges of the English nobility. Derived from the Latin *Magna Charta* (great charter), this is a major British constitutional charter forced on King John I by a baronial alliance at Runnymede (1215). The Charter was designed to prevent royal restrictions of baronial privilege and feudal rights and to safeguard church and municipal customs. It paved the way for constitutional monarchy.

Mahdī

Guide; leader; "The rightly guided one." Messianic figure that will appear at the end of the world and usher in a new order. He will come from Makkah and rule from Damascus. 'Ali, the fourth Khalif in Islam, reported that the Prophet Muhammad said, "Even if only a day remains for *Qiyāmah* [Day of Judgment] to come, yet Allah will surely send a man from my family who will fill this world with such justice and fairness, just as it initially was filled with oppression." The *Mahdī* will be tall, fair, and will resemble the Prophet Muhammad (SAS) in many ways. The title has been claimed by various individuals in history, including Muhammad Ahmad who founded a short-lived state in Sudan in the late nineteenth century. Scholars like al-Ghazzali and others avoided discussing the subject because of the fear of encouraging politically disruptive movements in the Muslim community.

Majlis

From the verb "*jalasa*" meaning to sit down, or to hold a session. Among the principal derivative meanings are "a meeting place", "meeting, assembly," a "reception hall" and "a session which is held there." From the pre-Islamic period, *majlis* designated an assembly or council of the tribe's notables and this institution is still alive. In contemporary age, the term refers to any council and more precisely to the legislative assemblies and parliaments in the Muslim countries.

Majlis al-shūrā

The name given to extraordinary, ad hoc consultative assemblies in the last century of the Ottoman Empire.

However, the meaning of the term, in the twentieth century, has expanded to refer to consultative council or the "Parliament" of the Islamic state. This body consists of '*ahl'l-ḥall wa'l 'aqd*' (literally those who loosen and bind) i.e., people of intellect and intelligence. The Imam or leader should consult this group of learned people on all important public matters. This principle indicates that Islamic government is a government by consultation and conference. Whenever there is call for a legislative enactment, the *Majlis al-Shūrā* must first look into the context of the Shari'ah for a guiding general principle. If such a principle is forthcoming, it is the duty of the legislature to legislate in consonance with that principle. But very often the *majlis* will be confronted with problems on which the Shari'ah is silent. In such instance, it is for the *majlis* to devise the requisite legislation, taking the spirit of

Islam and the community's welfare into consideration. All this presupposes that the members of the *majlis* are not only experts in the *nusus* (texts) of the Qur'an and Sunnah, but are also people of understanding and insight (*ūlu'l albāb*). The parliaments of the Islamic Republic of Iran and of the Islamic Republic of Pakistan are designated as *majlis al-shūrā*. See LEGISLATURE.

Majority, simple

Fifty percent of the votes plus one more vote. If 1,000 votes were cast, a simple majority would be 501 votes. The word majority by itself almost always means simple majority.

Majoritarianism

The doctrine or philosophy that majority rule should prevail in democratic decision-making. Majoritarianism can also mean a democratic system of government in which power is concentrated as much as possible in the hands of the majority. Majoritarians tend to think of majoritarian democracy as the only legitimate form of democracy, and to virtually equate democracy with majority rule. This majority, may be modified for constitutional amendments and for protection of vital group interests by, for example, requiring extraordinary or regional majorities to approve changes. See also *SHURA*, DEMOCRACY, CONSOCIATIONAL DEMOCRACY.

Makr

Cunning, graft, double dealing and deception or trickery. *Makr* signifies a secret strategy of which the victim has no inkling until the decisive blow is struck. Until then, the victim is under the illusion that everything is in good order.

Malikiyyah

Malikiyah is one of the four schools of Islamic jurisprudence, founded in Madinah by Anas Ibn Malik (d. 795 AD). Imam Malik's major contribution to Islamic law is his book *al-Muwattah* (The Beaten Path). The *Muwattah* is a code of law based on the legal practices that were operating in Madinah. The *Maliki* School emphasizes the relevance and the authority of the traditions of the Prophet (SAW) and the first Muslim community at Madinah. The Maliki School in Morocco took the local and prevailing conditions into consideration and thus brought these to the orbit of the *shari'ah*. Malikis are dominant in North Africa, Upper Egypt, and the Sudan

Mamlūk

Literally, "thing possessed," hence "slaves," especially used in the sense of military slave. However, the term is used to refer to a dynasty of rulers succeeding the Ayubid as governors of Egypt and Syria. The Mamluks ruled Egypt from 1250 to 1517 (648-922 H) and Syria from 1260 to 1516 (658-922 H).

Mandate

A call for a policy expressed through an election result. A mandate is rarely, if ever, self-evident from the election return itself. The existence of a mandate is based upon interpretation, and disagreements can occur. Mandate also refers to a system devised by the League of Nations to administer the non-self-ruling territories of the vanquished powers during World War I. Under the United Nations, the system is known as trusteeship.

Manisfesto

A document issued generally before a major election by a political party, outlining its policies and programmes.

Maoism (Mao)

The Chinese variant of Marxism-Leninism that stipulates that the revolution is permanent, not subject to replacement in the dialectical process. Named after the great Chinese leadèr, Mao Tse Tung who steered China ideologically away from the Soviet Union. He placed the peasants on par with the proletarians in the class struggle, emphasized continuing revolution and upheld that "power flows from the barrel of the gun."

Maqāṣid al Sharī'ah

Maqāsid is the plural of "*maqsid*" meaning intention, design, objective and goal. *Maqāṣid al Shari'ah,* therefore, means the objectives of the Shari'ah. The objectives (*Maqāsid*) of the *Shari'ah* consist of protecting the necessitites, (*Darūriyāt*), complimentary requirements (*Hājiyāt*), and the embellishments (*Tahsiniyāt*). Particular emphasis is laid on the necessities which consist of protecting the five essential values, namely religion, life, intellect, lineage and property. These five necessities are derived from Shari'ah as necessary and basic for human existence. Therefore, every society should preserve and protect these five necessities; otherwise human life would be harsh, brutal, poor, and miserable here and in the hereafter. Any measures which secure these values fall within the scope of *maqasid al shari'ah*, and anything which violates them is *mafsadah* (evil).

Marāsim

Official court ceremonies, both processional and non-processional. The whole range of ceremonial, including protocol and etiquette, is called *rusum.*

Market Socialism

An economy containing a mix of publicly-owned and privately-owned business, in which workers and the public exercise significant control over business decisions, but in which market forces greatly influence such things as the goods that are produced, the prices of these goods, and the wages of employees. See INDUSTRIAL SOCIALISM.

Marshall Plan

Named after U.S. Secretary of State George Marshall, who proposed the program in 1947. It refers to a U.S. postwar assistance programme that provided billions in aid to European countries to help them rebuild their economies following the devastation ofWorld War II. The plan helped the Industrial capitalism ofWest Germany, the working of a democratic system in Italy and France, the stabilization of Greek economy and the overall increase in production.The plan is also called the "European Recovery Programme."

Martial Law

Administration of a certain area by military authorities through executive edicts and orders superceding all civil law. It involves control by soldiers and drastic penalties for law and order offences such as rioting and looting. In strict dictionary terms, martial law is the suspension of civil authority and the imposition of military authority. When a region or country is said to be "under martial law," it means that the military is in control of the area, that it acts as the police, as the courts, as the legislature.The degree of control might vary; a nation may have a civilian legislature but have the courts administered by the military. Or the legislature and courts may operate under civilian control with a military ruler. In each case, martial law is in effect, even if it is not called "martial law." See DICTATORSHIP.

Martyr

This term refers to someone who dies for what he or she believes in. It should be noted that in Islam, any loss of life is regretted except for the sake of Allah (SWT) and in the true cause of justice. A martyr in the cause of Allah is Islamically referred to as *shahid.*

Ma'rūf (pl. *ma'rūfāt*)

Well-known; that which is good or beneficial; virtue; kindness. The term *ma'ruf* denotes all virutes and good qualities that have always been accepted as good by the human conscience. *Ma'rūfāt* are in harmony with human nature and its requirements in general. The Shari'ah classifies *ma'rūfāt* into three categories: (1) *Farḍ andWājib,* the mandatory, the observance of which is obligatory on a Muslim society and the *sharī'ah* has given clear and binding directions about them. (2) *Maṭlūb,* the recommendatory, those which the *sharī'ah* wants a Muslim society to observe and practise. (3) *Mubah,* the permissible, the things which have not been expressly prohibited by the *sharī'ah.* See *MUNKIRAT.*

Marxism

The ideas of Karl Marx and his followers that have been interpreted both as a science predicting an inevitable downfall of capitalism and the subsequent emergence of a communist society and as an ideology protesting private ownership of productive property and other liberal ideas, institutions, and practices. See COMMUNISM.

Marxism – Leninism

A political ideology based on the writings of Karl Marx and the Russian revolutionary V. I. Lenin. The ideology deals with the fundamental laws of development of nature and society, the revolutionary overthrow of the system based on exploitation and the building of communism, the world outlook of the working class and its vanguard, the Communist and workers' parties. The term communism is used synonymously with Marxism-Leninism.

Maṣlaḥah (pl. *maṣāliḥ*)

Public interest or welfare. The term is an abstract of the verb *ṣalaḥa* or *ṣaluḥa,* which means "repair or improve" something. It is used by jurists to mean "general good" or "public interest." When it is qualified as *maṣlaḥah mursalah,* it refers to unrestricted public interest in the sense of not having been regulated by the Law-giver and no textual authority can be found on its validity or otherwise. It is synonymous with *istiṣlāḥ* and is occasionally referred to *maṣlaḥah muṭlaqah* on account of its being undefined by the established rules of the shari'ah. Al-Ghazali defined *maṣlaḥah* as that which secures a benefit or prevents a harm but are, in the meantime, harmonious with the objectives of *sharī'ah.* The *sharī'ah* recognized *maṣlaḥah* as the ultimate purpose of the Divine Legislator.

Mass party

A type of party which though led by a small group of professional leaders has a large number of the electorate as its members. The mass party has a national headquarter and branches all over the country. Its programme provides a method for members to state policy preferences, select leaders, choose candidates for public office, and participate generally in the political process. The mass party arose from the expansion of the suffrage and political participation. See CADRE PARTY.

Massive Retaliation

A nuclear deterrence policy of the Eisenhower administration after 1954. The US would use all its nuclear arsenal at any time, anywhere, to forestall Soviet expansion. This strategy was possible because the US then had an overwhelming superiority in number, quality, and delivery of the nuclear weapons over the Soviets. However, as the Soviet Union achieved nuclear parity, Washington shifted its nuclear war strategy from massive retaliation to flexible response. See FLEXIBLE RESPONSE.

Materialism

A set of ideas associated with the view that the world is material, that matter, nature or being exist apart from and independently of human consciousness. It holds the view that matter is primary and the source of sensations, while consciousness is secondary and derivative and that only the material world explains all manner of mental phenomena. See SECULARISM.

Mayor

The head of town or city government, elected by councillors or by the voters and, in some countries, appointed by the central government. In some countries, mayors are simply chairmen of councils, but in others they have executive powers.

McCarthyism

Political style characterized by public hysteria over communism. Named for U.S. Senator Joseph R. McCarthy, whose broad public accusations that communists were infiltrating American institutions dominated American politics from 1952 until McCarthy's death in 1957.

Media

The main forms of large-scale public communication in contemporary society especially the so-called "mass media" of press, television and radio. These now extend to embrace a range of "new media" based on computers and telecommunications, especially the internet. Although politics and the media have their separate institutional existence, there is now an intimate and even inextricable interdependence between the two. The beginnings of modern democracy are associated almost by definition with freedom of the press to report and comment on proceedings of parliament and acts of government. However, the growing concentration of a commercialized press in the hands of powerful owners is considered as a threat to democracy. See AUTHORITARIANISM, DEMOCRACY.

Mediation

The activity in which a neutral third party, the mediator, assists two or more parties to help them achieve an agreement on a matter of common interest. Mediation differs from most other conflict resolution processes by virtue of its simplicity, and the clarity of its rules. It is employed at all scales from petty civil disputes to global peace talks. Mediation is typically one of the most important activities of diplomats, and should be a relevant quality of democratic politicians. In politics and in diplomacy, mediation is obviously a non-violent method of dispute resolution.

Mercantilism

An economic system based on the theory that the wealth of a nation is a function of the gold, silver, and other precious metals it accumulated. Under mercantilism, monopolies, tariffs, and running trade surplus became national economic policies. Adam Smith challenged this view, arguing that the true wealth of a nation was to be found in its productive capacity, not its treasure. See CAPITALISM.

Merit system

Refers to the selection, retention, and promotion of government employees on the basis of demonstrated technical merit. In most democratic countries today, all or nearly all civil-service employees are selected and promoted by some kind of competitive examination. Some countries, however, adopt seniority system for promotion. Still others combine the two for promotion purposes. See BUREAUCRACY.

Metaphor of the "ship of state"

A classical liberal metaphor for the governance of society. The term "ship" implies that government and society are made by man and not by God. It also implies that society may steadily progress towards some destination, that the "passengers" (the citizens) should decide this destination, and that the "captains" (qualified officials) should decide the best means of getting there. See GOVERNMENT.

Militant

A person very strongly committed to, and very active in support of, some cause. It could be, and sometimes still is, applied to almost any active supporter of a creed.

Militarism

The influence and sometimes predominance of the armed forces in the political and governing life of a country. The army holds a veto over a civilian government, intervenes in its affairs, or establish a military government. See COUP D'ETAT.

Military

The entire organization of armed forces (land, sea and air) whose primary function is to defend the state against external enemies or to enforce the will of the state against other states. They can sometimes be used internally, where the police cannot handle a situation. Excessive use of the military for maintaining law and order in the country may prompt the military to stage a coup.

Military Regimes

Autocratic governments where the military controls the country's political system usually following a coup d'etat. In military regimes the civil liberties of the subjects and normal political constitutional arrangements may be suspended. See DICTATORSHIP.

Militias

An organization that operates like an army but whose members are not professional soldiers.

Millah

Religion, sect, creed, faith or a spiritual community. In the Qur'an, it is used to mean "religion" and on eight occasions, the Qu'ran speaks of the religion of Abraham (*Millata Ibrahim*). With the article, *al. Millah* means the true religion and is occasionally used for *Ahl al-millah*, the followers of Islam as opposed to *ahl al-dhimmah*, the non-Muslims under the protection of Islam. In modern Persian and in Turkey, *millah* is used to mean "nation" or "people."

Minister

A person who is in charge of a particular government department. In the United States, the term refers to a foreign envoy below the level of an ambassador.

Ministry

A government department that deals with a particular area of administration within a country, for example, education, employment, and defence.

Minority

A group which is numerically inferior to the rest of a state's population, occupies a non-dominant position, possesses distinctive national, ethnic, religious or linguistic characteristics, and seeks to ensure its survival and development as a culturally distinct population. Muslims in India are an example of a minority living alongside the Hindu majority. See *AHL AL-DHIMMAH*

Minority government

A government supported by less than half the legislature under a parliamentary system of government. Understandably, such governments tend to be unstable and less effective than majority governments. Minority governments were a feature of the Weimar Republic in Germany (1919-1933) and the French Fourth Republic (1946-1958).

Missionary Parties

Parties whose principal aim is to win converts for their ideologies and not to maximize their votes so as to win elections. The party's electioneering activities seek not votes but converts. Their strategy to win power is to convert the masses gradually, over many decades or even centuries if need be. The Socialist Workers Party of the United States and the Jama'at-e-Islami of Pakistan may be cited as examples of missionary parties. See CADRE PARTY, JAMA'AT-e-ISLAMI.

Mīthāq

Covenant, agreement. The term is frequently found in the Qur'an and often linked with its synonym *'ahd*.

Mixed Economy

Economic systems with a mixture of both capitalist and socialist economies. Mixed economic systems characterize most developing countries. Their essential feature is the coexistence of substantial private and public activity within a single economy. Britain and France are also examples of mixed systems although the state is relatively larger in France and the market relatively more important in Britain. See WELFARE STATE.

Modernization

Literally, the processes whereby society becomes modern. In economic terms, the development of money-based exchange system, sizeable industrial sector, specialization of jobs and functions, and proliferation of specialized organizations. Politically, less definite meaning. Often refers to basing authority on a non-traditional, secular claim to legitimacy, developing a specialized modern-type bureaucracy, creating effective mass parties, and establishing a system of relatively peaceful and orderly leadership succession. Modernization was the avowed objective of most of the governments of the "new" states, an objective looked upon benevolently by the United States—the home of the modern—and anxious to maintain or expand its own influence and foster viable political systems after its own image (neo-colonialism) as a buffer against revolution.

Monarchy

The rule by a single person, generally as a result of inheritance (in the West normally primogeniture, sometimes preferring males over females) and in fewer cases, by election by dignitaries in councils (like the medieval Holy Roman Emperor or the King of Poland). It generally refers to a political system in which power is held by a hereditary aristocracy, headed by a king or queen.

Monetarism

A school of thought that focuses on money supply as a key determinant of the level of economic activity in a nation. Monetarists tend to view state economic actions as likely to disrupt domestic and international affairs. They tend, therefore, to be closely associated with economic liberals in the dislike of state influences.

Moral Autonomy

The right of individuals to make rational and ethical judgements about their conduct and its effect on others. Anarchists are particularly adamant that individuals should never surrender any capacity to make moral judgements to governmental authority.

Moral Majority

An organization of religious conservatives, founded in 1979, whose declared object is to safeguard traditional family and moral values on which America was built. It opposes abortion, homosexuality and pornography. The Moral Majority now acts as a subsidiary of the Liberty Federation (established in 1986) and focuses on what it calls strictly moral issues.

Most Favoured Nation (MFN)

Trade status under GATT where imports from a nation are granted the same degree of preference as those from the most preferred nations. A foreign policy tool that has been used by the United States to reward allies and to punish foes.

Movement

A loose coalition of individuals and organizations sharing similar interests and acting together to realize agreed upon political changes. Movements are much less structured than organizations.

Mu'āhadah

Arabic term meaning treaty, agreement or contract. *Mu'āhadah* or *'ahd* has sometimes been used interchangeably with *ittifāq* or *ittifāqiyyah*. The former is used generally to mean "contract" and the latter means more strictly "agreement." As used by politicians, the term *mu'āhadah* refers to a contract undertaken by two or more states, generally referring to defined aspects of commerce or other matters. See *'AHD*.

Mu'āmalah

In its strict and original sense *Mu'āmalah* refers to transactions concerning credit granted by a donor to a beneficiary. More generally, it refers to relations and dealings among humans. It refers to juridico-human relations and ensures that the Mulsim's behaviour conforms to juridico-moral theories.

Mu'āraḍah

Opposition, resistance. Also used to mean objection, exception, and protest. Islam stipulates the freedom of expression *ḥurriyyat al-mu'āraḍah* which is not just about the right of the individual but his duty to uphold truth.

Mufsidūn

The term refers to the corrupt people in society. It also denotes the evil, scandalous deeds, and malicious acts of people in the state. See *FASĀD*.

Muftī

Juriconsult learned in the Qur'an, the Sunnah and *fiqh*. The mufti is the only one who can issue a *fatwā*, which gives him the power of handling cases where there is doubt among other Muslim learned. In Islamic law, *muftī* is an attorney who writes his opinion (*fatwā*) on legal subjects for private clients or to assist judges in deciding cases. The recorded opinions of the *muftīs* are a valuable source of information for the actual working of Islamic law as opposed to the abstract formulation. Only in the fields of marriage, divorce, and inheritance are the *fatawās* binding precedents; on other subjects they might be set aside. In the Ottoman Empire the *muftīs* were state officials. The British, who retained the institution in some Muslim areas under their control, gave to the office of Husseini, the grand mufti of Jerusalem, great political importance. See *FATWĀ*.

Muhājirūn

The emigrants, primarily those Makkan Muslims who emigrated to Madinah either just before the Prophet Muhammad (SAW) or in the period up to the conquest of Makkah. In particular, the term refers to those who accompanied the Prophet (SAW) in the *ḥijrah*. See *ḤIJRAH*.

Muḥtasib

The person entrusted with the responsibility of *hisbah* is called *Muḥtasib*. In a classical meaning, the term is concerned with the control of the market and any other Institutions that have to do with social welfare. *Al-Muḥtasib* is literally a judge (*Qāḍī*) who makes decisions on the spot, anywhere any time any place at any time, as long as he protects the interests of the public. His responsibilities are almost open ended in order to implement the foregoing principle: commanding the good and forbidding the evil of wrongdoing. *Al-Muḥtasib* and/or his deputies as full judge (s) must enjoy high qualifications of being wise, mature, pious, well-poised, sane, free, just, empathic, and learned scholar (*faqīh*). He has the ability to ascertain right from wrong, and to distinguish the permissible (*ḥalāl*) from the non-permissible (*ḥārām*). See *ḤISBAH*.

Mujāhid (pl. *mujāhidūn*)

Fighter, freedom fighter; warrior. Someone who is active and fights for Islam. The warrior in the cause of religion. But in a broad sense, it is often used to denote someone who struggles to get or acquire something of value in society. The name frequently given in common parlance to resistance fighters in political struggles in Islamic areas of the world e.g., Aghanistan and Iran. See *JIHAD*.

Mujtahid (pl. *mujtahidūn*)

Diligent, industrious, one who exercises *ijtihād*. A legist formulating independent decisions in legal or theological matters, based on the interpretation and application of the four *usūl*. One entitled to give an independent judgement on a point of theology or law. In Iran, the title of *Āyatullah* has been applied to *Mujtahids* in recent times.

Mulk

Rule, reign, sovereignty, supreme authority, kingship, royalty, monarchy. It is used in Qur'ān to refer to Allah (SWT) to whom alone belongs *mulk* over heaven and earth as well as over the judgement. "Blessed be He in Whose hands is Dominion, Sovereingty, and He has power over all things." However, in the Arab monarchies of the last century, the term is used to refer to the actual area over which kingly power is exercised (*mamlakah*) like that of Saudi Arabia, Jordan and Morocco. See SOVEREIGNTY.

Multinationals

The shorthand for multinational corporations, large enterprises operating simultaneously in several countries. See MNCs.

Multiculturalism

Multiculturalism is an approach to education that focuses on the diversity and richness of the component cultures in the society and teaches respect and tolerance for cultural differences. Many contemporary conservatives reject this approach, because they view it as relativistic and unpatriotic.

Multilateralism

An approach to international affairs predicated on the premise that international cooperation for the management of conflicts of interest would benefit all parties involved. This approach lends itself to issues where there is a commonality of interest among the units of the international system. This doctrine became the hallmark in such post-war endeavours such as Bretton Woods, GATT, and the United Nations. Global multilateralism has, however, been challenged by the emergence of trade regional blocs such as NAFTA, the E.U., and APEC. Another challenge is the unilateral action and bilateral confrontation in trade and other negotiations followed by the world powers as a result of their frustration with failed consensus-building in multilateral forums. See BRETTON WOODS.

Multinational Corporations (MNCs)

Business firms that engage in production, distribution, and marketing activities and own assets beyond the jurisdiction of one state. These corporations have headquarters in one country but branch offices in a wide range of both developed and developing countries. Examples include Ford, General Motors, Coca-Cola, Philips, Exxon. They have political as well as economic impact on the international system because they move and control goods, services, money, personnel, and technology across national boundaries. MNCs have tremendous bargaining powers with governments and international organizations. The annual sales of MNCs are comparable to the gross national product of national economies. General Motors, for example, is bigger than the combined GNPs of Israel, New Zealand, and Venezuela; Ford is bigger than South Africa. MNCs promise investments, jobs, higher living standards, and the introduction of technology to assist developing countries to modernize and industrialize. In return, they demand political stability and concessions on taxation and government regulations. When national and corporate interests conflict, MNCs challenge the political decisions of governments from every possible vantage points. MNCs have the notoriety of having undermined the economies of many countries including Chile in the 1970s and Malaysia in the 1990s. Nationalists often condemn them because they are subversive of national cultures, and, more importantly, subversive of national sovereignty. Socialists perceive them as instruments of global capitalism. See INTERNATIONAL ORGANIZATIONS.

Multi-party Systems

A system consisting by definition of more than two parties. Multi-party system exists where three or more parties contest elections, gain representation, and form a coalition with the governing party. They are found in many countries like Malaysia, Pakistan, India, and most notably in Western European states. In the Scandinavian countries, Belgium, Holland, and Italy, for example, no one party is strong enough to win majority seats in the parliament. In these countries, the governments are usually formed by coalition of parties. See POLITICAL PARTY, BI-PARTY SYSTEM.

Multipolarity

A world political configuration with more than two centres of power; the existence of multiple hegemons, such a world in which there are five principal or major powers. See BI-POLARITY, BALANCE OF POWER.

Murtad

One who turns back, especially from Islam, an apostate. Apostasy is called *irtidād* or *riddah*; it may be committed verbally by denying a principle of belief or by an action e.g., treating a copy of the Qur'an with disrespect. A person is an apostate if he leaves a religion and either adopts another religion or assumes a secular lifestyle. Historically, Islam, Christianity and other religions have taken a very dim view of apostates. The penalty was often execution. Today, apostasy in Islam is a very complex and sensitive issue. There exists a range of beliefs among Muslims: Some believe that the punishment for the mere renunciation of faith is death. An adult apostate would typically be given three days to reconsider their decision before being executed. Some believe that this sentence is to be carried out whether or not the apostasy occurred in an Islamic State or not. Others believe in complete freedom of religion, such as is stated in Article 18 of the Universal Declaration of Human Rights: Everyone has the right to freedom of thought, conscience and religion; this right includes freedom to change his religion or belief. Apostates have been rarely executed in the 21st century. However, Muslims feel a powerful sense of rage when one of their number forsakes the community. They consider it a profound insult to Allah and to all Muslims

Musāwah

Equality, equivalence, equal rights and equality before the law. The term presupposes equality of all—equality in rights, liberties, opportunities and public duties. These are to be enjoyed by all irrespective of race, language and creed. There is no room for privilege under a system which subjects all equally to the identical law. The Qur'an recognizes no grounds for the superiority of individuals or nations to one another except that of moral rectitude and piety.

Musta'min

A person who temporarily resides in a foreign country, by its permission. There are, in Arabic, no different terms which distinguish between a Muslim going to non-Muslim territories and a non-Muslim coming to Muslim territories nor even between a subject of an allied state or unallied or even belligerent state. All are called *Musta'min* which literally means one who seeks protection. Such a foreign resident in Muslim territory is as safe at the outbreak of war between his State and the Muslim State as before. According to the terms of the passport he might return home whenever he liked; he might even take with him all his property. If a *Musta'min* acts as a spy, he forfeits his immunity. This also happens if a *Musta'min* of a belligerent state becomes an ordinary belligerent immediately after leaving Islamic territory, and his immunity that he enjoyed during his stay in the Muslim territory comes to an end.

Mustabid

This refers to arbitrary, high handed, autocratic and tyrannical or despotic behaviour in society. It may denote a despot, tyrant and an autocrat.

Mustakbirūn

The term is mostly used to denote the arrogant, supercilious behaviour of people. Sometimes, it refers to the people of haughty, quarrelsome, self-willed and stubborn nature.

Mu'tazilah

Literally, those who "separate" themselves or "stand aside" from others. *Mu'tazilah* is the first major school of "dogmatic theology." Arising as a theological school in the early part of the eighth century CE, the *Mu'tazilah* stood primarily for three principles: absolute unity of God (*tawḥīd*) (hence anything besides

God, including the Qur'an, could not be co-eternal with God and was therefore considered to be temporal or created), God's justice (*'aḍl*) (allowing for human free will), and Divine reward and punishment (*al-w'ad wa-al-wa'īd*) (in the Hereafter). *Mu'tazilah* was founded by Wasil b. 'Ata' in the first half of the period between second and eighth centuries.

Mutual-Assured Destruction (MAD)

The cold war nuclear strategy of the U.S. and the Soviet Union where each had sufficient military power of lethal weapons to destroy the other even if destroyed itself, thus assuring that neither country could realistically win a nuclear war. As a theory based on deterrence, MAD kept a fragile peace between the superpowers during the cold war era.

N

Nadwah

Council, debating group, study group, club and sometimes parliament or chamber of deputies. Specifically, the *Nadwah* or *Dar al-nadwah* is a kind of town hall in Makkah in the time of the Prophet (SAW), situated near the *Ka'bah*. It was the gathering place of nobles. All matters of import to the *Quraysh* are said to have taken place there up to the coming of Islam. During the Umayyads and the first Abbasids, it served as a residence during their pilgrimages. At the end of the ninth century, it was incorporated as an annexe to *al-Masjid al-Ḥaram*. In South Asia, *Nadwah* refers to the famous institution of Muslim theologians, founded in 1891, in India and is known as *Nadwat al- úlamā'*.

Nahḍah

Raising, awakening: actualisation of potentialities latent in the child. Derived from the Arabic root *nahaḍah*, to rise. This term is applied to the renaissance of the Muslim world in general. In this renaissance, the substance, which is Islam, remains the same. Its potentialities and capabilities are receiving increasing recognition by the Ummah such that they are struggling to apply them to their contemporary problems. See ISLAMIC REVIVAL, *TAJDĪD*, PAN-ISLAMISM

Nahy

Prohibition, illegality. It is also used to imply a mere reprehension, guidance, reprimand or supplication. Being the opposite of a command (*amr*), *nahy* is a word which demand avoidance from doing something addressed from a position of superiority to one who is inferior. See *AMR*.

Nation

A political and/or cultural community. Sometimes used as a synonym for "state" and "people," nation is often used to describe an ethnic, linguistic or cultural community, or even a race. The word nation is of Latin origin. In its original meaning, it signifies the geographical origin of persons, their birthplace. The use of the term has proliferated since the French Revolution. The revolutionaries used it to designate the body of associated citizens who were ruled by the same laws and represented in the same legislature. Reciprocal bonds of loyalty were seen to exist between the nation and the citizen. But a concurrent understanding emerged which stressed the existence of traditions and a common language. See NATIONALISM.

Nation-building

The process by which loyalty to the state is developed within the general population.

Nation-building tasks are undertaken by a wide variety of agencies ranging from the executive branch of government to public school systems. Sometimes nation-building involves deliberate policy on the part of rulers, sometimes they are instigated through things like threats of invasion.

Nation-state

A political institution combining the concepts of nation with state. It refers to a state inhabited by people who identify themselves as a community because of shared culture, history, language, ethnicity or other factors. The French, Dutch, Chinese and Japanese people all constitute a nation as well as a state. Not all nations like the Kurds (Turkey, Iraq and Iran), and Palestinians (West Bank and Gaza, Lebanon, Jordan) are fortunate enough to have a state of their own. The structure of the nation-state system demands the promotion of its own interests to the exclusion of and, at times, at the cost of all others. The Qur'an demands of the *ummah,* instead, promotion of virtue and eschewing of vice, to cooperate for the good and to prevent evil, to avoid crime and stop aggression. See STATE, NATION.

National Socialism or Nazism

An ideology most clearly articulated by the German National Socialist Workers Party (Nazis) under Adolf Hitler between 1920 and 1945. It proclaimed the racial superiority of the "Aryan race," sought to create a "greater Germany" composed of such people, and pursued this goal through policies of military domination. The regime advocated a brand of state socialism which was antithetical to classical socialism developed by Karl Marx. The militaristic focus of Hitler and his party inevitably led the country to WW II. Germany's defeat in the war in 1945 led to the de-Nazification of the country. The post-war emergence of various right-wing movements have been characterized by some analysts as neo-Nazi groups.

Nationalism

An ideology in which a people, regardless of their race, class, or religion, feel that they have more in common with each other than they have with other people and give their highest loyalty to a state they live in. Nationalism holds that humanity is naturally divided into nations that are known by characteristics such as race, language, religion, common traditions, and feeling of being together, and that only national self-government is legitimate. More generally and ambiguously, nationalism involves a belief that distinct cultures deserve some kind of political recognition. Nationalism that feeds and fattens on hatred and anger directed against a competitor group is against the teachings of Islam which enjoins the believers to promote brotherhood and peace with all. See IDEOLOGY, PATRIOTISM.

Naturalization

Legal process by which a person can acquire a new nationality or citizenship. States differ widely in their attitude toward admitting aliens to citizenship by formal grant of naturalization. Citizenship conferred by this process is gratuitous concession on the part of the State to which naturalization is sought and it may be granted under prescribed conditions or may be refused for any reason which the State considers sufficient. In some states, the process is made easy and resident aliens are encouraged to acquire citizenship; in others the process is so difficult as to discourage the admission of new citizens. See CITIZENSHIP.

Natural Law

A view dating back at least to the time of the ancient Greeks that posits that there exists a principle or body of law supposed to be innate, discoverable by natural human reason, and common to all people. Under this philosophy, human or positive law, though changeable and culturally dependent, must, if truly just, be derived from the principles of natural law. The concept is rooted in Greek philosophy and Roman law. Particularly in the Christian philosophy of Thomas Aquinas, natural law — the sense of right and wrong implanted in humans by God — is contrasted with revealed law. It lies behind Hugo Grotius's ideas on international law (17th century). It was used as a basis for ethics, morality and even for protests against tyranny by Spinoza, Leibniz, Locke, Rousseau, and many others. Since then, some scholars have dealt with natural law as a means to develop a body of international law to govern the relations among nations. However, with the development of scientific philosophies in the nineteenth century, natural law largely lost its influence.

Natural Rights

The idea that nature bestows on each individual ownership of his or her own life and that each person is thus entitled to pursue his or her own understanding of happiness using the resources (mind and body) that nature has bestowed upon him or her. Classical liberals argue that the natural entitlements of life, liberty, and the fruit of one's own labour cannot be curtailed by government except to secure or protect similar rights for other individuals.

Neo-Colonialism

A system of relations between two unequal countries in which a strong nation exerts political and economic hegemony over an independent nation or an extended geographical area without necessarily reducing the subordinate nation or area to the legal status of a colony. It also refers to the residues of colonial rule—language, administration, economic dominance—perceived to hinder the progress of new nations toward self-sufficiency. In any case, neo-colonialism is the continuation of colonialism and direct exploitation by other means. It exists in the form of bloc system or satellite system and economic shackles or ideological subversion. The essential objective of neo-colonialism is to maintain the flow of imperialist profits from former colonial territories and other weaker nations after they have been granted independence. Neo-colonialism found its scholarly expression in dependency theory and modern world system theory. See COLONIALISM.

Neo-conservatism

A conservative reaction to liberal and radical movements of the 1960s. Neo-conservatism includes a strong anticommunist thrust, acceptance of the welfare state but concern that government has become too large and intrusive, emphasis on freedom as opposed to equality, and support for religion and traditional values. See CONSERVATISM, LIBERALISM, NEOLIBERALISM.

Neo-corporatism

A new version of corporatism that emerged in the last three decades of the twentieth century as reflected in the writings of a new breed of corporatist writers, who sought to divorce their new model of corporatism from the old models which had fascist underpinnings. Neo-corporatism is a system in which all interests are organized and the government deals directly with all affected interests at all stages in the making and administration of policy. Under neo-corporatism, the government does not merely respond to the interest groups' pressure but actively involves the groups in the job of governing. The Scandinavian states approach the neocorporatist model more closely than any others.

Neo-imperialism

An element of the structuralist interpretation of capitalism. Core industrialized nations exploit the periphery and create dependency through financial and production structures in neo-imperialism. See IMPERIALISM.

Neo-liberalism

A spin-off from liberalism that occurred in the late 1970s. Neo-liberals accept many liberal values such as civil liberties, civil rights, and equality of opportunity. They, however, assert that they are concerned with economic growth more than with redistribution of income; that they favour an industrial policy in which government, business, and labour cooperate closely; and that they support a stronger national defense rather than a weaker one. The term neo-liberalism was coined by Charles Peters, the editor of *Washington Monthly*. See LIBERALISM.

Neo-marxism

The use and modification of a variety of Marx's concept and theories for the purpose of providing a critique of contemporary societies and international affairs, without necessarily accepting fully Marx's dialectical materialism of his prognosis of the coming revolution. See MARXISM.

Neo-pluralism

A variant of pluralism which recognizes the development of elite groups with more access to power. See PLURALISM.

Neutralism

From the Latin "*neuter*," meaning not to take sides. It refers to a policy of not taking sides in an international dispute or war nor join an alliance. Some states like Switzerland claim permanent neutrality. Others choose to be neutral, perhaps more accurately, non-aligned as a tactical choice that serves its interest at a particular time. Thus, the behaviour of states professing such a policy varies from one of relative withdrawal or isolation to a policy of independent action and the avoidance of alliance arrangements. Under international law, the boundaries and territorial waters of a neutral state must be respected. See NON-ALIGNMENT.

New Industrializing Country (NIC)

Also known as "Tiger economies." There is some debate and discrepancy about the membership of this grouping but four are generally identified: Hong Kong, Singapore, South Korea and Taiwan. These countries have attained rapid industrial and economic growth over the past three decades. These countries exhibit strong market orientations, heavy industrialization, and export promotion. They have a high level of entrepreneurial skills amongst their populations, an open economy regarding foreign investment and stable and controlled democratic structures. NICs have made the label third world inappropriate. It must be remembered that Hong Kong was a dependent territory, not a state. It has now been repatriated to China.

New International Economic Order

The solution proposed by supporters of the World Systems Theory to the problem of less developed countries' dependency. The countries of the core would provide substantial aid to the countries of the periphery. The core countries would also grant more favourable terms of trade to the countries in the periphery to promote their economic growth.

New Left

A political movement that was especially prominent on American campuses during the

1960s and that drew significantly on anarchist principles in questioning all authority and in criticizing many conventional arrangements. The "new left" was particularly critical of capitalism, militarism, and representative democracy. See ANARCHY.

New Right

The term is associated with a resurgence of the right in Western politics since the late 1970s. The New Right, drawing inspiration from the works of von Hayek and Friedman, among others, demonstrates three key characteristics: one, a commitment to laissez-faire and elimination of state intervention in all aspects of life; two, a reaffirmation of traditional values with regard especially to the family and community; three, a libertarian strand which stresses the need for individual liberty and responsibility. The New Right had influential roles in the administrations of Ronald Reagan in the USA and Margaret Thatcher in the UK.

New World Order

In contemporary usage the phrase is associated with President George H.W. Bush who popularized it in the aftermath of the Iraqi invasion of Kuwait on 2 August 1990. He defined the New World Order as "a new era – freer from the threat of terror, stronger in the pursuit of justice and more secure in the quest for peace, an era in which the nations of the world, East and West, North and South, can prosper and live in harmony." In the aftermath of the war, much of the US efforts related to a NWO centred on reforming the UN, strengthening the machinery for collective action and laying down the groundwork for US hegemony. In the wake of the September 11, 2001 incident, President George Bush re-interpreted the NWO and championed the policy of "American hegemony," "pre-emptive strike" and "unilateralism" in American foreign policy. Although the term is associated in the popular mind with the American invasion of Kuwait, calls for a new world order have regularly accompanied significant events usually the ending of general wars in international relations. Similar calls were made in 1815, 1918 and 1945-46. See BUSH DOCTRINE, PRE-EMPTIVE STRIKE.

Niẓām (Pl. ***Anẓimah***)

Proper arrangement, organization, system, rule, system of regulations. *Niẓām* was used as the honorific title which became a characteristic of the rulers of the Indo-Muslim state of Hyderabad. In modern political parlance, *al-Niẓām al Siyāsī* refers to the political system or the system of government be it a monarchy, a single-party or multi-party system.

No-confidence Motion

A Motion of No Confidence is a motion put before a legislative assembly, by the opposition or by an erstwhile supporter who themselves have lost confidence in the government, expressing no-confidence in government (i.e., the cabinet). The aim of the motion is to defeat or to embarrass a government. The motion is passed or rejected by means of a parliamentary vote. If such a motion is passed, the prime minister and the cabinet must resign and request the dissolution of parliament. In presidential systems, the legislature may occasionally pass motions of no confidence as was done against the U.S. Secretary of State, Dean Acheson, in the 1950s, but these motions have only symbolic effects. See COLLECTIVE RESPONSIBILITY.

Nomenklatura

A Russian term denoting top party and state apparatus which constituted the ruling elite of the former Soviet Union. Literally, however, the term refers to the process of choosing of appointees to different positions of authority from a list of candidates approved by the Communist Party of the Soviet Union (CPSU). That list of candidates is referred to as *nomenklatura*. *Nomenklatura* is the former Soviet Communist Party's system of controlling all important administrative appointments, thereby ensuring the support and loyalty of those who managed day to day affairs.

Nomination

The legal procedures by which election authorities certify certain persons as qualified candidates for office and print their names on the official ballot. Usually, the "nomination paper" is submitted which is then scrutinized by an election official. If all the regulations are met, then the nominee is declared a candidate. See ELECTION.

Non-alignment

A national policy repudiating alliance with either the US or the Soviet Union during the cold war period. The policy was formulated in 1955 when most of the Asian and African states met at Bandung and decided to follow a policy of neutralism and to work for decolonization. At their first meeting in Belgrade in 1961, they called themselves the Non-Aligned Movement. The collapse of communism and the end of the Cold War have thrown non-alignment as a strategy into some disarray. Non-alignment differs from neutrality in that it does not commit a state to non-aggression or non-involvement in local conflicts and, unlike neutrality, it did not become an important concept in internationals relations until after World War II. See ALLIANCE, NEUTRALITY.

Non-Governmental Organizations (NGOs)

Organizations independent of governments, and which have humanitarian or co-operative rather than commercial objectives. More restrictively, NGOs are defined as professionally—staffed non-governmental agencies which seek to aid constituencies external to themselves and are not directly accountable to their intended beneficiaries. More generally, NGO has become shorthand for the diversity of lobbying or interest groups and associations which perform advocacy or service functions and which have been increasingly frequent observers at and participants in international negotiations. Some NGOs are supported by foreign governments or corporations, by international organizations, or by NGOs based in Western/ Northern industrialised states. See MNCs.

Non-Proliferation Treaty (NPT)

A treaty signed by Britain, the USA and the USSR in 1968 which became operational in 1970. Under the terms of the NPT, powers possessing nuclear weapons agreed not to transfer such devices to any non-nuclear state, and non-nuclear states agreed not to acquire nuclear weapons. In April 1995, at the end of the treaty's first twenty-five years, a global review conference of 178 nations decided to extend the NPT permanently. Critics charge that many developing countries continue to see the NPT as an effort on the part of the nuclear *haves* to prevent the *have-nots* from acquiring nuclear weapons. Others still argue that the treaty cannot be expected to limit the proliferation of either nuclear weapons or knowledge about how to build them, especially as it becomes progressively easier to acquire nuclear capacity. Israel, India and Pakistan have had nuclear capability for some time, and it is believed that Iran and North Korea may also have it.

Non-State Actors

International actors not always recognized by states and inter-governmental organizations that stimulate international cooperation on all levels of human interaction. Multinational corporations, international banks, religious movements, trans-national political organizations, terrorist groups and private individuals are examples of non-state actors. The significance of non-state actors has increased tremendously with the onset of globalization. See INTERNATIONAL RELATIONS.

Non-Violent Action

The use of organized civil disobedience to protest and compel the remedy of political, economic, and social suppression and discrimination with a determined avoidance of violence. The use of non-violence runs throughout history. There have been numerous instances of people courageously and non-violently refusing cooperation with injustice. However, the fusion of organized mass struggle and non-violence is relatively new. It originated largely with Mohandas Gandhi in 1906 at the onset of the South African campaign for Indian rights. Later, the Indian struggle for complete independence from the British Empire included a number of spectacular non-violent campaigns. Perhaps the most notable was the year-long Salt campaign in which 100,000 Indians were jailed for deliberately violating the Salt Laws. According to Martin Luther King Jr., "non-violence is a powerful and just weapon.... which cuts without wounding and ennobles the man who wields it. It is a sword that heals." See CIVIL DISOBEDIENCE.

North Atlantic Treaty Organization (NATO)

A collective security alliance ofWestern states against the perceived threat of communist aggression in the North Atlantic area. Founded in 1949, NATO's 16 members—Belgium, Britain, Canada, Denmark, France, Greece, Iceland, Italy, Luxembourg, the Netherlands, Norway, Portugal, Spain, Turkey, the United States, and Germany—form the largest and most highly organized international defence system in the world. Hungary received associate status to the alliance in 1991. All the signatories of the North Atlantic Treaty agree that "an armed attack against one or more of the parties to the treaty in Europe or North America shall be considered an attack against them all."The supreme governing organ of NATO is the North Atlantic Council, chaired by the secretary general of NATO in Brussels. In 1994, NATO launched its "partnership for peace" program, which invites former members of the Warsaw Pact and the former Soviet republics to take part in a wide range of military co-operation arrangements. These arrangements do not necessarily imply full NATO membership or security guarantees. See WARSAW PACT, SEATO.

North-South

Terms meant to distinguish between the advanced industrialized nations of the northern hemisphere and the poorer states of the southern hemisphere. The South is also referred to as the Third World. Some scholars include the former Soviet Union and Eastern Europe as part of the North, but most others restrict the definitions to Western Europe, Japan and North America. Debate and discussion revolve around the question of how the North-South economic gap be bridged and what, if any, obligation the North has toward the South. The growing tension between the few developed economies of the North and the many developed economies of the South is known as North/South Axis. See NEW INTERNATIONAL ECONOMIC ORDER.

O

Oligarchy

The word oligarchy is from the Greek for "few" and "rule". Thus, it means rule by the few. To the ancient Greeks, the term also referred to the few who were wealthy. In modern times, oligarchy is a form of government where most political power effectively rests with a small segment of society (typically the most powerful, whether by wealth, military strength, ruthlessness, or political influence). Many political theorists, notably Robert Michels, have argued that all societies are inevitably oligarchies no matter the supposed political system. See ARISTOCRACY.

Ombudsman

A term originating in Scandinavian polities denoting grievance officer. Also known as "Paliamentary commissioner." An official appointed by a legislature to hear and investigate complaints by private individuals against administrators. The ombudsman is appointed to investigate and publicize instances in which administrators have used their powers wrongly or failed to act when they should. Any citizen may register a complaint with the ombudsman. Ombudsman may issue public censure or in the final analysis he or she may direct the public prosecutor to take the matter to court. For Islamic equivalent see *ḤISBAH.*

One-Party State

A state in which politics is dominated by a single party, e.g., communist party states. Other parties sometimes exist, but are not allowed to challenge the dominance of the ruling party in any serious way. See PARTY SYSTEM.

One-party system

A country in which only one political party exists and works and no other political organization is allowed to work. It is not an open organization in which any citizen can become a member. Rather, it partakes of the nature of a select club where admission and expulsion is based upon the approval of those holding control of its affairs. By limiting the membership, it seeks to maintain the militancy of its organization and discipline, and to ensure highly qualified and trained members. Some scholars contend that the notion of a one-party system is a contradiction because more than one party is required to make up a party system. Others argue that the term one-party system has empirical utility. They distinguish different kinds of one-party systems. It includes not only totalitarian parties in dictatorships but also dominant parties in democracies. See POLITICAL PARTIES.

Opinion Polls

A technique used to access people's perceptions about issues or candidates or other items of interest by asking questions to a representative sample of the population. Most polls are conducted by telephone, although personal interviews provide an alternative method. Polls occupy an important position in the analysis and measurement of public opinion all over the democratic world, in part because commercial polling businesses survey public opinion and publish their findings in newspapers. Two of such famous firms are the American Institute of Public Opinion (founded by George Gallup) and Louis Harris and Associates in the United States known as Gallup and Harris poll respectively. See ELECTION.

Opposition

The politicians and political parties, and groups that form part of a country's legislative assembly but are not in the government. Contrary to general understanding, the opposition is more than a spearhead for criticism and a searchlight for scrutiny. Today, governments are responsible for legislative policy, the preparation of bills and the delineation of priorities. The opposition is regarded as the alternative government: as such, it is expected to articulate its own legislative programme and to define its stand on the great public issues of the day. See PARTY SYSTEM.

Organization of African Unity (OAU)

A regional multi-purpose intergovernmental organization composed of 52 independent African states. The OAU was set up by the Conference of Independent African States held in Addis Ababa, Ethiopia, in 1963. It has a permanent secretariat in Addis Ababa. Its major aim is to promote unity among its members and improve economic and cultural relations in Africa. It vehemently opposed the minority government of South Africa and its policies of apartheid. It recognized the sovereignty of existing African states within their colonial frontiers, endorsed a policy of non-intervention in domestic affairs and did not encourage secession. OAU has been superseded by the African Union.

Organization of American States (OAS)

The most important intergovernmental organization within the inter-American system. Established by the Ninth International Conference of American states at Bogota, Colombia, in 1948, the OAS has its headquarters in Washington, D.C., where 35 regional states in the Americas meet to discuss regional economic, political, and military matters. The largest decision-making body of the OAS is the General Assembly which sits annually as a general conference of all members and has jurisdiction to consider any regional problem that a majority of its members wish to debate. The Permanent Council carries out directives of the assembly and performs pacific settlement functions when disputes among members are considered by the OAS. The OAS functions as a general regional multi-purpose IGO as well as a collective security defence organization. The United States has used the OAS to provide a multilateral legitimacy to the implementation of its foreign policy goals in the western hemisphere and has converted its unilateral actions to the status of regional international "peace-keeping" often without consulting the OAS.

Organization for Economic Cooperation and Development (OECD)

An international governmental body representing 24 of the most industrialized countries of the world, created in 1961 to develop trade and support in each other's growth and economic welfare. An administrative body, the Council, having representatives from each country, governs OECD. Its headquarters are in Paris, France. Apart from its major concern with economic development, OECD promotes multilateral world trade on a non-discriminatory basis.

Organization of Islamic Conference (OIC)

An international organization of Islamic States with a permanent delegation to the United Nations. It consists of 57 member and 3 Observer states and is based on the Charter of the Islamic Conference which came into force on February 28, 1973. Its principal policy-making bodies are constituted in the form of "conferences." The OIC describes itself as "an international organization grouping fifty seven States which have decided to pool their resources together, combine their efforts and speak with one voice to safeguard the interests and secure the progress and well-being of their peoples and of all Muslims in the world." The immediate catalyst which helped precipitate the first Islamic Summit Conference in Rabat, Morocco, in 1969 was the incident of the burning of the Al-Aqṣā Mosque. The OIC held its 10th summit conference in Putrajaya, Malaysia, in October 2003.

Organization of Petroleum Exporting Countries (OPEC)

A functional inter-governmental organization consisting of a group of thirteen oil-exporting countries that formed an intergovernmental cartel to regulate the production, distribution, and pricing of oil. Members include Saudi Arabia, Nigeria, Algeria, Venezuela, Libya, Kuwait, United Arab Emirates, Iran, Iraq, Ecuador, Qatar, Gabon, and Indonesia. Organized in 1960 with headquarters in Vienna, Austria, the cartel has four administrative sections, each with its own responsibilities, working toward the common goals of oil pricing and supplying world demands. OPEC, however, has not been successful in devising a strategy to keep the oil prices stable.

Ordinance

French *ordenance*, literally, act of arranging, from Medieval Latin *ordinantia*. Ordinance refers to an authoritative decree or direction, a law set forth by a governmental authority; specifically a municipal regulation. Generally, it refers to temporary laws issued by the executive branch of the government. See LAW.

Oslo Agreement

The outline peace deal worked out in negotiations between Israel and the Palestine Liberation Organisation, secretly conducted in Norway. The principles agreed were, in essence, the withdrawal of Israeli forces from the Gaza Strip and the West Bank and the Palestinian right to self-government within those areas through the creation of the Palestinian Authority. The agreement was sealed with the famous handshake between Yasser Arafat and Yitzhak Rabin on the White House lawn in September 1993.

Ostpolitik

A German political term, it literally means "Eastern policy." A foreign policy orientation of the Federal Republic of Germany initiated by Chancellor Willy Brandt in the late 1960s and early 1970s to normalize relations with the Soviet Union and its Eastern European satellites. Basically, Brandt accepted the principle of "two Germanys" which was acknowledged in an agreement signed in 1972. Ostpolitik led to substantial decrease of tension in Europe. Helmut Schmidt who succeeded Brandt as Chancellor followed that orientation with the same vigour. With the collapse of the Soviet Union and of the Berlin wall, this concept has lost much of its utility.

'Othmanli (or Ottoman)

The name of the rulers of the Turkish caliphate from the late thirteenth century to 1924 (late 7th to 1342 H) and for the culture that flourished under their rule. The name appears in Europe as "Ottoman," though it is more accurately rendered as "'Othmanli."The term is also used as an alternative name for the Turkish language. At its height, in the early sixteenth century, the Othmanlis ruled much of the Middle East, the Balkan Peninsula, and a large part of the Caucasus region. 'Othmanlis slowly declined in power, defeated in the World War I and carved up by the League of Nations in 1919. Mustafa Kemal Ataturk formally ended the 'Othmanli caliphate in 1922 and established a Turkish republic.

Overkill

A concept in strategic theory, relating to nuclear warfare. It means the capacity of a nation to destroy, by nuclear weapons, more of an enemy than would be necessary for a military victory.

P

Pacifism

Refusal to settle disputes with violence. Many pacifists are committed to achieving one's goals only through actively non-violent resistance or non-aggressive means. Other pacifists are not opposed, on principle, to all social use of violence in all cases, but believe that war is a category of violence which is never necessary nor acceptable. Pacifism is often induced by religious beliefs. Many Buddhists are pacifists, as are Mennonites, Church of the Brethern, Amish and some other Christian groups. Opinions are divided among Christians over whether Jesus Christ advocated pacifist teachings. Pacifism as a distinctive belief is not at all common. See NON-VIOLENCE.

Palestine Liberation Organization (PLO)

An organization recognized as the sole legitimate representative of the Palestinian people by the Arab heads of state. The organization was sponsored allegedly by President Gamal Abdel Nasser along with other Arab states, under the leadership of Ahmad ash-Shuqayri in 1964. The objective of the PLO ultimately was to create a Palestinian state following the liberation of Palestine from Israeli occupation. The PLO pressed the doctrine of the necessity of armed struggle, particularly after the defeat of Arab armies in June 1967. In 1969, Yasir Arafat was elected chairman of the Executive Committee of the PLO. During the 1970s and 1980s, the PLO was sidelined during the war and the peace process that followed. By the late 1980s, the situation changed when Yasir Arafat confirmed the PLO's recognition of the right of Israel to exist. The U.S. opened the dialogue with the PLO. On 13 September 1993 in Washington, D.C., Yasser Arafat and Israeli Prime Minister Rabin signed an agreement for the implementation of limited autonomy in the West Bank and the Gaza strip. However, basic differences continue to cloud the prospects of that agreement.

Palestine National Authority

The interim government of the Palestinian territories headed so far by Yasser Arafat, and manned almost exclusively by PLO officials. It is a semi-autonomous state institution nominally governing the Palestinians in West Bank and the Gaza Strip was established as a part of Oslo accords between the PLO and Israel. Though not explicitly stated, there was an unwritten understanding on both sides that it would become the basis of an independent Palestinian state in the process of the final settlement. The Palestinian Authority enjoys so far an international recognition as the organization representing the Palestinian people (albeit a limited one). It has an observer status in the United Nations. Israelis, who do not recognise a Palestinian state, always drop the word 'National.' See INTIFADAH, OSLO AGREEMENT.

Pan-Arabism

The idea that Arabs constitute a distinctive group of people with strong bonds of a common language, history, and cultural attributes. As an ideology, pan-Arabism emerged first in the former Arab provinces of the Ottoman Empire. It was preceded by Pan-Islamism which was encouraged by the Ottomans. However, following the collapse of the Ottoman Empire and with the imposition of the Mandate system at the expense of Arab aspirations, pan-Arabism emerged with the more narrowed focus on the Arabs rather than on Muslims. It was an expression of resistance to the colonialism of Britain and France which had territorially atomized the Arab world. As a secular ideology, pan-Arabism played a dominant role up until the humiliating defeat of the Arabs by Israel in 1967. From that point on, this ideology began gradually to lose credibility with more and more people turning to Islam as a political alternative.

Pan-Islamism

Pan Islamism is an ideology that calls upon believers to cast aside the veils of secular nationalism and racial, linguistic, and tribal loyalties to reunite the long-divided ummah. In this sense, Islam asks for more than personal devotion and submission to the will of God; Islam demands the devotion and submission of the community of believers to the precepts revealed in the Qur'an and set forth in the *shari'ah*. Pan-Islamism aspires to provide a supranational ideal transcending individual states as a focus of identity capable of shaping ends and means of foreign policy. In practice, however, while Pan-Islamism continue to exert real influence as a cultural force, the independent state as part of a framework of inter-state relations constituted according to the norms of international law continues to dominate the politics of the Muslim world. Thus, pan-Islamism is not a political reality but it retained a psychological one. Muslims throughout the world continue to feel a special bond with their co-religionists, without regard to race, tribe, language, or even nation.

Parkinson's Law

The view advanced by Professor Northcote Parkinson suggesting that the size of a bureaucracy increases not because of the impetus of new programs and greater enforcement but because of a natural tendency of organizations to expand. Parkinson analyzed the size of the British Colonial Office and discovered that as the British Empire declined, the number of people employed in the British Colonial Office actually increased. He concluded from this and other data that Parkinson's Law applies to organization. Some critics question the validity of Parkinson's law.

Parliament

A consultative assembly. The word is mainly of English usage and is applied in the context of parliamentary systems. It is a multi-membered body which considers questions of public policy and has constitutional powers to make law. The key function of the parliament is representation. The other functions include making and dismissing governments; passing laws and scrutinizing the executive; and recruitment and socialization of political leaders. See LEGISLATURE.

Parliamentary Dismissal

The procedure to remove the executive from office by an elected parliament. Procedures for parliamentary dismissal of the executive (or the Government, as it is called in Britain) differ somewhat among countries and over time. In some countries simple defeat for any official government measure is enough to bring resignation, but in other cases formal parliamentary passage of a motion of censure or no-confidence is required.

Parliamentary Immunity

Immunities granted to the members of legislature from the legal consequences of speeches made and acts committed in the chamber. In UK and Commonwealth countries, legislators enjoy freedom from criminal or civil action for what is said or done in the course of debate or legislative proceedings.

Parliamentary Privilege

Special rights or advantages given to members of the House of Parliament collectively or individually. These rights enable the parliament to maintain its independence and the dignity of its position. Some of the parliamentary privileges include the freedom of speech and right of publication.

Parliamentary Question Time

An amount of time given to members of parliament to raise questions when parliament is in session. Question time provides members of parliament the opportunity to ask a question to any member of the government. Asking questions is one of the methods by which rank and file members of parliament can review and criticize the actions of the civil service and the ministers and also to take part in the governing process. The questions are put in both oral and written form. They may be simple requests for information or may require the ministers to explain and justify actions taken by their departments. However, members are required to give the ministers one or two days' notice before asking the question.

Parliamentary Sovereignty

The principle that declares parliament to be supreme over all other governmental institutions including the monarch and the judiciary. The parliament, in a parliamentary system, can pass any law, on any subject, and the law of parliament is the supreme law of the land. A parliament can, if it so chooses, suppress civil liberties or suspend elections without fear that its acts are unconstitutional. Parliamentary supremacy prevents judicial review of local domestic law. That is, no court can declare an act of parliament to be null and void. The principle of parliamentary supremacy was established over the 17th and 18th centuries during which time parliament asserted the right to name and depose a king. See PARLIAMENT.

Parliamentary System

A representative system that features "fusion" rather than "separation" of executive and legislative institutions and powers. The executive (prime minister, premier, or chancellor, and cabinet) is elected by the popularly—elected house of parliament and may be removed from office by parliamentary vote. United Kingdom and Malaysia are two of the many examples. The executive remains continually accountable to the people's elected representatives in parliament. Although more than three-fourths of existing democratic systems are parliamentary, there are important differences in how they operate. In some countries, the government is normally backed by a majority of its own party in parliament known as majoritarian parliamentary system. In others, the government almost always represents a coalition of several parliamentary parties known as representational system. In some parliamentary systems, ministers take part in the activities of parliament (UK, Malaysia), in others ministers are not allowed to be members of the legislature (France, Netherlands and Norway). Under the parliamentary system the roles of head of state and head of government are more or less separated. In most parliamentary systems, the head of state is generally a ceremonial position, often a monarch or president, however, sometimes retaining duties without much political relevance, such as Civil Service appointments. See FUSION OF POWERS.

Participatory Democracy

A broadly inclusive term for many kinds of consultative decision making in a democracy. There are many varieties of participatory democracy including: Deliberative democracy; consensus democracy; anticipatory democracy; semi-direct democracy and non-partisan democracy. The term, though related, should not be confused with direct democracy. See DEMOCRACY.

Partition

The division of a sovereign territory into two or more autonomous states. As a means of conflict resolution, it is a mechanism designed to allow self-government to minority groups who, because of persecution, economic exploitation or the threat of cultural assimilation, are demanding statehood. Although the cause of most partitions is ethnic division or nationalism (India, Ireland, Palestine etc.), some partitions (of Germany and Korea) were the result of the conflict between the two superpowers, the US and the Soviet Union, who divided a homogeneous people for territorial and strategic gain. See INDEPENDENCE.

Party convention

A special meeting held by a political party to select its leadership candidates, write a platform, choose a national or provincial committee, and conduct party business. See POLITICAL PARTY.

Party Identification

(also called party affiliation or partisan affiliation). A feeling of loyalty or psychological attachment to a political party. Party identification is usually related to voting behaviour. It is an inner psychological feeling or attitude, not an outward formal dues-paying attachment to a party, such as party membership.

Party Membership

Formal attachment to a political party of one's choice. It usually involves the assumption of obligations to the party and receiving privileges from the party. See POLITICAL PARTY.

Party Organization

Structural configuration through which political parties perform their various functions. This structuring creates units of organization at the national and local levels at which elections are conducted.

Party Systems

Patterns of party relationships that exist within a political unit. It refers to the interaction of parties with each other and with the overall political system. Much of the health of a political system depends on the party system, whether it is stable or unstable, whether it has too many parties, and whether they compete to promote cohesion or disintegration of the system.

Passive Resistance

Non-violent resistance, usually characterized by acts of non-cooperation by individuals or groups despite physical threat or pressure. See CIVIL DISOBEDIENCE.

Patrimonialism

Term coined by Max Weber to describe a political system in which the object of obedience is the personal authority of the individual which he enjoys by virtue of his traditional status. The organized group exercising authority is based on relations of personal loyalty cultivated through a common process of education. The person exercising authority is the chief; his administrative staff consist of personal retainers; those subject to authority are his traditional comrades or his subjects.

Patriotism

Love for and loyalty towards one's own country. All nation-states encourage and promote patriotic respect for national symbols, such as the flag, independence day and the national anthem.
See NATIONALISM.

Patronage

The distribution of government jobs and favours in return for support in an election campaign. The patronage power is available in key positions in the government hierarchy and thus often the key to success at the polls. Many of the appointments to the post of judges, ambassadors and the like made by chief executives in the U.S. and other Western countries and, indeed, in most of the developing countries are based on services rendered during past elections.

Pax Americana

From Latin, meaning "American Peace". The term denotes the period of relative peace in the Western world since World War II, that placed the United States of America in the role of a modern-day Roman Empire (based on Pax Romana). During this period, the USA has been involved to a greater or lesser extent in various regional wars (probably most famously, the Vietnam War), and has maintained espionage and covert operations in many other areas. In general, the term "Pax Americana" is used to describe the US effort to suppress countries which do not cooperate with American policy (so called rogue states). This usage implies that the Roman Empire was immoral in some way and so is the attempt to establish Pax Americana. See BUSH DOCTRINE, NEW WORLD ORDER.

Periphery

The less-developed countries or areas of Asia, Latin America, and Africa. In the dependency literature, the periphery is dominated by the core or centre which consists of the economically and politically dominant countries of the world. The literature on the capitalist world-system has applied the concept of periphery back to the origins of capitalism in Europe. The periphery plays a subordinate but important role in a worldwide capitalist division of labour by providing raw materials and cheap labour. As capitalism expanded, countries that at one time were part of the core slipped into peripheral or semiperipheral status.

Permanent Revolution

It refers to the theory of how to sustain Communism within a backward state. The term is most closely associated with Leon Trotsky but the call for Permanent Revolution is first found in the writings of Karl Marx. In communist theory, this involves a continuous process of transforming a feudal or colonial society to a communist one, without establishing a distinct capitalist society for any prolonged period. See COMMUNISM.

Peter Principle

The idea formulated by American executive Lawrence Peter, that every employee tends to rise to his or her level of incompetence. For government organizations, the implication is that no one who is doing a job well is permitted to remain in that position, and that at a given moment, most jobs are occupied by incompetents. See PARKINSON'S LAW.

Platform

An official statement of Party principles, policy, and programmes. Platforms are not considered strict promises to voters though in principle a party's nominees are supposed to endorse them. Platforms are probably best viewed as statements reflecting the philosophy of those who are influential in a party.

Plebiscite

The vote by which the people of a political unit determine autonomy or affiliation with another country. In 1956, British Togo land, a former League of Nations mandate, voted to become part of Ghana instead of joining with French Togo land. See REFERENDUM.

Pluralism

A system in which all interests organize and compete freely and no one group is able to dominate. The government is open to pressure from the interest groups, and politics consists largely of the competition among these interest groups to see that the policies they favour are adopted by the government. There is no state that is perfectly pluralist; the term is an abstraction. The United States is often cited as an example of pluralism at work. Pluralism also refers to the view that non-state actors (bureaucracies, individuals, groups etc.) are important entities in international relations and that the agenda of world politics is extensive and goes beyond security concerns. In short, international relations is the result of a multiplicity of factors and actors. See DEMOCRACY.

Plurality

(also known as first past the post system). In an election, a winning margin that is less than a simple majority (50 percent plus one more vote). If in an election, candidate A gets 40 percent of the vote; candidate B, 30 percent; and candidate C, 30 percent. Candidate A is therefore elected by plurality. See ELECTION.

Plutocracy

From the Greek "ploutos" meaning wealth, plutocracy refers to a government system where wealth is the principal basis of power. It is a system which is governed directly by the wealthy classes or is controlled by the wealthy classes by financial contributions or by bribing the governors. There are not many examples of a "true" plutocracy in history as such. In the present era, there are numerous cases of wealthy individuals exerting financial pressure on governments to pass favourable legislation. Most western partisan democracies permit the raising of funds by the partisan organisations, and it is well-known that political parties frequently accept significant donations from various individuals (either directly or through corporate institutions). Some critics describe these donations as "bribes," although legally they are not. See ARISTOCRACY.

Pocket Veto

The decision of the president to not take action on the signing of a bill near the end of a session of congress. If congress adjourns within a ten-day period, the bill is killed without the president's formal veto. See VETO.

Political Idealism

A school in international relations that assumes the essential goodness and changeability of human nature. It trusts in education, reform and the periodic use of force to remedy defects. It believes that a rational and a moral political order derived from universally valid abstract principles can be achieved. See POLITICAL REALISM.

Political Party

A group of people, however loosely organized with a label, seeking to win office through elections and gain control over machinery of government. When out of office, usually present persistent and more or less organized opposition to policies of party or coalition in power. In the West, political parties function mostly as electoral devices to get a group of leaders elected. In a Muslim society, a political party has to function not just as an electoral instrument but also as a social service organization to help improve the condition of the people. See ELECTION, OPPOSITION, PARTY SYSTEM.

Political Realism

A perspective on international relations that assumes that the world, imperfect as it is, from the rational point of view, is the result of forces inherent in human nature. To improve the world one must work with these forces, not against them. This being inherently a world of opposing interests and of conflict among them, moral principles can never be fully realised. The patriarch of the philosophy of realism was Reinhold Niebuhr. Its chief representative, however, is Hans J. Morgenthau. The main element of political realism is the concept of national interest which is defined in terms of power. The assumption is that statesmen think and act in terms of interest defined as power. Power is not only a tool of analysis but also a guide to policy. It is the perennial standard by which political action should be judged. Thus, according to this school, a foreign policy should concern more with the political requirement of success rather than anything else. It should eschew the preoccupation with ideological preferences of political actors.

Polarised Pluralism

A multiparty system of more than five parties in which there are three poles, including a centre pole. This concept was coined by Giovanni Sartori to characterize a political system in which two or more extremes are the predominant feature. See PARTY SYSTEM.

Police State

A political system where the government maintains strict control over society often with the use of a force of secret police. This implies that the control by the government contradicts the will of the people being controlled. It is a state in which the police are free to act without restriction. Many totalitarian systems have relied heavily upon special secret police concerned with such crimes against the state as speaking and working against the regime. The best known examples in recent years have been the Nazi Gestapo, the Savak of the former Shah of Iran and former Soviet agencies such as KGB. Thus, a police state is inherently anti-democratic. It is similar to martial law. See MARTIAL LAW.

Policy Analysis

A critical examination of public policy to ascertain the nature of its constituents and evaluate its effectiveness. Policy analysis includes all stages of policy formation, including implementation. Analysis concentrates on programmes, is often interdisciplinary and takes a comparative approach. Policy analysis is of major interest to political scientists especially those involved in the area of public administration.

Politburo

In theory, executive committee of the Central Committee of the Communist Party of the Soviet Union. First formed in 1917, the politburo dominates the central committee and the general congress of the Soviet Communist Party. It is a relatively small body of about a dozen full members and a half-dozen nonvoting or "candidate" members. In reality, it is the autocratic and supreme decision-making and policy-deciding body in Soviet political system; chaired by general secretary of the party.

Political Attitudes

Learned attitudes that relate to political issues, events, personalities, and institutions in either a favourable or unfavourable manner and usually in a consistent or characteristic way. In recent times, the concept of political culture has been used in the examination of people's attitudes to their own political system.

Political Beliefs

Deeply held convictions about political reality that are based on one or more fundamental assumptions about human behaviour, e.g., humans are basically selfish and governments should legislate and enforce the sharing of resources in a complex society.

Political Campaign

The activities of a political candidate (and those working for him/her) that are designed to motivate other citizens to take the time and effort to vote, and to vote for him or her. Political campaign involves a complex combination of popular appeals, communicated by various means to voters through the utilization of manpower and money. It is a process in which candidates and those who assist them acquire a number of resources and use them so they can be converted into votes. Vital to all political campaigns are two final ingredients, people and money: People to communicate a candidate's message calling for votes and money to pay for the campaign costs. Anyone who has too little of either is unlikely to do well in a modern political campaign, particularly for major national offices. See ELECTION.

Political Community

A community of people who share a sense of allegiance to the same government. The members of a political community are willing to work together to settle their differences in a peaceful manner. The political community will be much stronger if its members share group identification, an in-group or we-group feeling.

Political Conflict

Struggle among people to achieve a particular value allocation from public authorities. It is a conflict over type of rules the government should pursue. No society is entirely without political conflict. Political conflict is not an unfortunate and temporary aberration from the normal state of perfect cooperation and harmony.

Political corruption

A knowingly exploitation of the public office for personal and private gains. Political corruption is identified with behaviour of public officials who (1) in violation of the norms and contrary to the accepted rules and standards for the conduct of public office (2) and in a manner which harms the interests of the public, (3) knowingly exploits the office for clear personal and private gains. In short, it refers to the exploitation of public political power for extralegal material advantage.

Political Culture

Popularized by Gabriel Almond and G. Bingham Powell, it is defined as the pattern of individual attitudes and orientations toward politics among members of a political system. It is made up of political attitudes, values, feelings, information and skills possessed by members of the political community. It is reflected in a nation's ideology, in attitudes towards political leaders, in the duties of citizenship, in the conduct and style of political activity, in what is considered political and what is not. Political scientists have identified four types of political culture: parochial, subject, participant and civic.

Political Development

Defined in several ways. Central to all theories of political development is the notion that all societies have passed, or are in the process of passing from a condition in which a bundle of related characteristics which can be broadly classified as "traditional" predominates, to one in which modern characteristics predominate. Theorists of political development share many attitudes: they are concerned with the increasing complexity and differentiation of political institutions as either an inevitable or desirable feature of political development; they take the Anglo-American polities as approximating the model of a developed political system, and they see masses as disruptive and reactionary and hence hampering progress and development. Muslim political scientists would point to the dynamic role of the masses, because of the progressive, egalitarian features of "traditional" society; they would warn of the dangers of elitism and stress the need for leaders to be in constant touch with the masses and responsive to their needs; and they would argue against too much preoccupation with institutional complexity and differentiation, which are just breeding grounds of corruption and of no relevance to general population. See MODERNIZATION.

Political Economy

The attempt to merge economic analysis with practical politics, i.e., to view economic activity in its political context. Political economy is an approach which searches for economic determinants of political life. It suggests that the proper starting point for the analysis of the distribution of power in a society must be the economic relations within that society. The main motor force of social change is considered to be economic, more especially technological change; and such economic change is alleged to determine the most significant changes in social relations, values or ideology, and political structure. The political economist's emphasis on economic factors, class struggle and exploitation generally goes hand-in-hand with a moral commitment to radical change.

Political Education

The learning process undergone by citizens in a political set-up. Political education includes both formal and informal education, including imparting an understanding of the history of one's country and the values underlying its procedures and tradition. Such an education is considered an essential component in the training of a democratic citizenry. However, political education is also part of a totalitarian political system.

Political Efficacy

The belief that one's political views and actions can affect the operation of the political system. Political efficacy is an important determinant of political participation. Almond-Verba study of political culture found that better educated people are more characterized by political efficacy than the less educated ones.

Political Equality

The principle that each adult citizen has the same opportunity as every other adult citizen to take part in the political decision-making process. This means "one person, one vote." This is a logical consequence of the principle of popular sovereignty.

Political Geography

The geography of states and substate units. Early scholars suggested a correlation between types of climate and categories of political systems. Others have tried to imply an association between the types of soil and the behaviour of voters. Such writings on ecological determinism have been attacked from different quarters as fallacious and flawed.

Political Influence

A style of power that is particularly indiscernible. It often is exerted in conversations between two people in back rooms. Formal power-holders such as ministers may seek the information and opinions of those held to be well-informed, wise and experienced. Such people are influential. The extent to which influence is important will depend on a country's political culture and the values of its politicians.

Political Integration

The condition of making politically whole or complete by bringing together political parts. It is the uniting of the distinct part of a polity into a workable and viable whole. The parts of the political system which are normally included under this umbrella are the formal institutions of government, the party system, the electoral system, elite groups taking an active and direct part in the making of political decisions such as the military, the public servants, the top economic managers and labour leaders, and pressure groups. Political integration describes either a process of unifying these institutions into a cohesive whole over time or a condition of political cohesion. Political integration may also occur between two or more polities. More often, political integration may occur between two or more subdivisions or component parts of a national political system.

Political Obligation

A theory which seeks to explain why and under what circumstances, citizens are required to obey their governments. There are various explanations for this, although an important one is the idea that the existence of government and the powers which it exercises are based on the consent of the governed.

Political Participation

A term to denote the actions by which individuals take part in the political process. Debate centres on two issues: the value of political participation to individuals and the political system, and the causes of participation and non-participation.

Political Prisoners

People detained in prison or kept under house arrest because their political views differed from those held by the ruling authorities in a given country. In many cases, a veneer of legality is used to disguise the fact that someone is a political prisoner. Sometimes false criminal charges are brought against them for long-term imprisonment and they may be denied bail unfairly, or special powers may be invoked by the judiciary.

Political Protest

Any form of political opposition/dissent which registers dissatisfaction with or opposition to the procedural consensus established by a society without calling for the total destruction or transformation of its political system. Protest phenomena range from mild forms of political opposition, such as an open vote by a party member against one's own party, to extreme forms of political dissent, such as widespread and violent acts of rebellion against the political system or its leaders. Political protest is specifically directed against some aspect or symbol of the political system of a society and it is frequently rationalized in terms of a well-ordered set of ideas about the nature and organization of the polity, its injustices and inefficiencies. Political protest may assume both violent (involving the threat or use of physical force) and non-violent (that does not involve the use of physical force and consequently does not result in physical or human destruction) forms. See STRIKE, DEMONSTRATION.

Political Psychology

A study of the behaviour and motivation of political actors by relating it to factors of a personal nature. This is much easier to study in the case of political leaders as their memoirs and biographies are available. It is very difficult to use the sophisticated questions psychologists want to ask in sample survey work. Most empirical work of a behavioural kind in this area has investigated the authoritarian personality.

Political Revolution

A sudden, out of the ordinary political change the objective of which is to destroy the existing government and to create a new and supposedly more legitimate one in its place. The American Revolution (1775-1783) is a clear example of a political revolution.

Political Rights

Those rights that assure an individual freedom of expression, opportunity to participate in the political process, fair treatment in criminal proceedings, and equal treatment under the law. See CIVIL RIGHTS.

Political Science

An academic discipline that studies ideas, behaviour, institutions and policies related to public politics and government. It concentrates most on how people compete for and use public governmental power. Empirical and quantitative methods have become increasingly important in political science. However, qualitative and evaluative approaches remain significant. According to Aristotle, it is the master or supreme science. According to Muslim philosopher al-Farabi, political science aims at leading people to true happiness through right actions. See POLITICS.

Political Socialisation

An aspect of the general process of socialization which every person to some degree undergoes. It is basically the process of teaching and learning about all aspects of the political system. Through the process of political socialization, children and, to a lesser extent, adults absorb attitudes, beliefs, information and judgments regarding politics. This process is carried out through various socialization agencies including family, school, peer groups, media, adult experience, and, in the case of Islam, mosque. See POLITICAL CULTURE.

Political Sociology

Often called political behaviouralism, it is an approach which attempts to investigate the influence of society on politics. The major assumption of political sociology is that politics is, at least in part, if not predominantly, determined by the social environment of the political actors. Political sociology tries to find the answer to the question: In what way do the social relations of men help us to understand the way they think, act and react politically? Political sociology is therefore interested in exploring the societal roots not only of how men act, but also of how men think politically.
See BEHAVIOURALISM.

Political Succession

The transfer of leadership and the exercise of power from one person or group of persons to another by violent or nonviolent means. See ELECTION, REVOLUTION.

Political System

An expression sometimes used as a synonym for country. However, the term is associated with David Easton and refers to the relationships, processes and institutions through which authoritative allocations are made for the whole society. Thus, the Malaysian political system consists of "inputs" from society to the formal institutions of government, in the form of public opinion, pressure group activity and so on, while the institutions of government process these inputs to produce outputs in the form of laws, policies and even norms and values. See STATE.

Political Theory

It serves as a kind of underpinning for all political science study. It deals with major concepts, ideas, and values. Throughout the ages, major political theorists have asked the question: What constitutes a good government and how can it be established? Political theory speculates about what ought to be rather than what is. In the behavioural phase, political theory is defined as a collection of law like statements aimed at explaining and or predicting a political phenomenon. See POLITICAL SCIENCE.

Political Values

Shared beliefs that provide standards for judging human thought and action. Political values may be viewed as pressures that motivate social behaviour within a political culture. Politics results from the interplay of values among individuals and groups pursuing different goals for their own benefit.

Political Violence

Rebellion, rioting, looting, sabotages, terrorism and physical conflicts between groups. Group conflict includes communal violence, usually between different ethnic and/or religious groups which, at its worst, can descend into civil war and massacres. Internal extremes of poverty and plenty are often associated with political violence, especially where economic difference is linked to ethnic differences. See CIVIL DISOBEDIENCE.

Political Will

A determined, deliberate, purposeful, independent decision, conclusion, or choice upon a course of action by persons in political authority, such as elimination of inequality, poverty, interest-based economy, political exploitation, and unemployment through various reforms of social, economic, and political structures. Lack of political will is often said to be one of the main obstacles to development and the main reason for the failure of many development plans and Islamization programme.

Politics

Efforts, both successful and unsuccessful, by some people to gain and exercise power over others. Politics consists of people acting politically, by organizing political interest groups and trying to induce governments to act in ways that will promote their interests over those of their opponents. Within every society or among societies, politics is the process of competition and co-operation by which values gain priority. These priority values are authoritatively allocated by the political system in order to legitimize their binding effect on the lives of the majority of people. Politics, then, is the process that settles claims people make on their political system so that they feel part of the same set of shared social values. Politics is necessary for the continuation of a decent existence. See POLITICAL SCIENCE.

Polity

The political organization of a society, its citizens, and the institutions and procedures through which the state governs. Often used as a synonym for political system. See STATE.

Polyarchy

It refers to a system in which the society is controlled by a set of competing interest groups with the government as little more than an honest broker. The term was introduced into the vocabulary of political science by Robert A. Dahl and Charles E. Lindblom. Polyarchy is characterized by elected officials, frequent and fairly conducted elections, universal adult franchise, freedom to contest in elections, freedom of expression, alternative information and associational autonomy. See DEMOCRACY, CIVIL SOCIETY.

Popular Sovereignty

The principle that requires that the ultimate power to make political decisions in the country is vested in all the people rather than in some of them or one of them. This principle forms the nucleus of the concept of democracy. See DEMOCRACY.

Populism

From the Latin word *populus*, which means *people*. At the most basic level, it refers to the belief that the instruments of the state need to be grasped from the self-serving elite and be used for the benefit and advancement of the oppressed masses as a whole. Generally, it means making an appeal to the people, variously understood, against the established structure of power and the dominant ideas and values within a polity that is formally democratic. For many analysts, populism became a convenient general term to cover any kind of radicalism based on or aimed at rural rather than urban populations. See RADICALISM.

Positivism

A philosophical doctrine which sees meaningful discourse as being possible only in reference to observable phenomena or in so far as it is susceptible for verification. Its adherents argue that philosophy should aspire to the same sort of rigor as science. Logical positivists assert that statements are meaningful only insofar as they are verifiable, and that statements can be verified only in two (exclusive) ways: empirical statements, including scientific theories, were verified experiments and evidences. Analytic truth statements are true or false by definition, and so are also meaningful. Everything else, including ethics and aesthetics, was not *literally* meaningful, and so belonged to "metaphysics." Thus, statements about God, good and evil, and beauty are neither true nor false, and thus should not be taken seriously. See BEHAVIOURALISM.

Post-Colonial State

States that have passed through the process of decolonization. Post-colonial states share many things in common. Their economic programmes are often unrealizable in the globalized economy and their judicial and police systems are unable to control the level of political violence which is often the result of tribal and ethnic conflicts. See COLONIALISM.

Post-Materialism

A political outlook that takes material well-being for granted and concentrates on "higher-order" values, for example life style issues such as ecology, nuclear disarmament and feminism. Post materialism tends to be stronger among younger, better off, well educated people.

Postmodernism

Literally, beyond the modern, and suggesting a fragmentation of modernist beliefs, identities and certainties. Emerging in 1968, the leading intellectuals of postmodernism are Foucault, Barthes, Lyotard and Derrida. There is diversity in their thought; but it can be summarized as a reaction against universal explanations and grand theories. Postmodernism is more an attitude to life and living than a system of ideas.

Power

Defined as the ability to make someone do something which he or she otherwise will not do. It is the capacity of some persons to produce intended and foreseen effects on others. This ability need not be accompanied by coercion (force or threat of force). See INFLUENCE.

Pragmatism

The philosophy that judges institutions and policies by their practical consequences. This philosophy was developed by William James and John Dewey. They believed that neither science nor politics is engaged in a search for absolute truth, but that both are interested in making improvements, through experimentation, on what we know and on what exists. Pragmatists do not ask, "is this true or is this best?" But rather ask, "Does this serve better than what we already know or have?"

Pre-emptive War

A war that is waged in an attempt to prevent other conflicts in the future, rather than in response to a direct attack or provocation. It is at the heart of the Bush Doctrine; the first example was the war in Iraq and current U.S. occupation. See BUSH DOCTRINE.

Preferential Treatment

Policies, like affirmative action and the use of hiring quotas, that favour the traditionally disadvantaged groups they target in ways that amount to reverse discrimination. Some argue that preferential treatment is unfair and undemocratic while others argue that democracy requires equality which is possible through preferential treatment.

Prerogative

An exclusive right inherent within an office or position that may be constitutional or may have developed out of custom and tradition.

President

A person who occupies the highest political position in the state. The president may simply perform ceremonial functions mostly in parliamentary systems, as in India, or may be the real executive, as in the presidential system, formulating and deciding public policies. In the U.S., the president is the chief executive and also the head of state. See HEAD OF STATE.

Presidential System

A system in which the responsibilities of leadership are vested in the chief executive, the President, elected for a fixed term and independent of the legislature. In it, the President is both the chief executive and the head of state. The United States is the principal example of the presidential system of government. The main features of the American presidential system are: separation of powers and checks and balances; decentralization of political parties; a written, rigid constitution; and judicial review.

Pressure Group

An organized group of people whose aim is to persuade a government or other authority to take a particular course of action, for example, to change a law. Some people consider it as a negative term to describe an interest group.

Prestroika

A Russian term meaning "turning around" or "restructuring." It refers to a set of reforms instituted by the last Soviet premier, Mikhail Gorbachev, that were intended to reduce the centralized power of the Soviet bureaucracy, reconsidering all soviet institutions, economic and political, and reforming those that do not work. Under this idea, Mikhail Gorbachev dismantled much of the Marxist-Leninist political structure in the Soviet Union. See GLASNOST.

Primary

(sometimes called the direct primary). An election in which ordinary members of a political party decide who will be the party's candidate in the upcoming general election. This is largely practiced in the U.S. Sometimes only people who have pre-registered for a political party may vote in that primary, and such a contest is known as a closed primary. The system which allows any registered voter to vote in any party's primary is known as an open primary. See GRASSROOT POLITICS.

Prime Minister

The chief executive in a parliamentary system. The prime minister is uniquely powerful because of his or her prerogative to call for an election to gain public visibility, to advise the dissolution of the parliament, to lead a political party, and to form a government. See, PARLIAMENTARY SYSTEM, PRESIDENT.

Private Law

It is that portion of law which determines the relation among individuals and creates the rights of one individual against other individuals and duty of one individual to other citizens of the state.

Privatisation

An umbrella term for many different policies loosely linked by the way in which they are taken to mean a strengthening of the market at the expense of the state. It is most commonly used to refer to the selling of nationalized or publicly owned industries and enterprises to the private sector and individuals. However, more limited forms of privatisation have also been pursued, such as "hiving off" or "contracting out" segments of the public sector to private enterprise, or inviting the private to participate in joint ventures with public services. Privatisation is a truly global phenomenon, pursued by governments of virtually all political complexions.

Programming-planning-budgeting system or PPBS

Output budgeting wide ranging management technique introduced in the mid 1960s by Charles J. Hitch and is based on the industrial management techniques of program budgeting. In U.K., it is often called output budgeting. PPBS is in effect on integrating a number of techniques in a planning and budgeting process for identifying, costing and assigning a complexity of resources for establishing priorities and strategies in a major program and for forecasting costs, expenditure and achievements within the immediate financial year or over a longer period.

Proletariat

In Marxist theory, the proletariat are those belonging to the industrial working class who do not own the means of production (land, factories, banks, natural resources) and who are solely dependent for their livelihoods on the ability to sell their labour to the bourgeoisie. They are property-less, rootless, poor, and mobile, and have nothing but to sell their labour to the bourgeoisie.

Proliferation

An excessive, rapid spread of nuclear weapons. One of the most important concerns about nuclear weapons, particularly after the end of the cold war, is the possibility of proliferation or the spread of nuclear weapons beyond the major powers that have held them for the past 30 to 50 years. Fear of proliferation is that it could lead to a nuclear war, nuclear accidents, or even nuclear terrorism. However, there has been some debate about whether non-proliferation is necessary or even a good idea. Some argue that "managed proliferation" which would spread nuclear weapons gradually to major European powers like Germany, might be Europe's best guarantee of future stability. Others suggest that the proliferation of nuclear weapons throughout the world could well become a stabilizing force in a multilateral world.

Propaganda

The term originally referred to the propagation of the faith in Catholicism, but refers today to the way in which governments subordinate knowledge and information to state policy. In general, it means the use of mass communications to influence public opinion in a country. Most major powers use propaganda. The United states, for example, maintains the U.S. Information Agency to present the U.S. point of view in the most favourable light. The CNN and other media controlled by the U.S. are active in influencing public opinion in target nations so that its people will insist that their officials will act as the U.S. wishes.

Proportional Representation (PR)

A democratic parliamentary election system with multimember districts; in a few cases the whole country is the only voting district. Seats in parliament are allocated to parties according to their proportion of the popular vote within each district. The systems of PR differ in detail, but they are designed to enable each party obtain approximately the same percentage of seats in parliament as its percentage of the countrywide popular vote. The system is designed to, and generally does, produce a more equal relationship between votes and seats than the various majority systems.

Psephology

The study of elections and of electoral results by means of statistical analysis. It is derived from the Greek "psephos," the pebble thrown into one another to cast a vote in Athens. Psephology broadly takes two forms, defined by the character of the evidence studied. Geographical psephology analyses elections results at constituency and regional levels and examines their correlation with census and other official data. Survey-based psephology analyses the electoral behaviour and attitudes of representative samples of individual citizens. See PARTY SYSTEM.

Public Administration

A sub-discipline of political science concerned with the bureaucratic process: how governments conduct themselves, the norms and values of government officials, the organization and accountability of bureaucrats, their relationships with politicians and the public, and the system they use to make and implement decisions. Public administration, in short, is concerned with describing and analysing administrative rules, practices, performances and personalities. See PUBLIC POLICY.

Public Law

As distinguished from private law, public law is that portion of law which determines a state's character and its relations to its citizens. See PRIVATE LAW.

Public Choice

Theories which argue that people make choices according to economic scarcity based on marginal utility. Public choice theories are concerned with what choices political actors—voters, politicians, bureaucrats and pressure groups—make and how they interact with each other in making their choices. The initial premise is that, like economic actors, people in politics act rationally and selfishly in pursuit of maximum satisfaction.

Public corporation

A corporation chartered for a public purpose. It is created by a statute passed by the legislature which specifically empowers the corporation to undertake a specific public purpose. In Commonwealth countries, a public corporation is usually called Crown Corporation.

Public Opinion

Opinions that people hold about matters of public concern which governments find it prudent to heed. It is the sum of all private opinions of which government officials are aware and take into account in making their decisions. Public opinion has two dimensions: preference and intensity. The preference dimension measures the property of being for or against some party, candidate, or policy, and the intensity dimension measures how strongly people feel about their preferences. Democratic governments depend for their existence on public opinion through formal and regularised institutional devices like elections, interest groups, and other organizations claiming to represent opinion to influence public policy. See DEMOCRACY.

Public Policy

The authoritative allocation of values for society. Public policy includes laws passed by legislative bodies, the pattern of implementation of those laws by executive branch officials, and the interpretation of laws and the constitution by the courts.

Putsch

A German word meaning a revolt or uprising especially one that depends upon suddenness and speed. It is a sudden attempt to get rid of a government by force. See COUP D'ETAT.

Q

Qaḍā'

The Arabic word for adjudication, or judicial decision-making, literally execution, that is, of the ruling, or *ḥukm*, of the *sharī'ah.* The literal meaning of *qaḍā'* is also reflected in its juridical application where *qaḍā'* is defined as declaring the *ḥukm* of the *sharī'ah* concerning a dispute in a manner that binds the disputing parties. The prompt enforcement of valid judicial decisions is a basic postulate of *qaḍā'* in Islam. Judicial decisions should not therefore be delayed, as an unwarranted delay could be prejudicial, and may well undermine the substance of justice. See JUSTICE.

Qadhf

Literally, *qadhf* means "throwing" words of abuse at others. Thus, it would comprise all forms of abusive words including slander, libel, insult, and cursing. However, the Qur'an uses it in a more specific sense to mean either accusing another person of committing the act of adultery *(zinā)* or denying the legitimacy of his or her child. If the accuser fails to provide evidence, then he becomes liable to the punishment of *qadhf.* The Qur'an prescribes a mandatory punishment for slanderous accusation, besides a handful of other offences, collectively known as the *ḥudūd*. The accusation of adultery, if unproven, carries the prescribed punishment of eighty lashes. See *HUDŪD*.

Qāḍī (Pl. *qudāh*)

Judge, magistrate, justice. *Qāḍī* is the Islamic judge, appointed by the political leader and entrusted with the execution of justice in all matters of religious law, such as marriage, divorce, inheritance, and religious endowments (*awqāf*). Originally, the *qāḍi* was meant to handle civil and criminal cases, too, but the tendency through out the centuries has generally been to leave these to the civil authorities, who were not of the *'ulmā'*. The ideal requirements for being a *qāḍi* are stringent and include having a blameless character and life, possessing a thorough grounding in the legal sciences, and even having the ability to act as a *mujtahid*. It is the *qaḍī*'s sworn and sacred duty to be fair and balanced in his deliberations, regardless of the status and power of the parties to litigation. See *IJTIHĀD*.

Qawm

Qawm means nation or *sha'ab* (people), and it can also mean Ummah. Nation has a specific connotation. *Qawm* is bounded by a common identity, having some form of common unifying force, which is why it can also be used to describe a nation unified by race, hence the noun *qawmiyyah* (nationalism). *Qawm* is used loosely, denoting any nation, not necessarily along racial or ideological lines. Thus, it applies to all collective groupings of people. See NATION.

Qiṣāṣ

Retaliation in cases of killing and wounding, most especially in pre-Islamic era. Islam limited its application to certain events and freed it from tribal customs. Retaliation for killing is known as *Qiṣāṣ fi'l-nafs* (blood-vengeance); for wounds which are not fatal is known as *Qiṣāṣ fī-mā dūn al-nafs*. Under certain cases the payment of blood money (*diya*) can take place. A distinction between deliberate and accidental killing is made: in the latter the application of *Qiṣāṣ* is excluded. See *ḤUDŪD*.

Qitāl

Fight, struggle, combat, battle, killing or putting someone to death. *Qitāl* means fighting with a weapon in hand with the aim of defeating, and if necessary, killing the enemy. This word occurs, with its variations, 33 times in the Qur'an. *Qitāl* can be undertaken for the sake of Allah and carried out according to the instructions of the Qur'an. *Qitāl* can take place when there is an Islamic state to carry it out. *Qitāl*, however, is not an objective of Islam nor is it the normal course of Muslims. It is used only as a last resort and in the most extraordinary circumstances when all other measures have failed. See *JIHĀD*, *ṢULH*.

Qiyās

Literally, measurement, comparison, correlation. Generally, reasoning by analogy, the fourth source of Muslim law. It can indicate inductive reasoning (*istidlāl*), and even deductive (*istinbāṭ*). It is the method adopted by the Muslim jurisconsults to define a rule which has not been the object of an explicit formulation. The establishment of *qiyās* as a judicial source responds to the need to find solutions not foreseen in the texts (Qur'an and *Sunnah*) and to define rules applicable to new situations. For *qiyās* to be effective, four elements are necessary: (1) the appearance of a new case which causes a problem; (2) a basic case (aṣl) governed by a *ḥukm* defined by a text; (3) a raison d'etre of the law (*'illāh*); (4) a result which is the *ḥukm* applied to the derived case.

QUANGO

Non-governmental organizations given operational autonomy. Used with the term "quasi-government" about organizations with an arms-length relationship with government. There is concern that such organizations have been unaccountable for and open to political patronage. See NGO.

Qudrah

Faculty, power, strength, capability, omnipotence of God. *Qudrah* is a term used for a person's freewill to act by his/her own capacity. Generally, it refers to all means, ways and instruments that enables a person to perform an act that has been ordained. Sometimes the term is attributed to Allah as in *Qudrat Allah* i.e., Allah's power. See POWER.

Quorum

Minimum number of members who must be present before an organization can legally transact business. This number, or proportion, varies with the constitution or by-laws of the organization concerned; legislative bodies usually can not pass laws unless a majority of their members is present.

Qur'ān

The *Qur'ān*, the last revealed Word of God, is the prime source of every Muslim's faith and practice. It is the principal source of the *Shari'ah*. It is literally the word of Allah (SWT), purely divine, incomparable and inimitable. It was revealed in a piecemeal fashion to facilitate the understanding of the text, appreciate its relevance, implant gradually but firmly its norms and to smooth the path of its implementation. This revealed book was preserved, word for word, in its complete and original form to serve as a source of guidance for all times. The Qur'ān contains three types of instruction: the articles of faith, the ethical and legal instructions, and the regulations concerning state and society. It provides a general theoretical framework for Islam, containing universal and particular rules, principles, exhortations and commandments which are manifest, sublime and blessed. Being divine, it is sacred, eternal, unconditionally binding, and irrevocable for the faithful. The Qur'ān has 114 chapters of varying length and form called *suras*, which are divided into a number of verses (*āyāt*) ranging from 3 to 287.

Quwah

Strength, power. Used frequently in the Qur'ān as the capacity to act, to fight, to win. It applies either to communities or individuals. The term is attributed to Allah (SWT) with the sense of *Qudrah*. See POWER, *QUDRAH*.

R

Rabb

Lord and Master, Sustainer, Provider, Supporter, Nourisher and Guardian, and Sovereign and Ruler, He who controls and directs. A person's *Rabb* is one whom he looks upon as his nourisher and patron; from whom he expects favour and obligations; to whom he looks for honour, advancement and peace; whose displeasure he considers to be prejudicial to his life and happiness; whom he declares to be his lord and master; and lastly, whom he follows and obeys. Allah is *Rabb* in all the above sense of the term. The rational of the basic Qur'anic message "serve none but God" is that since God is man's *Rabb*, He alone should be the object of man's worship and service. Politically, it includes the ideas of having just claim to the possession of something and, consequently, having authority and power over it. See ALLAH.

Race

A subdivision of the human species, characterized by a more or less distinctive combination of physical traits that are transmitted in descent: the Caucasian race, the Mongoloid race, the White race. The concept of race provides distinctions that are useful in the scientific study of the human species, its dissemination and adaptation to different environments throughout the world. It can also provide useful clues for historians and cultural anthropologists into a people's development.

Racism

An ideology or a belief that human races have distinctive characteristics that determine their respective cultures involving the idea that one's own race is superior and therefore, has the right to rule others. Racism is based on the false notion of biological and mental differences between races and used by reactionary forces to justify racial and national discrimination in their own countries. Islam firmly rejects this philosophy.

Radical Feminists

Feminists who are most critical of liberal societies. Some promote socialism as a remedy for the inequalities facing men and women in liberal capitalist nations. Others insist that women must separate themselves from males if they are to discover the full potential of being women.

Radical Parties

Parties advocating extensions of suffrage and reforms of the political system. European radicals in the twentieth century have been parties of the centre left. In France and Italy, radical parties have been anti-clerical. See POLITICAL PARTY.

Radicalism

From the Latin "radix" meaning root, in the nineteenth century was used to describe a trend to drastic reform. Radicals advocate fundamental changes in the political, legal, and economic structures of the state; often, but not necessarily, by extreme means. For many years attached to ultra-left movements, the radical label today fits, and is even claimed by the extreme Right.

Raīs

The "chief, leader" of a recognizable group (political, religious, juridical, tribal, etc). See *RIYĀSAH*.

Raison D'etat

Fundamental principle of geopolitics that divorces politics from ethics in matters concerning the welfare of the state, leading to the conclusion that end justifies the means.

Rashwah

The legal term for "bribe" which is strictly forbidden by law. Prophetic traditions prohibiting bribe-taking and/or bribe-giving are categorical.

Ratification

Formal approval required by many constitutions which set up elaborate systems of checks and balances. Ratification seeks to make certain kinds of constitutional amendment difficult without a substantial measure of political unanimity. Ratification also means the issuance of a formal declaration (usually by a head of state or by an authoritative body) confirming the acceptance of a treaty or agreement.

Rational Choice

A choice commensurate with logical reasoning. In political theory it is assumed that every individual and state behave rationally in all activities. Rational Choice theory is a way of looking at deliberations between a number of potential courses of action, in which "rationality" of one form or another is used either to decide which course of action would be the best to take, or to predict which course of action will actually be taken. Usually, "rational" is defined in a formal, mathematical way.

Rationality

A concept which places the individual actor at the centre of analysis, policy-making being determined by individual choice. Rationality is one of the foundations (with regard to people's behaviour) upon which Western political and economic theories are built. A rational person is one who will always attempt to maximize satisfaction or profits, or minimize costs. The notion of rationality as one of the modernization ideals means the replacement of age-old traditional practices by modern methods of "objective" thinking and logical reasoning in all economic and political activities.

Reactionary

A pejorative term to describe someone who is opposed to social and political change. It should not be applied to moderate conservatives who advocate slow, incremental changes. Reactionaries usually advocate reverting to patterns of a bygone age.

Realignment

A redefinition of the relationship between political parties and key social groups within society which has a fundamental impact on their relative strength. The formation of new relationships is usually confirmed in what is termed a "realigning election" which is seen as the start of new patterns of political behaviour. See ELECTION.

Realpolitik or Realism

A German term referring to power politics. Realism is a theoretical perspective of international relations that focuses on the anarchic aspects of the international system. It assumes that states compete with each other over a number of finite resources in the world, from territory to market share to control over strategic waterways. Conflict is thus seen as inevitable. Realism, therefore, counsels that states pursue their interests (defined as power) while preparing to defend themselves against outside threats. It emphasizes policies based more on practical power considerations and less on moral or ethical considerations. The attainment and maintenance of state security in a hostile world through power or balance of power politics is viewed as the primary goal of leaders. To the Realists, politics is "the struggle for power" both at the national and international levels. See IDEALISM.

Recall

The removal of an elected official by calling for a special election. Such an election must usually be demanded in a petition of a specified number of qualified electors. Recall also refers to summoning back or withdrawal of diplomatic officials from a country.

Referendum

Deciding on a policy or constitutional issue by means of a popular vote at the request of a government or a legislature. In some states, it is required that important issues, such as amendments to the constitution, be submitted to voters on a referendum. Switzerland has been by far the heaviest user of national referendums. From 1866 to 1991, the Swiss held 420 referendums followed by Australia with 45, and France with 21. The United states never held a national referendum, but a number of American states have held many state wide referendums. See INITIATIVE.

Refugees

People who temporarily take refuge in another country to escape persecution, military action, imprisonment or death. The mass exodus of refugees has become quite common as a result of ethnic hatreds resulting in massacres. The United Nations considering refugees as a world problem set up a High Commission for Refugees. There are approximately 22 million refugees in the world and most of them are from poor countries taking refuge in other poor countries. The developed countries have introduced stricter rules to bar their entrance.

Regional integration

The processes by which states in particular regions of the world come to bring together aspects of their economies and politics. There is much debate about the stimulus for such developments, with some seeing the cause as residing in the more or less sovereign preferences of states themselves. Others argue that integration occurs because of the operation of powerful dynamics beyond the control of nation-states. Economists believe that economic integration spurs higher rates of growth and efficiency in using scarce resources.

Representation

It has many meanings depending on the context under which it is being used. Originally, the verb "to represent" was used to mean "to act for" i.e., as in the case of one person acting for another. Then the term acquired the meaning of a single legal person representing a group of clients. The last development in the meaning and perhaps the commonest usage is in reference to an accredited deputy or a member of a legislature. Generally speaking, there are two modes of parliamentary representation and a system based on majoritarianism.

Representative

A person who represents a community or constituency in a legislative body.

Representative Government

A system of government in which citizens elect representatives as their agents for law-making, law enforcements, and decision-making. In a representative government all members of society have a say in making political decisions, either directly or indirectly. The term is used synonymously with democracy. It is a form of democracy and theory of civics wherein voters choose representatives to act in their interests. Globally, in 2003, a majority of the world's people live in representative democracies including constitutional monarchy with strong representative branch—the first time in history that this has been true. See DEMOCRACY.

Republic

From Latin res publica, or "public affair," suggesting an ownership and control of the state by the population at large. Thus, republic is a form of government in which the head of state is neither a monarch nor a hereditary ruler but is elected by the people. The concept of democracy, however, is not implicit to that of a republic. The republican form of government may involve a limited democracy, where such rights are available only to a limited group of people, as is the case in many dictatorial or totalitarian states. The term is also broad enough to include many of advanced democracies. Generally, a republic implies the notion of elected representation and democratic control by the people. See REPRESENTATIVE GOVERNMENT.

Republicanism

A tradition of political theory that advocates an active role in the political process for the different elements within a republic. It refers to the adherence to the principles of republican government in which the supreme power of decision making rests with the body of citizens entitled to vote and is exercised by the representatives chosen directly or indirectly by the qualified electors. See POLITICAL THEORY.

Reselection

The renomination, usually by a local party organization, of an incumbent representative. It is common for incumbents to be reselected. The term de-selection has been used in case of a representative who has not been reselected.

Residual Powers

Also called reserved powers, these are powers that are potentially broad in scope and may be constitutionally or judicially allocated to the central government or the provincial or sub-national units. Residual powers are associated with a federal form of government. See FEDERALISM.

Right of Return

This phrase refers to one of the Palestinians' key demands in the peace process: the right of some 4 million Arab refugees and their descendants to return to their pre-1948 homes in Israel and the occupied territories. The demand is rejected outright by Israel, which has its own right of return, i.e., the automatic right of every Jew in the world to settle in Israel. See PALESTINE, REFUGEES.

Rogue State

A controversial concept used by the United States government to refer to a government which does not abide by US-defined international norms of civilized behavior and whose leadership is considered hostile or irrational to the extent that conventional methods are ineffective in persuading it to conform to standards set by western powers. Thus defined, rogue states are almost always ruled by authoritarian regimes that restrict basic human freedoms. They are generally hostile to the West and its allies and are often accused of sponsoring terrorism or of seeking to acquire or develop weapons of mass destruction. The threat posed by alleged rogue states to the security of other countries has been used to justify US aggression. North Korea and Iraq have been suggested as "rogue states," along with Iran, Syria, and Libya. Some scholars argue that "rogue state" merely means any state that opposes the U.S. Other opponents accept the concept, but accuse the U.S. of being a rogue state itself, whose foreign policy is sometimes accused of having the sort of brutality and capriciousness of those it considers "rogue states."

Russian Revolution

The uprising in Russia in March, 1917 in which the Czarist government collapsed and a provisional government was established. This provisional government was overthrown by a coup d'etat on November 17, 1917 establishing the Soviet government.

Revenue Sharing

The distribution of national revenue from a specific tax to different levels of government by a legal formula. It is especially common under federal government.

Revisionism

Any account or statement of opinion that revises a hitherto accepted interpretation. Originally, the term was applied to socialists who accepted the authority of Marx's writings, but they interpreted them less literally and deterministically than orthodox Marxists. They believed that Marx did not foresee the political, economic, and social changes that enabled capitalists to resist the predicted overthrow of capitalism. They also believed that a socialist, egalitarian society could be approached through democratic, rather than revolutionary, means. Eduard Bernstein (1850-1932), one of the parliamentary leaders of the German Social Democrats, was among the most prominent revisionists. See MARXISM.

Revolution

A term which suggests profound change involving dramatic events over a short period of time, rather than evolution through stages or incremental adjustments to existing social, political and cultural arrangements. Revolutions have played an important role in the evolution of democracy, and revolutions have recently played an important role in the transition from authoritarian to democratic regimes. A recent example of such a transition is the Iranian revolution of 1979 which replaced monarchy with an Islamic republic. See ISLAMIC REVOLUTION OF IRAN.

Ribāṭ

A fortified Islamic monastery. This institution is connected with the duty of the holy war, the defence of the lands of Islam and their extension by force of arms. The *ribāṭs* are primarily fortresses, places of concentration of troops at exposed points on the Islamic frontiers. Like Western Castles, they offer a refuge to the inhabitants of the surrounding country in time of danger. They serve as watch towers from which an alarm can be given to the threatened populace and to the garrisons of the frontier and interior of the country who could support the efforts of the defenders.

Riddah

Apostasy. It refers to the renunciation of one's religion i.e., apostasy from Islam. It is customarily considered a vice, a corruption of the virtue of piety in the sense that when piety fails, apostasy is the result. One who is guilty of apostasy is called a *murtad* (apostate), or one who apostatises. In Islam, along with certain other faiths, the punishment for apostasy is death. *Riddah* also refers to the situation that developed during the early period of Islam. When the Prophet Muhammad (SAW) passed from the scene, Arab tribes near and far began to reassess the close associations that they had maintained with Islamic state under the Prophet's leadership. This development came to be called *riddah*, and where it took the form of withdrawal from the Madinah-centered Islamic rule, it was met by stern military measures on caliph Abu Bakr's initiative and, even more, 'Umar's, who emerged as the real power broker.

Riyāsah

Leadership, leading position, Presidency, Supervision. In its broad sense, it is the act of administering or managing something. The headship or leadership of a recognizable group (political, religious, juridical, tribal, or other) is called *ra'is*. In contemporary Arabic usage, the President of the Republic is called *ra'īs al-Jumhuriyah*. See *RA'IS*.

Roll-call Analysis

A situation where an accurate record of all members of parliament whether present or absent is a requirement. Part of that requirement is to determine vote or abstention of each deputy. In the past, this was done by calling out each name; however, this is done now through the use of electronic recording devices. Roll call analysis is quite valuable in identifying voting blocs in parliaments where partisanship is not a reliable index of voting behaviour.

Rule of Law

A general idea proclaiming law as indispensable basis of government. It is the idea that abstract and general rules, the law, should confine people's behaviour and decide their futures, rather than the mere decision of a person or group deciding in a one-off manner. The idea is captured in the formulation, "the rule of laws and not of men." The rule of law is the essence of the democratic state. Reference to the importance of the rule of law abounds in many contexts, in both domestic and, increasingly, international politics. Given the paucity of effective and genuinely recognized international law and the weakness of mechanisms like the International Court of Justice, an appeal to the rule of law in international relations adds very little to a more general cry for decency in world politics.

Rule-Making

Reading and interpreting the abstract concepts of laws and their application to particular instances, such as filling in details of statutory provision.

Russian Revolution

Momentous political upheaval that changed the course of world history. It destroyed the autocratic Tsarist regime and culminated in the establishment of the Union of the Soviet Socialist Republics or the Soviet Union. Its roots lay in the economic and political backwardness of Russia, the chronic poverty of most of the people, and rising discontent in the Middle and lower classes. The Bolsheviks, led by Lenin staged an armed coup and seized Moscow. A Council of People's Commissars was established in the civil war (1918–1920), the anti-communist forces were defeated and the new Soviet Constitution made Lenin and the Communist party all-powerful.

S

SAARC

Acronym for South Asian Association for Regional Cooperation with ministerial council as its apex decision making body. Its members are Bangladesh, Bhutan, India, Maldives, Nepal, Pakistan, and Sri Lanka. It is patterned on the ASEAN, and its activities are limited to economic, technical and cultural cooperation.

Ṣabr

Ṣabr implies (a) patience in the sense of being thorough, dedicated and devoted, (b) constancy, perseverance, steadfastness and firmness of purpose, (c) disciplined and planned effort with confidence and belief in the mission itself and (d) a cheerful attitude of acceptance and understanding under suffering and hardship and in times of strife and violence, and thankfulness to God in happiness, success and achievement.

Safavid

The dynasty that ruled Persia from 1501 to 1722 (907–1135 H). The *Safavid* State was established by Shah Ismail I, that restored Persian sovereignty over the entire area regarded as the heartlands of Persia and declared Ithna 'Ash'ari form of Shi'i school of Islamic jurisprudence as the official religion of the state. The state reached the height of its power under Shah Abbas (996–1038/1588–1629). Under the *Safavid* rule, arts flourished, the economy prospered, and contact was established with European courts. Intrigues among princes of the ruling dynasty, persecution of ethnic and religious minorities, and the weakened military all resulted in the accelerated decline and fall of the state in 1135/1722.

Ṣaḥābah (pl. of *Ṣāḥib*)

Those who, in a state of belief, enjoyed the companionship of the Prophet(SAW). It means the act of becoming a companion, an associate, a comrade, and friend of other in a society.

Salafiyyah / Salafī

Derived from *Salaf* (early generation of Muslims), it is used to describe the early generations of the Muslims. The term was adopted by a modern group of Muslims led by al-Afghani and Muhammad Abduh at the turn of the century. Central topics in the *Salafiyah* literature, in addition to the necessity of a reform of Islam, were resistance to secularization, Western imperialism, Orientalism, Zionism and the danger of importing the ideas of Kemalism.

Salṭanah

Sultanate, sovereignty, ruling power. *Salṭanah* also refers to the type of state ruled by a *sulṭān*. The various dynasties that ruled in India from 1210 to 1526 is known as Delhi Sultanate. In contemporary times, sultanates are rare, e.g., the Sultanate of Oman in West Asia and Brunei Dar al-Islam in East Asia.

Samāḥah

Literally, generosity or kindness. Politically, it is used for liberality, permission, pardon, tolerance as well as the act of forgiveness.

Samanid

A Persian dynasty ruling Central Asia (Transoxania) and at times the Persian province of Khurasan from 819 to 1005 (204–395 H). The *Samanid* extended its rule from Bukhara as far south as India and west as Iran. Although Arab Muslim intellectual life still was centered in Baghdad, Iranian Muslim scholarship, that is Shi'ah school of jurisprudence, predominated in the *Samanid* areas at this time. By the mid-tenth century, the *Samanid* Dynasty had crumbled in the face of attacks from Turkish tribes to the north and from the Ghaznavids, a rising dynasty to the south.

Sanctions

Punitive measures taken against a state by another state, group of states, or international organizations. Sanctions can be diplomatic, economic, social and military in nature. Sanctions are part and parcel of the principle of collective security as embodied in both the League of Nations and the United Nations. Sanctions have been effective instruments of foreign policy and a major means of influencing state behaviour in the twentieth century. The historical record shows major successes against such countries as Chile, Rhodesia, and South Africa. In some cases, like Arab oil boycott in 1973 and U.S. trade sanctions against Cuba, sanctions have failed to achieve their goals. The most notable recent application of sanctions was against Iraq following its defeat in the Gulf war of 1991. Millions of Iraqi children died as a result of U.S. led sanctions against both Iraqi imports and exports.

Sanūsiyyah

Named after its founder, Muhammad b. Ali *al-Sanūsi*. The *Sanūsiyah* was a combination of Sufi organization and a free-ranging though basically orthodox *Sunnī*. The *Sanūsi* order was based on a network of *zāwiyas* in strategic places. The *Sanūsiyah* used social and military action to combat European, first the French and then Italian, colonialism.

Satellite

A state that exists in the close politico-economic orbit of a powerful foreign government which constantly exerts pressure on the satellite to pursue policies favoured by the foreign power. Constitutionally, the satellite state is independent and autonomous, but due to its very close dependence, either militarily or economically on the foreign power, it has no choice but to be dictated or else to face severe economic or military reprisals. East European countries like Poland and Czechoslovakia were satellites of the Soviet Union.

Sayṭarah

Domination, control, command. It is, therefore, used for the act of gaining power over something, to seize or take hold of something. Politically, it is used for supremacy, authority and having decisive influence on something.

Scientific Socialism

Engel's term for a study of the economic laws of history that show that a socialist, egalitarian society is not a question of moral goodness or desirability, but of historical inevitability. See MARXISM.

Secession

An act or an instance of withdrawal by part of a state from an alliance or federation and declaring itself to be an independent state. Bangladesh broke away from Pakistan and emerged as an independent state in 1970. Likewise, the Baltic republics seceded from the Soviet Union in 1991. However, the northern states of the USA fought a bitter civil war to prevent secession, so did Nigeria a century later to stop the Biafran breakaway.

Second Ballot

The ballot used to elect a candidate if the first ballot fails to get a winner. It is common in an electoral system with single member constituencies that prevents any candidate winning who does not gain the majority (50 percent + 1) of the total votes cast at a first ballot from winning. A second ballot is then held a week or two later. At the second ballot the one with most votes is elected. This type of electoral system is used for French, Austrian and Finnish presidential elections. See ELECTION.

Second Strike Capability

An essential component of the policy of mutual assured destruction (MAD). A country has a second strike capability if it can absorb an enemy's first strike and then retaliate and inflict unacceptable damage on the enemy. See MAD.

Secret Service

Agency created by a government to carry out intelligence gathering and espionage activities, both domestic and international. Almost all nations have secret services. The American CIA, the British M15 and M16 and the Russian KGB, and the Israeli Mossad are some of the examples of secret services. All secret services use foreign agents. See CIA, KGB.

Secular

Something not pertaining to or connected with religion or church. Stated differently, it refers to worldly things or things that are not regarded as religious, spiritual or sacred. The temporal in contrast to the spiritual realm.

Secular Humanism

The view that human rights, individual liberties, and shared concerns can be articulated and safeguarded without reference to, or worship of, the spiritual.

Secular State

The state whose organs and institutions are detached from the religious foundation. A commonly advocated position is that the government should be a secular institution; that is, have no state religion, have no legislation that outlaws or favours one religion over another, and have no religiously motivated regulations on the eligibility of the nation's politicians. A secular state has no power over the nation's churches and the nation's churches have no political powers over the members of the government. Many Western democratic nations place a high importance of the separation of church and state. Some nations, such as the United States of America and Canada even have specific clauses in their constitutions that forbid the government from favouring one religion over another. Other democracies, such as the United Kingdom, have the distinction between church and state, but is slightly more blurred. These nations may have a constitutionally established state religion, but are still very inclusive to citizens of other faiths.

Secularism

Policy of separating church from state. As a formal philosophical system, secularism was first proposed by Jacob Holyoake about 1846 in England. It argues that the ultimate aim of human beings should be sought with reference to the present life and social well-being and espouses a belief in the integrity and sanctity of the free individual upon inherent human rights to life, liberty and pursuit of happiness. Secularism, in origin, is non-divine. Its metaphysical basis lies in the ontological barrier separating Man and God. In contrast, Islam is all divine. Its basis is the Qur'an and the traditions of Prophet Muhammad. Its perspective is unitary: all aspects of life, as well as all degrees of cosmic manifestation, are governed by a single principle of *tawhid*, the unity and sovereignty of Allah.

Secularization

The government's promotion of secularism. The gradual transformation of people's values from the strict adherence of religious beliefs and practices to an increasingly secular, rational, and pragmatic orientation. Secularization has been a powerful political movement in Europe since the French Revolution. In England, secularization is less thorough than in France. The Queen is the head of the Church of England. In France, state education is militantly secular.

Secularization has proved to be a controversial process, particularly in Islamic states. The overthrow of the Shah of Iran in 1979, the political instability in Algeria and Egypt are all expressions of opposition by Islamists against the secularization of their societies. See SECULARISM.

Security

Freedom from care, and thus, in a political context, freedom from those anxieties which would, were they to dominate people's lives, prevent them from engaging in the relationships regulated by government to safeguard life and property. Security is the necessary basis for the achievement of any other political end and therefore the first claim on government. It is the duty of the state to preserve security by countering threats from without, such as foreign aggression, and threats from within, such as insurgency and communal strife and maintain order through making and enforcing laws.

Select Committee

A committee appointed for a specific purpose and for a limited time by a legislature. Select committees may include members from both the lower and upper houses. Their purpose is to consider specific issues outside the jurisdiction of a standing (permanent) committee. See STANDING COMMITTEE.

Self-determination

The right of nations to independence and to determine for themselves the state in which they will live and the form of government they will possess and operate free of interference by other nations or states. Self-determination is enshrined in the United Nations Charter as a principle of "equal rights and self-determination of people."

Self-government

A government or control of a country, or organization by its own people rather than by others.

Seljuq

A dynasty of rulers in Persia and Iraq from 1040–1194 (431–590 H). Originally of Turkish stock from the steppes north of the Caspian Sea, they became Muslims towards the end of the 10th century. Their influence ultimately spread over an enormous area.

Senate

The word senate is derived from the Latin word *senex* (old man), via the Latin word *senatus* (senate). Therefore, senate refers to any powerful authority characteristically composed by the eldest members of a community, as a deliberative body of faculty in an institution of higher learning is often called a senate. In political parlance, senate refers to the second chamber of a bicameral legislature, also known as the upper house. In most political systems they have a smaller membership and are elected on a different franchise from the lower house. The upper chamber in the United States is called Senate, In U.K., it is called the House of Lords, and in Malaysia it is called *Dewan Negara*. See BICAMERAL LEGISLATURE, BICAMERALISM.

Seniority System

A system in which status, priority, or precedence is based on length of service in a given job.

Separation of Powers

A system in which the power is distributed among three branches of the government and the three branches are kept separate in role and responsibility. The legislative power is in the hands of the legislature; the executive is given the responsibility of rule implementation and the judiciary is assigned the power of adjudication. It is based upon a philosophy which assumes that concentrated power is dangerous to liberty. The American form of national government is based on separate spheres of power. See PRESIDENTIAL GOVERNMENT.

Settlements

The term refers to the Israeli act of settling more than 170,000 Jews, since the six day war in 1967, in the Gaza Strip and the West Bank (which Israelis call Judea and Samaria), most in heavily fortified colonies. Many Jewish people, both religious and secular, believe the territories to be part of the ancestral Land of Israel.

Sha'ab (pl. *shu' ūb*)

People, nation, tribe. In modern political parlance, *sha'ab* is generally associated with nationalism, along with *ummah* and *waṭan*. It is capable of evoking strong popular emotions. The term appeared in the names of political parties like *hizb al-Sha'ab*. During the first half of the 20th century, reference to the *sha'ab* was also made in a different sense by thinkers advocating socialist or communist cause, signifying the common people, the deprived lower classes, rather than the whole community. Revolutionary regimes designated their legislatures as *majlis al-sha'ab* (people's assembly). Some states even incorporated the term in their official names, e.g., the People's Republic of Yemen.

Shadow Cabinet

(in the British parliament) a group of prominent members of the opposition who are expected to hold positions in the cabinet when their party assumes power.

Shāfi'iyah

The *Shāfi'iyah* school of Islamic law was named after Muhammad ibn Idris al-Shafi'i (767–819). He belonged originally to the school of Madina and was also a pupil of Malik ibn Anas (d.795), the founder of *Mālikiyah. Imām Shāfi'ī* systemized the main principles of Islamic jurisprudence. His innovation was to respect the prophetic traditions and to apply a rigorous rational criticism to them, verifying every link in the chain of knowledge transmission and establishing criteria by which to judge the transmitters. Shafi'is dominate in Lower Egypt, southern India, Indonesia, Malaysia, East Africa and several parts of Central Asia. Iran was largely *Shāfi'ī* until the sixteenth century, when the *Safavid* dynasty made Shi'ism a state religion. See *MĀ LIKIYYAH.*

Shahādah (Pl. *shahādāt*)

Testimony, witness, evidence. It is the "bearing of witness" to the unity of God and the prophethood of Muhammad (SAW) which reads *Lā ilāha illa Allāh, Muḥammadun-Rasūl Allāh* (I bear witness that there is no God but Allah and Muhammad is the Messenger of Allah). It is the first pillar of the Islamic faith. Saying the shahādah once in one's life, with belief, makes one a Muslim.

Shāhid (Pl. *Shuhadā'*)

Witness, martyr, one who is killed in battle with non-believers. A large body of traditions describes the bliss awaiting the martyr. There are two types of martyr: One, the battlefield martyrs. They are martyrs in this world and in the hereafter. They are accorded distinctive burial rites. Two, the martyrs in the hereafter. This category would include (1) violent or premature death, e.g., those murdered for their beliefs or those who die through disease or accident; (2) natural death, either while engaged in a meritorious act such as a pilgrimage or a journey in search of knowledge.

Shaikh (pl. *Shuyūkh*)

An elderly, venerable gentleman or a revered old man. It has come to be used to mean a leader or noble, especially in the Arabian Peninsula, where *Shaikh* became a traditional title of a tribal leader. It is also the title of the ruler of any one of the sheikhdoms along the Persian Gulf. For example, it was the term used to refer to the leaders of Kuwait's royal al-Sabah family until June 19, 1961, when Kuwait joined the Arab League, and the title Amir was adopted. The title is sometimes often more informally used to address learned men as a courtesy.

Shaikh al-Islām

Formerly, especially in medieval Egypt, this was the title of the Grand *Muftī*, later being bestowed more and more exclusively upon the *Muftī* of Constantinople in the Othmanli *khilāfah*. It is now the title of the chief mufti in Tunisia. It is also a title of honour bestowed upon religious scholars of great eminence like Ibn *Taymiyah*.

Sharī'ah

Literally, the way to the water hole; the code of conduct for humans in Islam. Shari'ah, the

Islamic legal system, is based on the Qur'an, the sunnah, ijma', qiyas or ijtihad. It is the totality of the Islamic system. Shari'ah should not be confused with the term "law" as is found in modern Western usage. Law in the Islamic sense is the entire scheme of moral and social guidance directed toward the divine purposes of the Creator. It covers every aspect of human behaviour and deals extensively with the intention as it does with rituals and civil and criminal matters. It is primarily normative and is designed for moral education as well as legal enforcement. See LAW.

Shawkah

Thorn, Sting, Bravery, Valour, Might. In Islamic political thought, *shawkah* is used to denote power. In some cases, it is used as a means of gauging and measuring the intensity of the divergence of opinion on religious matters.

Shī'ah

Partisans of 'Ali Ibn Abi-Ṭalib attached to the idea of the pre-eminence of 'Ali and his descendants. A much smaller group than the Sunnis, Shi'ites form the second largest branch of Islam. Most Shi'ites, such as those in Iran and Iraq, are known as the Twelvers: those who believe in the disappearance of the 12th Imam, the only rightful earthly leader, and await his return. Other forms of Shi'ism include: the Zaidis; the ghulat e.g., the Druze and Ismailis. See SUNNI.

Shūrā

Consultation, deliberation, taking counsel or advice. A political principle referring to the participation of people in governing themselves. Classical theory held that a leader should consult the notables of the community who had a duty to give advice. Modern scholars equate the institution of *shūrā* with that of parliament (*majlis al-shūrā*). The Qur'an indicates that in all affairs related to the people, shūrā is obligatory. However, *shūrā* is obligatory only in matters on which there is no clear and definite command in either the Qur'an or the *Sunnah*. If there is a definite and clear command on the matter in these two sources, it is not necessary not even permissible to consult anyone. See PARTICIPATORY DEMOCRACY.

Shurṭah

A military-administrative term translated as police. In its original usage, the term was applied to the elite units of the armed forces whose function was to maintain law and order and to uphold the authority of the newly-established state. Its establishment is variously attributed to Caliphs 'Umar, 'Uthman and Muawiyyah. The *shurṭah* remained primarily a pragmatic institution with no authority in the developing theoretical systems of the Shari'ah. The institution combined the preventive and repressive functions of a police and security force with the judicial functions of a magistracy and summary court.

Single Transferable Vote or STV

A voting system designed to accurately achieve proportional representation in multi-candidate elections. In this system, voters rank candidates. Any candidate over the quota on first preferences is elected, with the surplus transferred to the voters' second choice. When no candidate has reached the quota, the bottom candidate is eliminated and these votes are also transferred. These procedures continue until all seats are filled. Single transferable vote is used, among other places, for all elections in the Irish Republic and Malta, Australia to elect the senate. The government of Tasmania calls the single transferable vote the "Hare system" after Thomas Hare, an English solicitor who developed the system. See FIRST PAST THE POST.

Six Day War

In June 1967, Israel mounted a dazzling series of pre-emptive strikes against the Arab armies massing on its borders. In less than a week, the triumphant Israeli forces seized Jerusalem and the West Bank from Jordan, the Golan Heights from Syria, and the Gaza Strip and the Sinai Peninsula from Egypt. Sinai, the biggest conquest in land area, was returned to Egypt in the wake of the Camp David Agreement of 1978. See PALESTINE, INTIFADAH.

Siyādah

Sovereignty, legitimate control over territory, recognition by others of that control. It is the full and exclusive legal power to make and enforce laws for the nation. It denotes the supreme legal authority of each nation over its own affairs. It also refers to the independence and autonomy of states. See SOVEREIGNTY.

Siyar

The classical conception of external relations developed as a separate branch of the *sharī'ah*, applied to all matters appertaining to relations between Muslims and non-Muslims. Contemporary Muslim states, however, have joined the UN and have accepted general principles of international law as the basis of relations between states.

Siyāsah (pl. *siyāsāt*)

Administration, rule or governance, policy. It refers to administrative justice dispensed by the sovereign and his political agents. In a broader sense, it includes all actions pertaining to political activities in domestic or international arena. *Siyāsah* in its widest sense has five purposes: the protection of faith, life, intellect, lineage, and property. Thus, those in authority are empowered to uphold and protect the values and objectives of the *sharī'ah* and to order punishment for conduct that violates the sanctity of these values. A well-known jurist, Ibn Qayyim al-Jawziyyah, divided *siyasah* into two types: unjust, which the *sharī'ah* forbids, and just, which serves the cause of justice. See *ADL*, JUSTICE.

Siyāsah Shar'iyah

Literally, it means *shari'ah*-oriented policy or government in accordance with the *sharīah*. In its juridical usage, however, *siyāsah shariyah* implies decisions and policy measures taken by those in authority on matters for which no specific ruling can be found in the *sharī'ah*. In other words, *siyāsah shar'iyah* denotes the administration of public affairs in an Islamic polity with the aim of securing the interest of, and preventing harm to, the community, in harmony with the general principles of the *shari'ah*, even if this disagrees with particular ruling of the *mujtahids*.

Social Contract

Associated with Hobbes, Locke and Rousseau, it states that individuals join and stay in civil society as if they had signed a contract. In modern usage, it refers to the idea that the government is created with the consent of the governed as a means of combining individual freedom with the benefits of social cooperation.

Social Democracy

Attempts to build and sustain political majorities for reforms of economic and social institutions which counter injustice and reduce inequality. Thus, social democracy aims at combating injustice and inequality through democratic means. In its predominant modern sense, social democracy is constituted by its rejection of the revolutionary path, and consequently its commitment to a politics that largely respects the boundaries of established states. Social democracy has often been described as a movement rather than a doctrine or programme.

Social Movements

A sustained series of interactions between public authorities and persons who speak on behalf of a constituency lacking formal representation. The latter make publicly visible demands for changes in the distribution or exercise of power and back these demands with public demonstrations of support. Social movements are usually held to be characterised by mass participation in collective action and by informality of organisation. Social movements influence the development of democratic government through struggles for individual rights and the genesis of citizenship.

Social Security

Any of various programs designed to provide a population with income at times when they are unable to care for themselves. The model for modern government applying social security programs was developed in 1883 by Otto von Bismarck under the title *soziale Sicherheit*. In general sense, it means safety and freedom from fear and want applied to a society as a group of interrelated and interdependent people. In the United states, it is used primarily in the economic sense and has particular reference to the policies and programmes embodied in the Social Security act of 1935. In a broader sense, social security includes all legislation that has as its fundamental purpose financial protection for people who otherwise would be impoverished. When proof of financial need is required for the receipt of benefits, the programmes are known as public assistance, relief, or welfare. In some European countries, the term social insurance is used to such programmes but these do not involve a needs test. See SOCIAL WELFARE.

Social Welfare State

The welfare programs and policies provided by social democratic governments. Such programs are typically more extensive than those provided by liberal governments and often provide universal welfare rights to all citizens, in contrast to program targeted exclusively at the most needy. See SOCIAL SECURITY.

Socialism

An ideology that arose in reaction to the exploitative nature of capitalism. Socialists seek a society in which cooperation and fraternity replace the divisions based on class lines which characterize capitalist societies. There is, however, considerable disagreement concerning both the nature of an egalitarian society and how it would be created. Fundamentalist socialists believe that state control of all means of production is indispensable to the creation of an egalitarian society. They reject the free market and, instead, have historically endorsed the centralized planning of the economy and the nationalization of key industries to achieve this goal. Reformist (or revisionist) socialists, however, believe that an egalitarian society can be created by reforming the capitalist system. See COMMUNISM.

Southeast Asian Treaty Organization (SEATO)

Defence treaty signed by Australia, France, Britain, New Zealand, Pakistan, the Philippines, Thailand, and the U.S., after France withdrew from Indochina in 1954. The major goal of the treaty was to curb communist incursions in that part of the world. Its headquarter was in Bangkok, Thailand. There were no standing forces. The treaty was invoked by the U. S. in the Vietnam war (1946–1973). Pakistan withdrew in 1972. SEATO dissolved in 1977.

Sovereignty

The full and exclusive legal power to make and enforce laws for a particular people in a particular territory. This means that each nation has supreme legal authority over its own affairs and in that respect is fully equal to every other nation. It is known in international law as "the principle of the sovereign equality of nations." It is customary to distinguish between internal and external sovereignty. Internal sovereignty has to do with the state's authority over its subjects, while the second notion refers to the independence or autonomy of states. See SIYADAH.

Sovereign Equality

The principle in which all states are equal in law. It characterized the voting procedure at the General assembly of the United Nations and was an important element of self-government.

Speaker of the House

The presiding officer of the lower house of parliament. By residing over the debates and acting as the administrative head of the house, the speaker plays a central role in the legislative process. The Speaker is elected by the house for the duration of Parliament on the nomination of the prime minister. As the presiding officer of the house, the Speaker is expected to be non-partisan and impartial in applying the rules and procedures and in identifying members who want to debate. During each sitting of the house, the Speaker rules on time limits for debate, on parliamentary privileges when they are violated, and on motions of adjournment and closure. In case of a tie, the Speaker casts the deciding vote. See PARLIAMENT.

Spoils System

The system practiced chiefly in the United States, in which public offices with their emoluments and advantages are used to reward supporters of a victorious political party. It was President Andrew Jackson's friend Sen. William L. Marcy, who said in 1832 that "to the victor belongs the spoils," and the system soon operated on every political level. With the growth of a two-party system in the United States, political patronage increased.

Sphere of Influence

The area or territory in which a hegemon or major state has interest and sustains political, military, or economic influence. During the Vietnam war, it was common to refer to Southeast Asia as being in the US sphere of influence. Likewise, the Soviet Union considered Eastern Europe as its sphere of influence.

Stalinism

Political views advocated and practiced by Joseph Stalin who rose to undisputed leadership in the Soviet Union (1925–1953). The two major ideological innovations of Stalinism were: an emphasis on building socialism in one country—the Soviet Union—rather than promoting world revolution, and totalitarianism. Stalin sought to "Russianize" the Soviet Union, attempting to eradicate by force the separate identities of minorities. Dissent was met with a powerful secret police, informers, mass deportations, executions and show trials. Stalin lost his place of eminence in communist folklore after his death largely because of his obsession with a personality cult. See REVISIONISM.

Standing Committee

A committee created on a permanent basis that deals with a major area of legislative concern. They consider bills and conduct hearings and investigations. They constitute the heart of the committee system because they have an ongoing role in the legislative system. Standing committees commonly have many subcommittees. See LEGISLATURE.

Standing Order

A general order of indefinite duration that remains in effect until modified or rescinded. Such orders are most often issued by military commanders to their troops, or by bodies operating under parliamentary procedure. Standing orders are necessarily general and vague since the exact circumstances for execution occur in the future under unknown circumstances.

State

A legal and a political entity that is not subject to any higher political authority. It can simply be defined as a human association in which sovereign power is established within a given territorial area. In ordinary language, the terms state, country, nation and government are regarded as synonymous although they are analytically different. The legal criteria for statehood are generally: (a) a permanent population; (b) a defined territory; (c) government; and (d) capacity to enter into relations with the other states. However, some have questioned whether these criteria are sufficient. Sometimes, the term state is used to refer to the major political-administrative subdivision of a federal system and as such is not sovereign but depends on the central authority for resource allocation, defense and foreign affairs. See FEDERALISM.

State Building

The creation of political institutions capable of exercising authority and allocating resources effectively within a nation.

State of Nature

An imaginary society in which people lived before civil society was formed. For Thomas Hobbes, a condition in which no effective government exists to enforce law and order. Competition for power and its benefits is unrestricted, producing a state of virtual war in which everyone's life is "solitary, poor, nasty, brutish and short." For Locke, people in the state of nature lived in equality and tolerance with one another. But their property was uncertain and hence they contractually formed civil society and thus secured "life, liberty and property." For Jean Jacques Rousseau, life in the state of nature was good; people lived as noble savages. However, life can be improved through a just society that would be a voluntary community with the general will. In such communities, humans gain freedom and dignity.

State Planning

A term for control and guidance (to varying degrees) of the economy by governments. Comprehensive "Soviet-style" planning involves the government's providing some incentives and disincentives for private actors to act in ways supported by governmental leaders. An intermediate level of planning, is practiced by social democratic governments, including extensive state influence over private investment decisions.

State Terrorism

Acts of terrorism carried out directly by, or encouraged and funded by, an established government. The massacre of the Palestinians carried out by Israel in 2002 is a clear case of state terrorism which earned Israel the label of a "terrorist state." See TERRORISM.

Statute

A law formally enacted by a legislature following proper legislative procedure. Some statutes merely amend or repeal previous laws, others may codify earlier legislation on a subject. A distinction is often made between statutes and laws. The latter includes common law, and administrative decrees and regulations. The legislature monopolizes the making of statutes while laws are made by other branches of government. See LAW.

Statutory Law

All the rules enacted by the legislature that command or prohibit some form of behaviour. In most countries, statutes are collected and published in "codes" or books of "statutes in force."

Strategic Arms Limitation Talks (SALT)

SALT represents the first round of Strategic Arms Limitations Talks between the United States and the former Soviet Union over a two-and-a-half year period from 1970 to 1972. The SALT I Anti-Ballistic Missile (ABM) Treaty prohibited the United States and the former Soviet Union from constructing ABM defence systems at more than two sites. Both parties further agreed to freeze the number of offensive ballistic missile launches at their existing levels until 1977. The SALT II ABM Protocol, signed in Moscow in 1979, further limited the superpowers to one defensive site and committed both parties to limit the number of warheads they carry. SALT II was never ratified, due to the Soviet invasion of Afghanistan, by the U.S. Senate, even though both Jimmy Carter and Ronald Reagan were committed to arms limitations.

Strategic Arms Reduction Talks (START)

The acronym START was coined by the Reagan administration in 1980 to begin a new round of nuclear arms negotiations as distinguished from SALT I and SALT II. The START brought the Americans and Soviets to the bargaining table in Geneva in 1982. These talks involved not only weapons deployed by the superpowers, but also the intermediate nuclear forces (INF) in Europe. After six years of intensive negotiations, the U.S. and the Soviet Union signed the Intermediate-Range Nuclear Forces treaty in 1987, eliminating an entire class of nuclear weapons from Europe and from the rest of the world. In 1991, START was finally signed in Moscow by Presidents Bush and Gorbachev. In the treaty the two superpowers agreed to reduce their strategic nuclear delivery systems by 40 percent and their total number of war heads by 30 percent. START II (1993) mandated even further reduction of strategic nuclear weapons. Even though the treaties generated a reduction in the numbers of strategic nuclear arsenals, both states retained a massive nuclear capability. Most of the weapons possessed by the former soviet Union are now located in Belarus, Kazakhstan, Russia, and Ukraine.

Strategic Defence Initiative (SDI)

Controversial programme developed by the U.S. government in 1983 to develop a space-based shield against nuclear missile attack. Commonly called "star wars," the programme was to rely on satellites and lasers to destroy incoming missiles before reaching their targets. Its opponents argued that it was impractical and costly.

Strategy

From a Greek root that literally means "generalship." It is a plan to deal with every possible move by the other actors. In a war context, it refers to the overall plan to defeat a foe, where a distinction is made between the "strategic" and the "tactical." Strategy is the utilization during both peace and war, of all a nation's forces, through large scale, long-term planning and development, to ensure security or victory. Tactics deal with the use and deployment of troops in actual combat. The term has also economic connotations: strategic resources are those which have national security value to a nation e.g., oil. Strategic trade policies are efforts on the part of the state to create comparative advantage in trade by such methods as providing subsidies to help an industry achieve great production efficiency than foreign competitors.

Strike

A concerted cessation of work or withdrawal of workers' services by a group of employees to achieve certain goals. The goals may include demands for higher wages, better working conditions, shorter work hours, and more benefits. Trade unions may play a role in strikes. Workers may strike to force the employer to recognize a certain union as their bargaining representative. Strikes are intended to create a financial loss for the company in goods produced or services rendered, thus prompting earnest negotiations. See VIOLENCE.

Subversion

Covert action designed to overthrow an established government. Subversion can take many forms, including secret financial and military help to rebel forces in the target nation and efforts to damage the reputation and popularity of the target government's leaders. It is well established that major powers, especially the United States, use espionage, sabotage, infiltration of the nations' governments, and even assassination to promote their foreign policy objectives.

Successive Voting

A voting procedure prevalent in some Western parliaments e.g., Norway. Proposals are rank ordered using some criterion. Each proposal is compared with the status quo in succession beginning with one of the extremes until one of the proposals wins a plurality of votes against the status quo. The term is also used to refer to the situation of the proportional representation system where the candidate with the highest votes qualifies for the best position, the second most popular for the second best position, and so on. See VOTING, ELECTORAL SYSTEM.

Ṣulḥ

Peace, reconstruction, settlement. Peace is a fundamental and dominant theme in Islam. Peace and Islam are derived from the same root and may be considered synonymous. One of God's names is Peace. The concluding words of the daily prayers of every Muslim are words of peace. The daily salutations among the Muslims are expressions of peace. The overriding concern of an Islamic state in its relations with other states or nations is to maintain peace, with exchange of goodwill missions and mutually honest endeavours for the sake of humanity in which all people share equally. War becomes a necessity only when someone violates the rights of the Islamic state, or disturbs its peace, or endangers its security or exploits its peaceful policies. See *JIHĀD.*

Sulṭah

Power, might strength and authority. Sometimes it is used in the sense of dominance, dominion, influence and even sovereign power.

Sulṭān (pl: *salāṭīn*)

Power, might, strength, rule, authority. By the 4th/10th century, sulṭān came to mean "holder of power, authority." It could then be used for provincial or even quite petty rulers who had assumed de facto power alongside the caliph. In the 5th/11th century, the term was used by the Great Saljuks in the sense of dominant power. In Ottoman Turkey, *sulṭān* was an elevated title. In Persian it was used as a title for officers and governors. Muslim rulers in the South-East Asian archipelago usually maintained the title of *raja* or *maharaja*, who later assumed the title of *sulṭān*.

Sunnah

Consists of all authentic reports of the acts, utterances and silent approval of the Prophet (SAW). Initially, there existed a distinction between the term Sunnah, referring to the practices of the Prophet (SAW), and the *ḥadīth* denoting his utterances as narrated by his companions. Gradually, however, the entire *sunnah* was reflected in the *ḥadīth* to such an extent that, by the fifth century AH, the two terms became completely synonymous. Mostly recorded in the six *siḥah* (authentic collections), the *sunnah* forms the second fundamental source of the *sharī'ah*. The *sunnah* is better seen not as "another" source but as an explanation and detailed elaboration, through words and deeds, of the general principles enshrined in the Qur'an. See *ḤADĪTH*.

Sunnī

Literally, "a follower of *sunnah*," a follower of mainstream Islam. Sunni is the popular name of the Muslim majority, which is technically known as *Ahl al-Sunnah wa al-Jamā'ah* meaning "the people of the established custom and the community" (in the sense of a single, normative political entity). See *SHI'AH*.

Supranationalism

Decision-making in international organizations, where power is held by independent appointed officials or by representatives elected by the legislatures or people of the member states. Member-state governments still have power, but they must share this power with other actors. Furthermore, decisions are made by majority votes and the decisions are binding upon all member-states even if it is against their will. Except for European Union, few international organisations today operate on the basis of supranationalism. See INTERGOVERNMENTALISM.

Supreme Court

The highest court of the nation, the *court of last resort*, with the authority to adjudicate all cases arising under the law. The rulings of the Supreme Court cannot be appealed. In most countries and subordinate states with constitutions, the Supreme Court interprets the constitution for its area of jurisdiction.

Surplus value

In Marxist theory, surplus value is the difference between the actual values of what laborer produces and what the capitalist makes from the production process.

Syndicalism

From French "sindicat" meaning "labour union." It refers to a revolutionary labour movement aimed at the possession of means of production and distribution, and ultimately at the control of the society, through strikes, sabotage, and violence. The movement originated in late 19th century France from the theories of Pierre Joseph Proudhon and Georges Sorel. Syndicalists agreed with Marxist class analysis but like anarchists rejected any state organization. Syndicalism was strong in France and Italy in the early 1900s and found U.S. expression in the Industrial unionism of the Industrial Workers of the World. World War I and the advance of communism overtook the syndicalists; their influence lasted longest in Spain, where it was destroyed in the civil war (1936–39).

Synthesis

An integration of two or more pre-existing elements which results in a new creation. In dialectics, synthesis is the final result of attempts to reconcile the inherent contradiction between thesis and antithesis. Along with the similar concept of integration, synthesis is generally considered to be an important element of modern philosophy. See THESIS, ANTI-THESIS, SYNTHESIS.

T

Ta'āwun

Cooperation, Mutual help, Working together for a shared purpose. The purpose, according to the Qur'an, must be good, for promoting social justice. *Ta'āwun* includes: mutual responsibility, mutual protection and mutual cooperation. There can be no *ta'āwun* in matters of sin and injustices of any kind.

Tanzīmāt

A plural noun meaning "ordering, setting in order, regulating." In modern Turkish and other Western languages, it is used to refer to reforms. In Othmanli history, Tanzimāt is employed to designate the sum of reforms from November 1839 until some time between 1871 and 1881. Almost all the reforms involved a greater or lesser degree of Westernization. See OTHMANLI *KHILĀFAH*.

Ta'zīr

Discretionary punishment, e.g., by the judge (*qādī*), for the offences for which no *ḥadd* punishments is laid down.

Tactical Nuclear Weapons

These are small, low-yield nuclear devices designed to be used on the battlefield itself. Warheads that could be fired several miles and explode without endangering one's own troops. Such nuclear battlefield weapons have never been used in actual combat. This variety includes atomic but not hydrogen bombs.

Tafwīḍ

Entrustment, authorization, empowerment, delegation of authority. *Tafwīḍ* is handing a task over to a subordinate. Applied to the state, it refers to the delegation of administrative powers to a person in whom the *imām* or the caliph has the fullest confidence. A person to whom power is delegated is called *wazīr al-tafwīḍ* or the Minister of delegation. However, the imam still retains the power of disallowing any act or policy formulated by the Minister of delegation.

Ṭāghūt

The one who exceeds his legitimate limits. In Qur'anic terminology it refers to the creature that exceeds the limits of his creatureliness and arrogates to himself godhead and lordship. In the negative scale of values, the first stage of man's error is *fisq* (i.e., disobeying God without necessarily denying that one should obey Him.) The second stage is that of *kufr*, (i.e., rejection of the very idea that one ought to obey God.) The last stage is that man not only rebels against God but also imposes his rebellious will on others. All those who reach this stage are *ṭāghūt*. Figuratively, it refers to all those individuals and governments that have been corrupted by power. Ayatullah Khomeini often referred to the Shah of Iran as *ṭaghūt*. See ISLAMIC REVOLUTION IN IRAN.

Taḥkīm (pl. *taḫkimāt*)

Arbitration. Appointment of an arbitrator, arbitral decision. *Taḥkīm* denotes a mutually agreed appeal to arbitration by parties in conflict. Historically, the term *taḥkīm* refers to the arbitration which took place between the fourth caliph 'Ali and his governor over Syria Muawiyyah. Some of 'Ali's supporters protested the arbitration and thus emerged the first schismatic movement in Islam known as *Khawārij* (kharijites).

Ṭā'ifah (pl. *Ṭawāif*)

A group, party, troop, company of men as used in the Qur'an. In later usage, the term often refers to a professional or trade group or corporation. It may also be used to mean a political organization whose members have the same aims and beliefs. Sufis use the term to refer basically to "group" or part of a whole.

Tajdīd (pl. *tajdīdāt*)

Renewal, renovation, restoration, rejuvenation. *Tajdīd* is an effort, a movement, to re-establish Islam in its pristine purity and to reconstruct the fabric of life and society in a given space-time context in accordance with Islamic values and principles. It represents a continuation of the mission of the prophets to implement Islam. Its spirit is one of creativity. It is non-sectarian and avoids extremes of conservatism and modernism. It has a comprehensive scheme of reform and reconstruction for the transformation of society along Islamic lines. See ISLAMIC REVIVAL.

Takāful

Mutual or joint responsibility, solidarity, mutual agreement. From the root *Kafala* meaning to feed, to support and to provide family with basic requirement of life. *Takāful* allows people to act together and to contribute voluntarily with the intention of helping one another. See *TA'ĀWUN*.

Talibān

Seeker, Seeker of religious truth. In general, it refers to students or graduates of a *madrasah* (an institution teaching broad spectrum of Islamic disciplines which are taught by the *'Ulamā'*). Specifically, the Revolutionary Islamic Afghan regime that ruled Afghanistan from 1996 till its downfall in December 2001, caused by the US-led bombing campaign. *Talibāns* aimed at uniting Afghans under a strict version of *shari'ah*. They brought a measure of stability to Afghanistan that the people needed and wanted even though they adopted the most stringent and punishing interpretation and enforcement of Islamic law.

Taqiyyah

The action of covering and dissimulation as opposed to revelating, spreading information. It means to conceal one's true religious beliefs for fear of persecution or simply in order to keep the peace and not cause division in a community. *Taqiyyah* is of special significance for the *Shi'ah* and is considered their distinguishing feature. Among the shi'is, Ismailis are masters in the act of disguising their creed. See *SHI'AH*.

Taqwā

Piety, Godliness, devotedness. It refers to the awe of Allah (s.w.t), which inspires a person to be on guard against wrong action and eager for actions which pleases Allah (s.w.t). As used in the Qur'an, piety requires a proper use of the mind by grasping the truth of God and life, a proper use of wealth by spending in the way of God under all circumstances and a proper use of the spiritual as well as the physical abilities of man by observing the fundamentals of Islam. It also demands a high degree of self-control over one's anger and emotions, a moral capacity for forgiveness and patience, and a conscious urge to make the sinner return to God in regret and repentance. To be pious is to be a man of true and fine convictions, of determination and character, of will and courage and, above all, to be man of God. See *ISLAM*.

Tasalluṭ

Domination, mastery, sway, influence and supremacy or control over something or somebody. Generally, it means to have power and mastery over something or somebody.

Taṭarruf

Excessive, Extremism, Radical attitude, immoderation. The term is used since the 1970s in the Islamic and Orientalist literature for the phenomenon of militant religious-political groups. Unless its contents are analysed carefully, the term can easily be politicized and used indiscriminately. The extremist doctrine is generally characterized by certain structural patterns: claims to know the absolute truth, dogmatism, utopianism, conspiracy theories, fanaticism and activism. See GHULUW.

Tawḥīd

Indivisible, inalienable divinity of Allah (SWT). The principle of *tawḥīd* denies anyone, be it a human agency as with a Hobbesian monarch, or a legal fiction in the form of a state, as in John Austin, the right to order others in his own right to do or not to do certain things. For, as the Qur'an declares, "The command rests with none but Allah ...Who is the Lord of the universe." *Tawḥīd* may be divided into two categories: *tawḥīd* of cognition and affirmation and *tawḥīd* of purpose and deeds. The former refers to affirmation of the Oneness of the Creator and of His attributes (i.e., He is Unique in His being the only Creator and the only One with His names and attributes). *Tawḥīd* of purpose and deeds is *tawḥīd* of lordship or that none should be worshipped except Allah (i.e., He is the only One worthy of worship). Islam is, above everything, assertion of the certitude of Tawḥīd: the oneness of God. Tawḥīd is thus the metaphysical and theological principle par excellence which gives the religion of Islam its unique profile and its distinctive morphology. As an ethical rule, *Tawḥīd* dictates the acceptance of God as the only source of all values: not to do so would lead one to shirk, the negation of *Tawḥīd*—a cardinal sin in Islam. Thus, *Tawḥīd* inculcates a psychological and behavioral attitude that demands a relationship with the Only One. The Muslim is motivated by this quest, in whatever he does, thinks or feels. The identity of personal piety and ritual devotion, of theology and law, of politics and religion, of faith and deeds in Islam are all manifestations of the same all-pervasive principle of *Tawḥīd*. See ISLAM, SHIRK.

Territorial Waters

In international law, the belt of sea adjacent to a country and under its territorial jurisdiction. Important for control of shipping, seabeds and fisheries, such limits used to extend 3 miles (4.8 km). More recently 12 miles from low-water mark. The *Third United Nations Conference on the Law of the Sea*, on November 14, 1994, set the limit of territorial waters to 12 miles (19.3 km), in which area the controlling state is free to set laws, regulate any use and use any resources. Beyond the 12 mile limit there was a further 24 mile (38.6 km) limit, the "contiguous zone," in which area a state could continue to enforce laws regarding activities such as smuggling or illegal immigration. A 200 mile (322 km) limit has been accepted by some countries.

Terrorism

The systematic use of violence or the threat of violence against civilians to achieve political objectives. The term is taken from the "reign of terror" in the French Revolution in 1793–1794. Terrorism is used by nations and political groups that cannot accomplish their objectives by diplomacy and that are too weak to use conventional military force. Terrorism's object is to terrorize the people and the officials of the target government so that they will alter their policies as the terrorists wish. Some of the active terrorist groups include the provisional wing of the Irish Republican Army, the Japanese Red Army, the Palestinian Black September and recently the al-Qaedah network. September 11, 2001 attack on the Twin tower in New York is a recent example of terrorism meant to force the United States to end its unjust support of Israel and to lift sanctions against Iraq. Terrorism has been used as an instrument of foreign policy by many governments including the United States. See STATE TERRORISM.

Thaqāfah

Culture, refinement, civilization and even the level of education acquired by someone. Thus, the term refers to the advance stage of human development with a high level of art, religion, science, and government. A well versed and civilized person is called *Muthaqaf.*

Thaurah

Uprising, revolt, or revolution. Revolt against authority, in earlier times, was regarded with ambivalence and was outrightly condemned by those in authority as a potential source of schism and disorder (*fitnah*). The *fuqhā,'* however, commended it as a means of getting rid of a sinful ruler. The Abbasids used this principle to justify their forceful sezure of power from the Umayyads. Since the 20th century, the term has come to imply a praiseworthy venture, a legitimate struggle against alien domination. In the post-independent environment, the term *thawrah* was given an expanded meaning to denote a total transformation of the society eliminating corruption, remedying socio-economic ills and restoring national glory. See REVOLUTION.

Theocracy

A system of government in which power and authority are seen as derived directly from God, and rulers are considered either incarnations or representatives of divine power. In ancient times theocracy was widespread. During the middle ages in Europe the Pope claimed ultimate authority in governing based on his religious authority, and later kings used the "divine right of kings" to justify their absolutist rule. Early puritan colonies in New England like Massachusetts Bay and New Haven had leaders who claimed to derive their authority from God. Some people erroneously use theocracy to mean an Islamic state. See ISLAMIC STATE.

Thesis, Antithesis, Synthesis

Marx borrowed these terms from Hegel's theory of the historical dialectic to describe the three basic elements of dialectical materialism. The "thesis" embodies the existing dominant material and social conditions of a society (e.g. capitalism and the bourgeoisie class). The "antithesis" includes those material forces and social classes that stand in opposition to the thesis (e.g., the proletariat). The conflict between these two eventually results in a revolution leading to some new social form, a "synthesis," which is a kind of temporary resolution of the conflict. This resulting synthesis, in turn, becomes a new "thesis," opposed and complemented by a new, contradicting "antithesis."

Think Tank

A policy research institute, especially one employed by government, whose job is to assist in the strategic planning of government policies, establish priorities, recommend new policy options, and make sure that all options are considered and that the one that yields the optimal result has been recommended. The term has also been applied to organizations with partisan interests that provide policy recommendations to its patron.

Third World

A term used to refer to many of the economically and politically less-developed or underdeveloped countries of Africa, Asia and Latin America because its industrial development followed the First World (the United States and its industrialized European allies, Japan, Australia and New Zealand) and the Second World (East Europe) countries. Some theorists have identified the poorest of the less-developed countries (e.g., some sub-Saharan states of Africa) as constituting a Fourth World. The term is looked upon by many as a pejorative term but is still in use. See FIRST WORLD.

Timurid

A dynasty of rulers in Central Asia (Transoxania and Persia) whose court was at Samarqand. Timur (Tamerlane to Europeans) was the founder of the dynasty in 1370. A product of both Turkish and Mongol descent, Timur claimed Genghis Khan as an ancestor. From his capital of Samarqand, Timur created an empire that, by the late fourteenth century, extended from India to Turkey. The turn of the sixteenth century brought an end to Timurid Empire when another Mongol-Turkish ruler overwhelmed the weak Timurid ruler in Herat in 1500.

Totalitarianism

The term was first popularized by Italian dictator Benito Mussolini, who used it to describe the all-encompassing state that his fascist movement aspired to create. Totalitarianism claims that governmental leaders should be given "total control" over all aspects of society, including the economy, religion, the art, and even family life, in order to achieve great transformations in social and human life. This attempt at "total control" may be mainly bluff, as was Mussolini's, or it may be extremely ruthless and thorough, as was the case with Hitler of Germany and Stalin of the Soviet Union. In a totalitarian state nothing is permitted that is not explicitly authorized. Totalitarian government is characterized by: an elaborate ideology, a single mass party, a secret police using terror to prevent challenges to authority, control of mass communication and the armed forces, and central direction of the economy. See AUTHORITARIANISM.

Tory

A member of a political party in Great Britain from the late seventeenth century to about 1832 that favoured the authority of the king over Parliament and the preservation of the existing social and political order. It was succeeded by the Conservative Party.

Trade Union

A continuous association of wage earners for the purpose of maintaining or improving the conditions of their working lives. In liberal democracies, trade unions frequently act as interest groups articulating and promoting their constituents' demands vis-à-vis government institutions (parliament, executives, bureaucracy, courts), influencing public opinion and forming alliances with sympathetic political parties.

Trade Unionism

The belief, held by Lenin and other communists, that the development of organizations (trade unions) by workers to engage in collective bargaining with capitalists undermines the proletariat's revolutionary consciousness, because unions are preoccupied with improving working conditions and remuneration within the capitalist system, rather than encouraging workers to overthrow the system entirely.

Traditional Conservatism

A political outlook that dominated Europe before the French Revolution and that strongly opposed the liberal and radical aspects of that upheaval. The central ideas of this outlook-the greater emphasis on society rather than on the individuals constituting it, the natural inequalities among people, the need to allow the most talented leaders to govern, and importance of following traditional wisdom rather than "abstract reason" – were best expressed by Edmund Burke.

Traditionalism

Traditionalism suggests the inclination on the part of some groups to revive or safeguard traditions (anything which is typical of the past, customary, or part of a cultural identity like, religious beliefs, linguistic practices or dietary habits) against non-traditional beliefs and values. Nationalism and religious revivalism are both strong expressions of traditionalism. Marxism and liberalism are progressive ideologies which abhor traditionalism. See CONSERVATISM.

Transparency

Disclosure, policy clarity, consistency or a culture of candour. In its commonest usage, transparency denotes government according to fixed and published rules, on the basis of information and procedures that are accessible to the public, and within clearly demarcated fields of activity.

Tribunals

Tribunals sit in judgement over a number of specialist areas, and frequently have appeals tribunals above them. For example, the Employment Tribunals (appeals to Employment Appeals Tribunal), VAT Tribunals, Land Tribunals etc. The tribunals will either give a right of appeal to the specific appeals tribunal (e.g., Employment Tribunal cases are appealed to the Employment Appeals Tribunal) which in turn allows appeals to the Court of Appeal or, in the absence of a specific appeals court, will have a right of appeal to the Queen's Bench Division of the High Court which has general authority over all lesser courts.

Trotskyism

A form of communism advocated by Leon Trotsky (1879–1940), a Russian revolutionary and one of the founders of the Soviet Union. He was Commissar of foreign affairs (1917–1918) and Commissar of War (1918–1925). Following Lenin's death in 1924, he lost power to Stalin and was deported in 1929. Trotskyism was vehemently opposed to Stalin's "Socialism in one country" thesis and advocated immediate, world-wide revolution by the proletariat. Trotsky founded, in 1936, a loose federation of small groups of radical socialists known as the Fourth International.

Trusteeship

A system of administration devised by the United Nations to supervise formerly dependent territories under the Trusteeship Council. A trustee nation was responsible for developing the trust territory and assisting it to independence. The Trusteeship Council helped the General Assembly and the Security Council supervise trust territories. See UNITED NATIONS, MANDATE.

Ṭugyān

Flood, Deluge, Tyranny, Oppression, Terrorization. In particular, it refers to the sin of arrogance and tyranny. A *ṭāgīn* (tyrant, oppressor, despot) not merely oppresses others but is overly confident such that he or she makes others feel small, uncomfortable or stupid.

Turnout

Percentage of legally-eligible voters actually voting in national elections. The voting turnout is calculated differently in different countries. In the United States, voting turnout is customarily calculated by dividing the number of persons voting by the number of persons of voting age. Most countries, however, figure the turnout rate as the number of persons voting divided by the number of persons actually registered to vote. The two methods would give two different turnout rates. See VOTING.

Two-party System

A system in which two major political parties are the principal contenders for power, and they alternate in office at periodic intervals. The Democratic and the Republican party in the United States, and the Labour party and the Conservative party in Great Britain are the two major parties almost alternatively ruling those countries. However, third parties do exist and play important roles in the political system. In some cases, minor party support of the larger major party has been a prerequisite for forming a government in many instances. See POLITICAL PARTY, PARTY SYSTEM.

Tyranny

In classical times, denoted a regime ruled by one man in which laws are made for the benefit of the ruler rather than for the common good. In broader sense, it usually implies harshly coercive autocratic rule in which concentrated governmental power is relentlessly exploited for personal gain by its rulers. The person who rules in such a manner is known as a tyrant. See DICTATORSHIP.

U

Ūlī al amr

Ruler, powerful leader. *Ūlī al-amr* is a term of wide connotation. It includes all those leaders of the Muslim society who control and administer its affairs in religious, cultural, political, economic, military and other spheres of life. The Qur'an enjoins Muslims to obey and follow those in authority as long as their policies and actions conform to the letter and the spirit of the *shari'ah*. See ISLAMIC STATE.

Umayyad/Umayyads

The dynasty of Caliphs ruling from 661 (41H) to 750 (132H). The founder of the dynasty (Mu'awiyah) moved the administrative capital from Madinah in Arabia to Damascus in Syria. Under the Umayyads, the contours of the Islamic world extended from the Atlantic in the west to India and central Asia in the east. Trade expanded greatly during this time, with many new products introduced into the area, such as paper from China. Following the defeat of the Umayyads and the establishment of the 'Abbasid caliphate in 132/750, one Umayyad family member, 'Abd al-Rahman, escaped to North Africa and subsequently founded in Spain a dynasty of Umayyad rulers who governed there from 756 (138H) to 1031 (422 H). See ABBASIDS.

Ummah

Community, group, group of people; Muslim community as identified by the integration of its ideology, religion, law, mission and purpose of life and group consciousness, ethics and mores. The *ummah* lies at the core of the Islamic political ideology. Ummah embraces all the believers without regard to their differences in origin, region, colour, language and blood ties. It also transcends all political boundaries and sets the community of believers in direct opposition to the modern concept of state as a geopolitical unit. The community in Islam is founded on the principle which designates submission to the will of Allah (SWT), obedience to His law and commitment to His cause. The historic role of the *ummah* is to be the true embodiment of the virtuous, the wholesome, and the noble. A truly Islamic community is the alert guardian of virtue and the bitter enemy of vice. See ISLAM, STATE, COMMUNITY.

Unicameralism

The practice of having only one legislative or parliamentary chamber. Many countries with unicameral legislatures are unitary states, which consider an upper house or second chamber to be unnecessary, in many instances having abolished the second chamber where one existed. This is either because an elected upper house has duplicated the lower house and obstructed the passing of legislation or because an appointed chamber has proven ineffectual. Unicameralists argue that the functions of a second chamber, such as reviewing or revising legislation, can be performed by parliamentary committees, while further constitutional safeguards can be provided by a written Constitution. See BICAMERALISM, PARLIAMENTARY SYSTEM.

Underground

Term generally used for any secret political movement that seeks to overthrow a country's existing government or military authority. Though underground movements have operated in many nations throughout history, they came to wide public attention during World War II (1939–45). They were especially effective in German occupied countries such as Yugoslavia, Poland, France, and the Netherlands.

Unilateralism

Literally, "one-sidedness," as an approach to policy it denotes a go it alone policy. A British movement which stood in opposition to domestic involvement with nuclear weapons, particularly during the 1980s in the ranks of the Labour Party. Other European peace groups are also considered as unilateralists. These groups campaigned vigorously against the NATO policy of deploying American nuclear missiles in Europe. These movements lost their support following the demise of communism and the end of the Cold War. In the twentieth century, the US, under President George W. Bush, has developed a distinctively unilateralist approach to international relations and invaded Iraq without the consent/authorization of the United Nations. American unilateralism signified a schism among the major Western allies. See MULTILATERALISM.

Unitary system

A system in which the central government has full legal authority over the lower levels and can regulate, modify, create, or abolish provincial or regional units as it sees fit. It is generally assumed that in a unitary system, there is complete centralization of legal authority within a state. In practice, the extent of centralization varies. In Britain, parliament has delegated extensive authority to elected local governments, while the French structure since Napoleon Bonaparte has been highly centralized. See FEDERALISM.

United Nations

An international organization of independent states founded after World War II. The UN charter was signed at the San Francisco Conference on 26 June 1945 by 50 nations. The broad purpose of the United Nations is to maintain international peace and security, to develop friendly relations among nations, to achieve international cooperation in solving international problems, to promote and encourage respect for human rights and for fundamental freedoms for all, and to be a centre for harmonising the actions of others. The UN is based on the principle of sovereign equality of all its members. Membership is open to all independent nation-states upon recommendation of the Security council. By 2002, the membership has grown to 190. The UN headquarters are in New York City. It makes its own rules, has its own flag, and operates its own police force. It uses six official languages: Arabic, Chinese, English, French, Russian and Spanish. It has six major organs: the General Assembly, the Security Council, the Economic and Social Council, the Trusteeship Council, the International Court of Justice, and the Secretariat.

The UN is not a supranational organization, nor is it a world-government. There are no citizens, taxes, or a regular army. It serves as the only intergovernmental organisation capable of global decision-making. See IGO.

Universal Suffrage

The extension of voting privileges to all qualified voters without distinction to race, sex, belief or social status. The first movements toward universal suffrage (or manhood suffrage) occurred in the early nineteenth century, and were focused at removing property requirements for voting. In the late nineteenth and early twentieth century, the focus of universial suffrage was intended to remove requirements against women having the right to vote. See FRANCHISE.

'Uqūbah

Punishment in all its forms, encompassing both discretionary punishments (*ta'zir*) and those designated by a text (*ḥadd*). There can be two basic types of 'uqubah: fixed punishments for crimes such as fornication, slander, alcohol drinking, theft and apostasy; punishments which are not legislated and hence left to the discretion of the judge. See *ḤUDŪD*.

'Urf

Custom, Usage, Practice, Convention, Tradition. *'Urf* and *'ādah* (tradition) are very ancient and important sources of Islamic law. As the pre-Islamic Arabs had no written documents or script, their social systems were regulated by custom and tradition. According to the available historical accounts, the *khulafā' al rāshidūn* retained many pre-Islamic social customs and traditions and also adopted and established some useful non-indigenous customs. Such borrowing was quite acceptable in their eyes, for the Prophet (SAW) himself had acknowledged the validity of some pre-Islamic customs that were compatible with the letter and spirit of the revelation.

Usūliyyūn

Those who conform to prevailing principles or those who adhere to the doctrine of going back to first principles. This term also refers to the scholars of legal methodology and those that specialized in theoretical jurisprudence often called "legal jurists." Within the Twelver

Shī'ah tradition, the term is applied to those of its adherents commonly identified as supporting application of the rationalist principles of jurisprudence, especially *ijtihad*, to interpret doctrine and practice during the occultation of the *imam*. Since the 1970s, the term usuliyyun has been generally used as the equivalent of "fundamentalism." See FUNDAMENTALISM, ISLAMISM.

Utilitarianism

A philosophy in the nineteenth century that advocated the concept of utility as the foundation of morals or the greatest Happiness Principle, which posited that actions are right in proportion as they tend to promote happiness, wrong as they produce its opposite.

Utopia

Comprehensive depictions of idealized communities or imaginary perfect societies. The concept comes from the Greek word meaning "nowhere," suggesting that these portrayals may help envision political possibilities, but are ultimately unattainable in their idealized forms. The ideal state depicted in Plato's *Republic* and Karl Marx's Classless Society are examples of utopia.

Utopian Socialists

The term that Marx and Engels used to describe early nineteenth century social reformers who believed that capitalism could be reformed by establishing utopias (ideal communities). These communities would be based on cooperation and social control over private property and wealth. These communities would be self-sufficient. Their leading proponents were Claude-Henri de Saint Simon, Charles Fourier, and Robert Owen. The utopian socialists eventually failed. See SOCIALISM, FABIANISM.

V

Values

A set of mental preferences, an object or situation deemed to be of intrinsic worth, something to be esteemed and sought. It is something one thinks is important and desirable, whether it be a car, passing grades, paying alms, performing regular prayers, or a brave new world. Values vary from one society to another. In some societies, great value is placed on wealth and material possessions, in others on religious status, and so on. There is a good deal of debate on the place of value in Political Science research. See BEHAVIOURALISM.

Vanguard of the Proletariat

A small revolutionary elite group to stimulate consciousness and indoctrinate the masses during the dictatorship of the proletariat. The vanguard is to make the proletariat conscious about its exploitation, of its need to organize as a class and of its role in history and thus usher in the classless society. The phrase vanguard of the proletariat is first attributed to Lenin. They were conscious of the "class-consciousness" doctrine of Marx. See MARXISM-LENINISM.

Vested Interest (groups)

Group of persons that have acquired rights or power in any sphere of activities within a nation or in international affairs which they often struggle to guard and maintain. Examples of powerful vested interest groups in developing countries include land lords, political elites, and wealthy private local and foreign investors.

Veto

A Latin term which means to prohibit, block or refuse consent to a proposed bill or policy.

Generally, it refers to the UN Security Council rule that allows any permanent member state (Britain, China, France, Russia, and the US) to defeat a substantive resolution by voting against the proposed policy. During the cold war, the excessive use of the veto by the two super powers, almost paralyzed the Security Council. Veto also refers to the power granted to the head of state to reject, and thus veto, any bill or joint resolution passed by the legislature. In the US, however, the Congress is empowered to overturn a presidential veto by a two-third votes in both houses of Congress. See SECURITY COUNCIL, POCKET VETO.

Vietnam Syndrome

A lesson the United States supposedly learned from having lost the Vietnam war: essentially, do not intervene in Third World nations unless U.S. vital interests are at stake, the US is assured of a quick and relatively inexpensive victory, and the US public will support the operation.

Vietnam War

The war fought by American forces in Vietnam since the early 1960s. In following with the Cold War policy of communist containment, US military advisors had been sent to Vietnam since 1954. However, the Kennedy administration increased the number of troops in Vietnam to 15,000 by the early part of 1963. When Johnson took over in office, the number of troops had grown to about 17,000 soldiers. In July 1964, Johnson sent another 500 troops to the Vietnam region. However, on August 4, 1964, a supposed attack on United States Navy destroyers in the Gulf of Tonkin shifted the role of the United States Military in Southeast Asia. However, Congress, at Johnson's urging, passed the Gulf of Tonkin resolution, which allowed Johnson the use of any measures necessary to repel any armed attack and prevent any further aggression against the United States. This measure was the key for the increased involvement in Vietnam by the United States. America lost some 60,000 soldiers in the war. Unable to stomach further casualties and to stem the tide of opposition in the U.S., the American government signed Peace Accords in 1973 and withdrew from Vietnam.

Vote

An individual's act of voting by which he or she expresses support or preference for a certain resolution, a certain candidate, or a certain list of candidates. A secreet ballot is seen as the standard way to protect voters' political privacy. See ELECTION.

Vote of confidence

Approval of a government's major proposals. If the government loses such a vote, the prime minister will be required to leave the office and the head of state will ask another person (if he has a majority) to form a new government or he will call for a general election.

Voting

A formal act of choice amongst a set of alternatives by an individual. The voting procedure might be secret, public or even recorded and published, as is done in many legislative assemblies. Votes are counted according to a variety of methods ranging from varieties of pure Proportional Representation to the simplest "first past the post" plurality system. Voting is a basic feature of democracy, but universal adult suffrage is recent. See ELECTIONS, FRANCHISE.

Voting Behaviour

Forces and factors influencing people's decision to vote or not vote. This is one of the most advanced areas in political science that deal with questions of what makes people prefer one party over other parties and candidates and what makes people decide to vote or not vote. Voting behaviour is shaped by many factors, some long-term and some short-term. Long-term factors include changes to the social structure or the extent to which people identify with a political party; these change only gradually but may provide the basis for an eventual shift in voting behaviour. Short-term factors include the particular political issues, events and personalities associated with each election. The two sets of influences are not easy to separate and have differing impacts at particular elections. See VOTING, ELECTORAL SYSTEM, ELECTION.

W

Wahhabism

A reform movement founded by Muhammad Ibn Abd al-Wahhab (1703–1792CE) and its adherents are concentrated in contemporary Saudi Arabia and Qatar, where ruling families in both kingdoms have adopted and propagated the doctrine. Wahhabis initially objected to the term assigned to them by Westerners and preferred instead to be known as *al-Muwahhidūn* (monotheists or Unitarians). *Wahhabism* claims to restore Islam from what its adherents view as innovations, deviances, heresies and idolatries. Wahhabis revert back to the Qur'an and sunnah to establish an Islamic state on the *shari'ah* and classical Islamic principles. The aim of Wahhabism is the purification of Islam of accumulated practices perceived as counter to the strictest interpretation of the Qur'an and the law of *shari'ah*.They condemn ornamentation, music, dancing, and singing, denounce all accretions that have crept into Islam and engage in a perpetual *jihād* as their principal means of winning converts and redirecting wayward Muslims to the righteous path. See FUNDAMENTALISM.

Wakālah (pl. *wakālāt*)

Representation, deputyship, power of attorney. *Al Wakālah* means agency, or delegating duty onto another party for specific purposes and under certain conditions. Though a general concept, it is applied specifically in Islamic Banking. Under the concept of *Al Wakālah*, a bank will act as an agent on behalf of a company or an individual. The bank gives a written undertaking to a seller at the request and on the instructions of the buyer, to make payment to the seller on behalf of the buyer on sight or at a determinable future date, up to a stated sum of money within a prescribed time limit and against stipulated documents and in compliance with the terms and conditions of the letter of credit. An authorized representative or agent of certain transaction between two parties is called a *wakil* (agent). See DELEGATION.

Walī (pl. *awliyā*)

One who is close, like a friend, relative, protector, helper. Generally, *walī* refers to a learned *sūfī*, cleric, or saint who enjoys God's favour and consequently possesses significant power. In Islamic law, the *walī* is the guardian or legal representative of an individual. It is also one to whom a ruler delegates authority. Shi'ahs believe that Prophet Muhammad (SAW) made Ali the *walī* or imam over the *ummah*, a point disputed by Sunnis.

Waqf (pl *awqāf*)

Prevention, blocking of an account, suspension from duty. In Muslim legal terminology, it means prevention and protection of a thing from becoming the property of a third person. Generally, *waqf* refers to a charitable trust dedicated to some pious or socially beneficial purpose. It refers to charitable organizations operated by the government and/or private organizations that help mosques, schools, orphanages, and the poor and needy.

War Against Terror

An informal international cooperation against the terrorist threat all over the world led by the United States. Following the suicide attack and the resultant collapse of the World Trade Centre in New York, the United States took upon itself the responsibility of combating terror world wide and hence invited the world community to join in this crusade against terror. Some countries, like Pakistan, were coerced to join in with the threat to "be with us or against us," and they acquiesced. Internally, the US established a new Office of Strategic Influence to combat terror with wide ranging powers. The first casualty of war against Terror was Afghanistan which harboured Osama bin Ladin, the alleged mastermind of the attack on the Twin Towers. The Taliban government fell under constant bombardment from allied, mainly the US, planes and was replaced by an interim government backed by international forces.

Warsaw Pact

The military organization of Eastern Europe signed in Warsaw, Poland in 1955, by Albania, Bulgaria, Czechoslovakia, East Germany, Hungary, Poland, Romania and the Soviet Union. It was the communist counterpart to NATO. Warsaw Pact members were bound to assist each other in the event of an attack on any one of them. Albania withdrew in 1961. The Warsaw Pact members collaborated in the invasion of Czechoslovakia in 1968—the only time it took military action. The Pact was ended as a military alliance in 1991, when the demise of communism and the end of the Cold War made it superfluous.

Wasiṭ

Middle, intermediary, mediator and intercessor. Mostly, it is used for an agent, a go-between broker to solve any problematic issues between two parties. The Qur'an refers to Muslims as *ummatan wasatah* (the middle community or the balanced community).

Waṭan **(pl. *awṭān*)**

Homeland, home country, fatherland, nation. This is a concept borrowed from Western nationalism. See NATION.

Watergate

Refers to the scandal in the 1970s, during which President Nixon's supporters engaged in such illegal acts as break-ins and phone-taps against their Democratic opponents. Nixon was willing to dispense with the normal rules of the political game in order to ensure that he wins the election handsomely. In June 1972, five men from Nixon's re-election committee were arrested as they tried to plant electronic devices in the headquarters of the Democratic party national committee in the Watergate building, Washington D.C. Nixon and his senior aides were implicated in a massive abuse of power and the obstruction of justice. The House of Representatives Judicial Committee voted to impeach Nixon in July 1974, which was averted when Nixon resigned from presidency the following month. Nixon was granted a full pardon by his successor, President Gerald Ford.

Waves of Democracy

A group of democratic transitions that occur within a specified period of time and that significantly outnumber transitions in the opposite direction during that period. The term was coined by Samuel Huntington to describe the speed with which new democracies were created. It is broadly agreed that there have been three such waves in world history. The first long wave from 1828 to 1926 saw some thirty countries achieve minimal democratic institutions. The second wave from 1943 to 1962 was driven by anti-colonial struggles that in some cases led to new democratic regimes. The third wave began with the Portuguese revolution of 1974 and has continued to the present. See DEMOCRACY.

Wazīr (pl. *wuzarā'*)

Vezier, minister. The office of minister or advisor to the caliph. In modern political parlance, the word is used to mean a minister or a member of cabinet.

Weimar Republic

The German government (1919–1933) based on the democratic republican constitution adopted at Weimar in 1919. The constitution provided for a parliament of two houses and a popularly—elected president. President Paul von Hindenburg appointed Adolf Hitler chancellor of the republic in 1933, whereupon Hitler suspended the constitution and established a totalitarian regime.

Weapons of Mass Destruction (WMD)

Weapons designed to kill large numbers of people, usually civilians but also potential military personnel. They are generally considered to be of limited military use because their destructiveness is likely to trigger an extreme response. The phrase weapons of mass destruction is the source of various semantic disputes. The phrase originated in 1937 to describe the use of strategic bombers by the German Luftwaffe during the Spanish Civil War. During the Cold War, WMD exclusively meant nuclear weapons. Indeed, modern nuclear weapons are vastly more destructive than either biological or chemical weapons. In fact, the so called "weapons of mass destruction" account for a small proportion of overall deaths due to weapons in general. The U.S.A. and Britain invaded Iraq to destroy a non-existent WMD under Saddam Hussein.

Welfare state

A state which uses its power to modify the normal play of economic forces so as to obtain a more equal distribution of income for every citizen, a basic minimum irrespective of the market value of his or her work and property. The state plays a prime role in ensuring the provision of a minimum standard of welfare to all citizens. The main aspects of welfare are medical care, education, housing, income maintenance and personal social services. Countries like France and Japan include a statement of welfare rights in their constitutions.

Westminster model

The system of institutions and procedures for democratic legislation that was practiced at Westminster in London and was promulgated as the dominant form of government throughout the British Empire. In this model the head of state has considerable reserve powers which, have been limited in practice by convention rather than explicit constitutional rule. As the phrase "the Westminster model" suggests, Britain was the homeland of majority democracy and it was exported to many commonwealth countries such as Australia, Canada, New Zealand, and Malaysia. See PARLIAMENTARY SYSTEM.

Whig

It means different things in different countries. In American history, it refers to a member of the patriotic party during the Revolutionary period, supporter of the Revolution. It also referred to a member of a political party (1834–1855) which was formed in opposition to the Democratic Party. In British politics, it refers to a member of a major political party in Great Britain which, in general, held liberal principles and favoured reforms: later called the Liberal Party. Today, it refers to one of the more conservative members of the Liberal Party.

Whip

A member of a legislature who serves as an assistant floor leader of a party. Named after the "whippers" in the organization of the traditional English fox hunt who kept the hounds from straying, the party whip is chosen in a party caucus as special officer of the political party. His duties include: to be in touch with his partisan colleagues, to disseminate their views, and to ensure presence of sufficient members to carry the vote through in the legislative body.

White Paper

A document containing authoritative recital of facts issued by the government stating its views on a particular matter of serious concern.

Wilayat-e-Faqih

Guardianship, Government of the Islamic jurist. This term is attributed to Ayatullah Ruhullah Khomeini (1320/1902–1409/1989). He argued that a devout, learned, and just Islamic jurist ought to be the supreme guardian of the Islamic state during the absence of the awaited twelfth Imam. In Iran, Khomeini was the *Wilayat-e-faqih* for much of the 1980s. See AYATULLAH

Will of All

Sum of the wills or wishes of individuals who voted in their own selfish interest and constitute a majority; opposite of the General Will.

Wiṣāyah

Literally, the appointment or designation of someone to assume specified responsibilities. Among *Shī'ahs*, the term refers to Prophet Muhammad's designation of 'Ali as his successor as the religo-political leader of the entire Muslim world. See *WALĪ*.

World Government

The age-old concept of a global set of governing institutions that would make laws binding on all national and international actors which would surrender many of their sovereign rights to a supranational authority. The massive destruction caused by World War I and World War II has led to a revival of the concept. Supporters see the creation and effective leadership of the United Nations as a positive model and a stepping stone for a world government. Globalization is also seen as hastening the emergence of a world-government.

World Trade Centre

Twin towers each 110 stories rising 1368 feet and 1362 feet respectively over lower Manhattan in New York City. At the time of their completion in 1973, the WTC towers were the two tallest buildings in the world and symbolized the financial might of America. Two years later, it was surpassed by the Sears Tower in Chicago. In 1996, the Petronas Twin Towers in Kuala Lumpur, Malaysia seized the coveted title of the tallest building in the world. The WTC towers were unable to survive the effects of a direct hit by two hijacked commercial jetliners during the attacks on the morning of September 11, 2001. The collapse of the Twin towers set into motion an international crusade against terrorism.

X

Xenophobia

An extreme fear of people from other countries, sometimes accompanied by a pathological hatred of strangers, which can lead to racism and ethnic cleansing.

Y

Yellow-dog Contract

An agreement, whereby an employee as a condition of employment, agrees that as long as he is in the employment, he will refrain from joining a labour union.

Youth Movements

Movements organized either by youths or adults to channel the energies of the youth in certain direction. Many churches set up youth groups in the hope of retaining the allegiance of their worshippers' children. The Boy Scouts aim at socializing their membership in civic values such as tolerance, obeying the law, public service and the like. Political parties have youth movements guided by their elders. Totalitarian parties organize the young from an early age with the purposes of indoctrinating them and selecting leadership cadres from amongst them.

Young Marx

Karl Marx's early writings contain philosophical and humanistic aspects that his later, more economically deterministic writings or do not. Some interpreters prefer to emphasize the philosophical and idealist writings of the "young Marx," rather than the "more scientific" and "materialistic" strains of his later work.

Z

Zakāh

Legal almsgiving, calculated on the basis of one's wealth. It is not the same thing as charity, *sadaqah*; the latter should be dispensed spontaneously and continually. The word *zakāh* is derived from the word "*zaka*" meaning purification, growth, and sweetening. Hence, *zakāh* is referred to as the compulsory 'purifying' tax on wealth which is one of the five pillars of Islam.

Zandaqah

Atheism, heresy. This is the act of holding a belief against what is generally accepted in religion. A free-thinker, an atheist or an unbeliever is called *zindîq*, which is a term of opprobrium in Mediaeval Islamic history.

Zero-sum Conflict

Conflict in which one side's gain is necessarily the other side's loss. Since compromise is impossible, this kind of conflict tends to be intense and even violent.

Zero-sum Game

An activity where gains by one party created equal losses for others. This is the typical mercantilist understanding of international trade, as opposed to the economic liberals who view international trade as a positive-sum situation that would benefit all participants.

Zionism

A movement which was originally concerned with the creation of a Jewish homeland in Zion (a Hebrew word for Israel) i.e., a state in Palestine for Jewish people. The first World Zionist Congress was established in 1897 by Theodore Herzl, after which Zionist groups were established all over the world. In 1903, the British government offered the Jews a home in Uganda, but this was rejected. Leadership of the Zionist movement was assumed by Chaim Weizmann, who was largely responsible for the Balfour Declaration of 1917. The Zionists established the state of Israel on May 14, 1948, the fact that led to profound sufferings of Palestinian Arabs. With the state established, the Zionist movement is now concerned with territorial expansion and development of the state of Israel by force of arms at the expense of the Palestinians in particular and the Arabs in general. See PALESTINE, INTIFADAH.

Ẓulm

Wrongdoing, injustice, tyranny; acts transgressing limit or bound; cheating. The word also embraces the act of performing and/or forcing others to perform unlawful acts.